CUSTOMER
DATA
PLATFORMS

MARTIN KIHN
CHRIS O'HARA

CUSTOMER

USE PEOPLE DATA TO TRANSFORM

DATA

THE FUTURE OF MARKETING ENGAGEMENT

PLATFORMS

WILEY

For general information on our other products and services or for technical support, please contact our Customer Care Department within the United States at (800) 762-2974, outside the United States at (317) 572-3993 or fax (317) 572-4002.

Wiley publishes in a variety of print and electronic formats and by print-on-demand. Some material included with standard print versions of this book may not be included in e-books or in print-on-demand. If this book refers to media such as a CD or DVD that is not included in the version you purchased, you may download this material at http://booksupport.wiley.com. For more information about Wiley products, visit www.wiley.com.

Library of Congress Cataloging-in-Publication Data is Available:

ISBN 9781119790112 (Hardcover)
ISBN 9781119790136 (ePDF)
ISBN 9781119790129 (ePub)

Cover Design: Wiley
Author Photos: (Kihn) Chae Kihn Photography / (O'Hara) Courtesy of the Author

SKY10022262_110420

Contents

Introduction   **1**
   The Pizza Challenge   1
   The Perils of Personalization   4
   Rise of the Avoidant Customer   5
   The Disconnected Data Dilemma   6
   Crossing the Customer Data Chasm   7
   Customer Data Platform (CDP)   8

CHAPTER 1
The Customer Data Conundrum   **11**
   Data Silos   11
   Known Data   14
   Customer Relationship Management (CRM)   15
   Customer Resolution   15
   Data Portability   16
   Unknown Data   16
   Cross-Device Identity Management (CDIM)   19
   Connecting the Known and Unknown   20
   Data Onboarding   21
   People Silos   22
   Customer-Driven Thinker: Kevin Mannion   24
   Summary: The Customer Data Problem   26

CHAPTER 2
The Brief, Wondrous Life of Customer Data Management   **29**
   Customer Data on Cards and Tape?   29
   Direct Mail and Email: The Prototypes of Modern Marketing 31
   A Brief History of Customer Data Management   32
     Relational Databases   34
   The Rise of CRM and Marketing Automation   35

    Marketing Automation   36
    Improved User Interface (UI)   37
    The Multichannel Multiverse of the Thoroughly Modern
      Marketer   38
    The Growth of Digital   38
    Today's Landscape   40
    Today's Martech Frankenstack   41
    Customer-Driven Thinker: Scott Brinker   43
    Summary: The Brief, Wondrous Life of Customer Data
      Management   44

CHAPTER 3
What Is a CDP, Anyway?   **47**

    Rise of the Customer Data Platform   47
    What Marketers Really Want from the CDP   51
    The Great RFP Adventure   52
    "We Want a Platform, Not a Product"   53
    Building a Platform Solution   54
    CDP Capabilities   54
    Data Collection   54
    Data Management   55
    Profile Unification   56
    Segmentation and Activation   56
    Insights/AI   57
    The Two (Actually Three) Types of CDPs   58
    A System of Insights   58
    System of Engagement   60
    The Third Type: Enterprise Holistic CDP   62
    Known and Unknown (CDMP) Data Must Be Unified   62
    A Business-User Friendly UI   62
    A Platform Ecosystem   63
    The Future Is Here   64
    Customer-Driven Thinker: David Raab   65
    Summary: What Is a CDP?   66

CHAPTER 4
Organizing Customer Data   **69**

    Munging Data in the Midwest   69
    Elements of a Data Pipeline   71
    Data Management Steps   72
    1 Data Ingestion   72

2 Data Harmonization 74
  Using an Information Model 75
3 Identity Management 76
  Benefits of Identity Management 77
  Spectrum of Identity 78
  Identity Management in Practice 79
4 Segmentation 79
  The Importance of Attributes 82
5 Activation 83
Getting It Done 84
Different Spheres of Influence 84
Customer-Driven Thinker: Brad Feinberg 86
Summary: Organizing Customer Data 88

CHAPTER 5
Build a First-Party Data Asset with Consent **91**

Privacy-First Is Customer-Driven 91
Privacy Police: Browsers and Regulators 93
Web Browsers and Standards Bodies 93
  Intelligent Tracking Prevention 94
  Enhanced Tracking Prevention and Brave 94
  Google's Chrome and AdID 94
Government Regulators 95
The Mistrustful Consumer 96
  How Can a Marketer Gain Trust? 98
Attitudes Around the World 99
The Privacy Paradox 100
  What Exactly Is the Privacy Paradox? 101
  How Do You Solve the Paradox? 101
Four Privacy Tactics to Try 102
Customer-Driven Thinker: Sebastian Baltruszewicz 103
Summary: Build a First-Party Data Asset with Consent 104

CHAPTER 6
Building a Customer-Driven Marketing Machine **107**

Know, Personalize, Engage, and Measure 107
  Know ("the Right Person") 108
  Personalize ("the Right Message") 109
  Engage ("the Right Channel") 111
  Measure (and Optimize) 113
Organizational Transformation 114

The CDP Working Model   114
   Team   114
   Platform   116
   Use Cases   116
   Methodology   117
   Operating Model   118
The People at the Center (the Center of Excellence Model)   119
   Marketing   120
   IT/CRM   121
   Analytics   122
How the COE Works   123
How to Get There from Here: A Working Maturity Model   124
   Channel Coordination Stages   126
   Engagement Maturity Stages   126
   Touchpoints: That Was Then   127
   Journeys: This Is Now   127
   Experiences: This Is the Future   128
Summary: Build a Customer-Driven Marketing Machine   128

CHAPTER 7
Adtech and the Data Management Platform   **131**
The Magic Coffee Maker   131
Background/Evolution of the DMP   132
Five Sources of Value in DMP   133
Advertising as Part of the Marketing Mix   134
Role of Pseudonymous IDs in the Enterprise   135
Advertising in "Walled Gardens" with First-Party Data   135
End-to-end Journey Management: The CDMP   136
Customer-Driven Thinker: Ron Amram   137
Summary: Adtech and the Data Management Platform   138

CHAPTER 8
Beyond Marketing   **141**
The Expanding Role of Customer Data Across the Enterprise   141
   Service: Frontline Engagement with the Customer   144
Commerce: The Storefront and the Nexus of Response   146
   Use of Commerce Data for Modeling and Scoring   147
Sales: The B2B Context, and What That Means for Customer
   Data   149
   Sources of Truth   150
   Householding   150
   Targetable Attributes   151

Marketing: The Brand Stewards, Revenue, and the
   Engagement Engine   151
Customer-Driven Thinker: Kumar Subramanyam   152
Summary: Beyond Marketing: Putting Sales, Service, and
   Commerce Data to Work   153

CHAPTER 9
Machine Learning and Artificial Intelligence   **155**
Once Upon a Time ... in *Silicon Valley*   155
Deep Learning and AI   156
   Back to the Hot Dogs   157
   Cast of Characters   157
Customer-Driven Machine Learning and AI   159
Data Science in Marketing   160
   Machine Learning Vs. Artificial Intelligence?   161
   What Does a Marketing Data Scientist Do?   161
Customer Data and Experimental Design   161
Customer Data, Machine Learning, and AI   162
   What Is a Model?   162
   Labeled Vs. Unlabeled Data   162
   Fitting a Model to Data   162
   Making Predictions   163
      Regression   163
      Classification   163
   Finding Structure   164
      Clustering   164
      Dimensionality Reduction   164
   Neural Networks   164
Applying Machine Learning and AI in Marketing   165
   Machine-Learned Segmentation   165
   Machine-Learned Attribution   167
   Image Recognition and Natural Language Processing (NLP)   168
Importance of Customer Data for AI   169
AI/ML in the Organization: Data Science Teams   170
Customer-Driven Thinker: Alysia Borsa   171
Summary: Machine Learning and Artificial Intelligence   173

CHAPTER 10
Orchestrating a Personalized Customer Journey   **175**
The Rise of Context Marketing   175
Prescriptive Journeys   177
Predictive Journeys   178

Real-Time Interaction Management (RTIM) Journeys   180
Customer-Driven Thinker: Laura Lisowski Cox   181
Summary: Orchestrating a Personalized Customer Journey   183

CHAPTER 11
Connected Data for Analytics   **185**

Customer Data for Marketing Analytics   185
Analytical Capabilities   188
Analytics Data Sources   188
Beyond the Basics   189
Key Types of Analytics   190
   Marketing/Email Analytics   190
   DMP Analytics   191
   Multitouch Attribution (MTA)   192
   Media Mix Modeling (MMM)   193
   Marketing Analytics Platforms   194
   Enterprise Analytics/BI   195
Customer-Driven Thinker: Vinny Rinaldi   197
Summary: Connected Data for Analytics   199

CHAPTER 12
Summary and Looking Ahead   **201**

Summary   201
Looking Ahead   204
Category Shake-Out!   205
Aggregate-Level Data and "FLOCtimization"   206
A Fresh Start for Multitouch Attribution   206
AI Finally Takes Over   207
The Future   208

Further Reading   **209**

Acknowledgments   **211**

About the Authors   **213**

Index   **215**

Introduction

THE PIZZA CHALLENGE

Art Sebastian had a problem. The affable, Chicago-born VP of Digital Experience at Casey's convenience stores joined a team on a journey to transform the company into "a more modern, contemporary and digital brand" – one that recognized each guest as an individual with their own preferences and needs.

"With retailers in the digital era, what consumers want is more relevance," he said. "They don't want marketing that goes to everyone but rather relevant promotions, messages that speak to them as individuals."

The problem? In a word: *data*. Not a lack of data, but a lack of connection, organization, and accessibility. A frustrating inability to create a customer profile that can be used to deliver a seamless digital experience.

"We had made some good progress," said Sebastian, "but with the progress, we accumulated more data. We have a website and mobile app that collect purchase behavior. We collected pizza orders in one system and loyalty in another. We spent a lot of time thinking about how to unify these multiple data sets."

Casey's logo is well known across the Midwest and the South, boasting 2,200 locations in 16 states and counting. It has a customer base devoted to its heart-of-the-community convenience stores, which are famous for comfort foods, like the tasty Taco Pizza, and friendly staff that treat you like their neighbor.

"Half of our stores are in small towns with a population of 5,000 or fewer," said Sebastian. "We really play a central role in those towns. We're the grocer, the restaurant, and the place where people meet. We support the local high schools and nonprofits some of the area's bigger companies don't focus on."

Like many retailers, Casey's aspired to deliver a better digital experience to its guests, one that paired relevant promotions with the soul of the brand. "When you look at all the things that people love about Casey's," said Sebastian, "it's authentic to be friendly and relatable."

Pulling insights from his customer research team, Sebastian knew that most customers actually bought the same or similar items every time they dropped in or ordered online. This was particularly true for pizza buyers, who nearly always bought the same pie.

1

What would happen if Casey's could personalize the emails to customers based on their pizza preference? Specifically, what if they could put an image of the customers' usual choice in the email, rather than the generic pepperoni they'd been using?

The challenge: Casey's email system was not integrated with its point-of-sale system. This mattered because it was not possible to know what a person's preference was without the point-of-sale data, showing what they bought. Lacking a connection, the email system could not personalize the message or offer.

"There was a lot of data stitching," said Sebastian, "but we did manage to do it."

His team ran a test in email using different pizza images, all featuring $3 off a large pie with a promo code. The image selected was based on the most recent pizza type each guest had purchased.

The results? There was a very significant 16% lift in conversion rate compared to the previous generic image.

"It feels almost silly to be talking about this in a world where people are doing so many sophisticated things," admitted Sebastian. "But we've been able to build on it for other initiatives, like better default settings on the website. Everything improves as we're able to hone in on the guest more and get more personalized."

Personalization works. Casey's story is repeated dozens of times by many customers we've met, and doubtless thousands of others across the globe. The value of relevant, personalized communication cannot be overstated and companies who don't provide it risk seeing their response rates decline and more organized competitors – or nimble startups – eat their pizza.

Although results vary based on factors such as the industry, product, and starting point, studies show that using key customer data – such as product purchase history, in Casey's case – to build more personalized messages yields results. For example, conversion rates on e-commerce websites rise an average 15–20% and engagement rates rise 30% after implementing better personalization. Personalized emails have at least a 6% higher open rate. Targeting ads on social networks based on website visits can increase click-through rates by a factor of two. Multiple studies estimate going from large segments to more one-to-one targets – even in a simple, incremental kind of way – quickly raises average customer lifetime value 20% and engagement rates 30% and more.

How do consumers feel? Our research shows that they not only tolerate but actually *expect* some level of personalization from brands. Salesforce runs a number of global surveys each year, enlisting thousands of consumers and marketing leaders around the globe and across industries, including business-to-consumer (B2C) and business-to-business (B2B) buyers and practitioners. These surveys, compiled into detailed annual reports, tell a compelling story of empowered consumers and marketers battling to keep up with their demands.

As should be obvious by now, customers are increasingly willing and able to move their business when a brand lets them down; they are in control. Across the globe, we see customers exerting their power in reasonable ways, demanding better products and services, and above all better *experiences*, built on data. Starting in 2018, 80% of customers told our researchers that the experience a company provided was as important as its products and services. And even more (84%) said that some level of personal treatment was key to winning their business.

Defining concepts like "personalization" and "1:1" is not as easy as it seems. But it is clear from the data that at a basic level, personalization requires different brand channels to behave in concert. According to our "State of the Connected Consumer" report, 69% of customers say they expect "connected experiences." They believe that behaviors and preferences expressed in one channel should be reflected in others; that they won't have to enter the same data twice, and so on. The same report showed that 57% of consumers said they had already stopped buying from a brand because a competitor had a better experience. Loyalty is an increasingly fragile asset.

Loyalty to consumer brands continues to decline, as the importance of in-the-moment experiences outweighs brand equity (or the psychological-emotional value of a logo). The consultancy Interbrand, which tracks changes in brand equity over time, showed the average equity of consumer product brands (e.g. Coca-Cola, Pepsi, Kellogg's) declined by 4% in recent years, and retail brand equity declined further. (The study was done prior to the impact of COVID-19.) Meanwhile, equity in the big four platform brands – Google, Apple, Facebook, and Amazon – went *up* almost 10% in the same period.

Why do proprietary ecosystems such as Facebook and Amazon see their perceived value climb while traditional brands suffer the opposite? In part, because these platforms have a personalization advantage. They treat a universe of mostly logged-in, repeat users, about whom they have amassed a deep data file. For example, Facebook and Instagram see about three billion monthly active users globally; and, astonishingly, more than half of those users access the platforms *every day*. About 62% of US households are members of Amazon Prime, and they spend an average $1,400 per year.

Having more data, these platforms can provide more personalized marketing and experience on channels such as websites and mobile apps. Greater personal depth yields a beneficial flywheel effect, as experiences yield data and loyalty, which increases over time – even as competitive brands, who generally lack the customer data and the ability to personalize, fall behind. Research shows, for example, that Amazon's product recommendations, based on greater customer-level information, perform about 2x better than those of other large retailers.

Few brands today would deny the benefits of deeper customer data, better insights, and the challenge of rising consumer demands for personalized experiences. Given these realities, and the competitive heft of large platforms such as Facebook and Amazon, we want to pose a simple question: Why doesn't everyone just start doing highly effective, one-to-one marketing now?

What's the problem, exactly?

THE PERILS OF PERSONALIZATION

Around 2010, Coca-Cola execs realized they faced a make-or-break moment. Sales of the #1 consumer brand were falling each year, around the globe, and there was no obvious solution. Aware of the experiential imperative outlined above, Coca-Cola wasn't sure how to act. It had the burden of being a mass consumer product that appealed to many people but lacked basic individual-level data about its customers. Its MyCokeRewards loyalty program was discontinued in 2017, after a decade of disappointment. If there was one brand that would never really be customer-driven, it seems, it was Coke.

But then somebody had an idea. The enterprising field team at Coca-Cola's Australian subsidiary had a brainwave. Sure, they couldn't hope to personalize at a one-to-one level, since they lacked that kind of relationship with customers. But they could approximate one-to-one marketing, couldn't they? They could get *more* personalized than they were; after all, anything was better than nothing.

So, they launched a campaign in 2011 called "Share a Coke." Aimed at reaching Australian millennials, it remade the iconic Coke cans by putting the 200 most common millennial first names on them. The hypothesis was that younger shoppers would be more likely to purchase a can that had their name, or the names of their friends, written on it in bold white-on-red. They were right. Extended to the US and other markets in 2014, the "Share a Coke" campaign drove Coke sales up for the first time in years.

When it comes to delivering a truly customer-driven experience, many companies find themselves facing a version of the Coca-Cola conundrum: not enough customer data, and not enough time. Roadblocks to the customer-driven future are fierce. Some of these are external and others, self-imposed. To provide a partial list, companies are:

■ confronted by consumers' own changing attitudes toward data collection, storage, and access

- shadowed by a systemic decline in trust, inspiring a rash of ad-avoidant and marketing-hostile behavior
- racked by rising regimes such as Europe's General Data Protection Regulation (GDPR) and the California Consumer Protection Act (CCPA)

And those are just the market-driven challenges; there are plenty within the walls of companies, too.

We face a moment of ironic tension, one that forces companies to think in creative, empathetic ways about customer data. What do we mean? We know that customers require unprecedented levels of personalized experience from all brands and are voting with their wallets if they don't get it. At the same time, these *same customers* are increasingly wary of providing access to the very information that is required to provide that experience – namely, behavioral, attitudinal, and demographic data at the individual level. It's a tension that researchers increasingly and aptly refer to as "The Privacy Paradox."

RISE OF THE AVOIDANT CUSTOMER

In recent years, marketers are counseled to shore up their customer data. Blue-chip consultancies such as McKinsey and Accenture wax on about the "customer data imperative" and the "first-party revolution." Just to compete with personalization powerhouses like Amazon and direct-to-consumer upstarts like Harry's and Casper, brands try to lure more customers to their channels, to sign up for newsletters and promotions, download mobile apps, and join social network communities. And consumers are more aware than ever of what these brands are trying to do.

It's not that consumers eschew data-sharing. It just has to be the *right* data, and the right recipient. Research shows that within certain parameters, we are okay with many forms of tracking. Salesforce's most recent "State of Marketing Report" revealed that 58% of customers are comfortable with their data being used "*transparently*." Yet only 63% of companies comply with this basic requirement, even as they become more attuned to consumers' needs. The percentage of marketers who admit to being "more mindful of balancing personalization with customer comfort" soared from 51% in 2018 to 81% in 2020 – meanwhile, the percentage of marketers who feel "completely satisfied" with their ability to do so fell from 30% to 28% from 2018 to 2020.

As we've seen, it isn't personalization *per se* that bothers people. Nor is "transparency," however defined, the only requirement for comfort. The dimensions are both context and openness. One study published in *Harvard Business Review* indicated that data collected based on behavior on a brand's own channels (what we call first-party data) was often acceptable for use. However, data inferred (via statistical methods), collected by unknown third parties, or collected without advance announcement, was not. In fact, if a consumer found out that one of these less-obvious methods of tracking were used, they were much less likely to buy.

Meanwhile, all brands wrestle with a secular decline in trust. Each year, the bellwether Edelman Trust Barometer plots a depressing death spiral. Trust in business (52%), media (43%), and government (41%) continues to drop. Established brands often share in the general malaise, suffering by proxy. For example, a recent Censuswide survey revealed that one-third of social network users have "little or no trust" in brand information they see on networks.

Given a general rise in paranoia and distrust in institutions, customers are unsurprisingly less and less receptive to marketing and advertising messages. A study sponsored by the Advertising Research Foundation (ARF) into the phenomenon of "ad receptivity" divides consumers into cohorts determined to have high, medium, low, or no receptivity to ads. In recent years, the high and medium-receptivity cohorts were down 3–8% in size, while the "Low Receptivity" group grew from 25% to 32% of the adult population. The group with "No Receptivity" grew to about 10%. In other words, about two in five consumers either don't respond at all or barely respond to marketing – and that group is getting bigger.

THE DISCONNECTED DATA DILEMMA

So much for the customer side of the customer-driven equation. Companies themselves tell us again and again that they face a host of challenges that can perhaps best be summed up in the phrase: *disconnected data*. As the customer experience mandate grows and companies fall over their picks mining customer data, they look at their own internal systems and see, in the words of one colorful customer we know, "a hot mess."

There's no doubt companies continue to grapple with more internal systems that contain data about channels, customers, prospects, and accounts (among other things). Our recent research showed that the number of significant data sources used by marketers alone grew 50% from eight in 2019 to twelve (projected) in 2021. Keep in mind these are major sources, and companies naturally host and/or manage many times more both inside and outside IT. In fact, other research showed that the average enterprise has about

900 different applications, an average of only 28% of which are integrated with a system of record.

So there's more places where data can sit, more complexity, more demands. It would be encouraging to report that this data was itself in good shape, properly formatted, harmonized, cleansed, and deduplicated. But companies tell us that is very much not the case. Across the board, in virtually every industry and region surveyed, we found that companies' satisfaction with the state of their customer data was low. Our research showed that the percentage who declare themselves "satisfied" with their data quality and hygiene (37%), timeliness (34%), integration (34%), consent management (34%), and identity reconciliation (33%) – all fall below thresholds for customer-driven success.

Even more disruptive, disconnected data both causes and is a symptom of disconnected organizations and teams. As channels appeared over the past two decades, teams were "spun up" to manage them, and these teams are often still operating as semiautonomous fiefdoms, compiling data and executing tactics with as little attention to hygiene and integration as the data substrate they're using. It's the disconnected team and disconnected data double threat that is inspiring so many so-called "Digital Transformation" initiatives among our customers.

CROSSING THE CUSTOMER DATA CHASM

What is a customer-driven company to do? That's the question at the heart of *Customer Data Platforms*, one we will try hard to answer. Various answers have been given in the past, as marketers and other departments applied technology solutions to their evolving business needs. We don't believe in rip-and-replace as a panacea, nor in the existence of a silver bullet; nor do we believe technology alone can solve people, process, and (especially) strategic issues. We believe the new paradigm of *Customer Data Platforms* is an evolution of what you've done before and is compatible with existing solutions. Our approach is one of compatibility and growth, not replacement and self-imposed crisis.

Since the 1990s, customer relationship management (CRM) has provided a great answer to many customer engagement needs. It has improved response rates, satisfaction, throughput, sales, market share, closing rates – in short, it's upped the game for many customer-facing disciplines well beyond marketing. At the same time, the category of CRM has expanded so far and wide that the leading analyst firm Gartner no longer covers it as a single market, instead dividing it into 190 distinct subcategories.

CUSTOMER DATA PLATFORM (CDP)

In the last few years, we've seen the rise of a category called the "customer data platform" or CDP. According to the Salesforce 2020 State of Marketing Report, 86% of marketers who use them are increasing or maintaining their use of CDPs, a sign of strong category adoption. Intended to help marketers and other customer-facing departments solve some of the dilemmas described above, the CDP has caused both excitement and confusion in C-suites around the world. Companies wonder if they need one, if they have one, and more importantly, what is this thing called a CDP, anyway? As we explain below, we don't believe the category is new; nor do we believe most vendors with the name "CDP" really sell one. In fact, one wide-ranging survey of marketing tech professionals found that 62% of them said they were using the "Salesforce CDP" before we even had one on the market.

It makes sense that a company known for pioneering CRM would be considered a CDP company. (After all, the "C" in both three-letter-acronyms stands for "Customer.") We will argue that CDP is just the latest evolution of the CRM category, with an emphasis on marketing use cases to begin, quickly expanding to other areas such as service, sales, and commerce. We will define the key components of the CDP, from data ingestion, processing, and identity management; to segmentation, machine learning, and artificial intelligence (AI); to cross-channel activation, reporting, and optimization.

Moreover, unlike other frameworks for this emerging and still undefined category, we'll argue for an expansive view, one that goes well beyond any single vendor's current feature set. One that encompasses the holistic customer journey, from pseudonymous (explained in Chapter 1) to known, and the holistic marketers' requirements, from real-time contextual personalization to traditional rule-driven campaigns.

In particular, we argue that a true enterprise-grade CDP *must* provide:

- *Anonymous to known.* Since customer journeys usually start with an anonymous ad viewer or visitor to a website, CDPs must start to capture data (with proper consent) in the anonymous or pseudonymous state. For this reason, we include capabilities associated with a data management platform (DMP) within the CDP.
- *Insights and engagement.* Researching marketers' real requirements – rather than vendors' press releases – we discovered that they actually encompassed two major systems:
  - *System of engagement:* Providing real-time engagement, such as channel optimization, next-best-offer management, and dynamic creative optimization

■ *System of insight:* Providing a more persistent "single view of the customer," or Customer 360, for the purposes of in-depth analysis, modeling, and measurement

Ultimately, our discussions with customers, our reading of the research, and our own broad experience tell us that marketers aren't looking for yet another application to build yet another customer-data silo. What they want is a long-term solution that lets them provide more personalized, trusted, one-to-one messaging and marketing, yielding a better customer experience.

In short, they want a trusted platform for marketing: one that is reliable, future-proof, and *customer driven.*

CHAPTER 1

The Customer Data Conundrum

Nobody but a farmer wakes up one morning and decides to build a silo – yet that's exactly what has happened, naturally, over the past decades. Starting with the best intentions, marketers and other divisions acquired applications and built customer data stores, then built patches and organized data lakes and marts, signed up with exciting start-ups and ... ended up with over a dozen (on average) separate databases storing data, often about the same customer. Meanwhile, organizations have built up around these silos, making the problem much worse. In this chapter, we discuss the current state of (disconnected) marketing and why it needs to be solved.

DATA SILOS

What's keeping marketers from achieving the "right customer, right message, right time" nirvana they've been chasing for decades? Put simply, it's the nature of customer data itself – it's siloed in different databases, stored in different formats, and used by different parts of an organization in different ways. It's constantly growing, pervasively available, and getting accessible in real time, but continues to defy brands' efforts to unify it and make it easily actionable.

Salesforce's sixth *State of Marketing* report surveys over 7,000 senior marketers across a wide swath of industries to find out what their top priorities and challenges are from year to year (the survey is conducted by a third party, and respondents are not aware that Salesforce is the sponsor of the research). In the most recent edition, two of the top five challenges were "unifying customer data sources" and "sharing a unified view of customer data across business units" (Figure 1.1). In this section, we will talk about why data unification continues to defy marketers' efforts – and discuss the challenges and opportunities for sharing customer data across your organization.

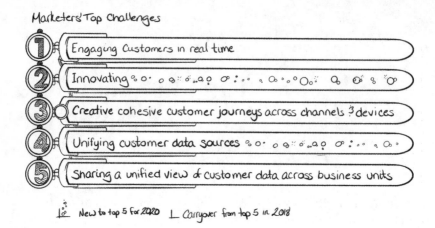

Marketers' Top Challenges

1. Engaging Customers in real time
2. Innovating
3. Creative cohesive customer journeys across channels & devices
4. Unifying customer data sources
5. Sharing a unified view of customer data across business units

1° New to top 5 for 2020 | Carryover from top 5 in 2018

FIGURE 1.1 Marketers' top challenges.
Source: Courtesy of Salesforce State of Marketing 2020.

Does this experience sound familiar? You start to carefully research new cars online, you "build" a few models on the website, research pricing and financing – even go to several dealerships and take test drives. After a few weeks or months narrowing down your choices, you pick the right vehicle and drive it home. Then for the next two years you get consistently blasted with emails, social media ads, and mobile ads for the car you already bought. What a tremendous waste of money! Despite all of the technological innovation driving marketing and advertising over the last 20 years, it seems like every brand who smells even the smallest whiff of purchase intent immediately starts a barrage of full-funnel marketing meant to overwhelm consumers into buying something.

The problem is not a lack of data. In fact, we have seen that marketers report using a median of 8 distinct data sources in 2019, and will expand that to 12 next year, a 50% increase. Think about the amount of data generated by a consumer in the car shopping process: online cookies generated through website visits that reveal the type and model of the car; web form data with name, phone number, and email address gathered from test drive request and finance forms; a user's mobile advertising ID from in-app experiences; and lead form data input at the dealership.

Put together, these data would reveal intent across the entire lifecycle of a car purchase – with attributes ranging from vehicle type, price range, color, location, financing type (buy or lease), and even past purchase history. With this type of data, a smart automotive marketer could move consumers from consideration to purchase in stages, close the deal – and continue the campaign post-sale with service deals and offers.

However, this rarely happens today. *The problem is not the amount of data being generated, but where that data is stored and who is using it.* The data from the website is not connected to the customer relationship management (CRM) system at the dealership. The "take a test drive" form never makes its way to the web marketing team to improve their targeting. The purchase data from the dealership and manufacturer's warranty data stay in silos and never get used to update the marketing team to prevent the company from trying to sell you a car you have owned for six months.

Over the years, we've built up a number of data silos, where critical customer information never gets the opportunity to enrich each other and lead to insights. How much money could a marketer save by simply turning off marketing for products a customer has already purchased? By using the carefully tuned buying propensity models from known customer data and applying them to unknown prospects coming to the website? By connecting what's happening on their e-commerce site to their email marketing? It seems obvious, but the problem of disparate, siloed customer data has only expanded and hardened over time.

Defining the problem space is simple: too many types of customer data, stored in different systems. But to start to solve it, we must look at the problem in two distinct ways, defined by fundamentally different data types: "known" and "unknown" customer data (Figure 1.2).

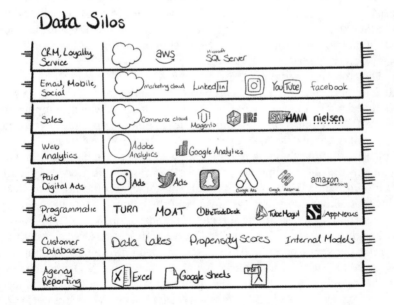

FIGURE 1.2 Data silos, organized by marketing function, across known and unknown data types.

KNOWN DATA

For simplicity, "known" data is any type of customer data that is personally identifiable, called "PII" or "personally identifiable information." This is where you fill out a web form, purchase something from a website, give the cashier your information at a retail store, subscribe to a site like the *New York Times*. This is the virtual gold of marketing – real information about real people that has been given with consent to a company you trust. It is increasingly rare thanks to privacy legislation (more on that in Chapter 5), and very expensive to obtain. In 2019, Mary Meeker's Internet Trends Report called out the increasingly high cost of customer acquisition as traditional brands start to compete with AI-driven direct-to-consumer startups, such that a customer's lifetime value has started to become less on average than the cost of acquiring them.

Depending on the industry, acquiring a new customer can cost anywhere from 5 to 25 times more than retaining current ones – and the cost will continue to rise as marketers attempt to stay afloat in a noisy digital marketplace. Two years ago, Comcast paid over $1,200 for every net-new wireless subscriber. The cost to purchase email can range anywhere from $200 to $600 per thousand addresses (CPM, or *cost per mille*), depending on the accuracy and granularity of the list. Real "people data" is expensive, and most companies have put a lot of energy into organizing and optimizing it, starting with its use in traditional CRM systems by sales, email systems by marketing, and service applications by call center employees.

The problem, however, is that even when the brand has a customer record, it lives in those silos (sales, service, commerce, marketing) and rarely gets unified in such a way that can power a customer journey. A typical company may use one CRM application to power its sales operation, another to keep track of customer service details, and yet another system to store data used for marketing. In addition, they maintain a data warehouse or data lake to create a "golden record" of customer data, and use it for things like propensity scoring and lifetime value (LTV) modeling. But a customer record may be replicated four times across those four systems – and the company may have multiple instances of data across different regions, brands, or operating companies.

Imagine how great it would be if Joe Smith in the service system (Joe returned the shoes he bought) could be unified with the Joe Smith inside the marketing system (don't email Joe about these shoes)? Or the Joe inside the data warehouse (Joe has a high propensity to buy) could be connected to the sales system (call Joe now)! This seems like a fairly straightforward problem to solve – why not just create a single system with one record? As above, most "stacks" are like old rambling houses, featuring additions built over many years – they're almost impossible to renovate.

CUSTOMER RELATIONSHIP MANAGEMENT (CRM)

The CRM system is the operating system for customer data that the sales organization plugs into, and is in many ways the organization's true "source of truth," going well beyond sales records. The service system in the call center is where tickets are opened and logged, and call center reps own a relationship with customers and prospects that may start on Twitter, go to the phone, and end up on email or text message. That system is the operational heart of the call center, and the "source of truth" for how customers move through specific parts of the funnel. Marketing and commerce systems are their own closed ecosystems, complete with different ways of identifying customers, storing their data, and analyzing it. Customer data is the lifeblood pumping through those systems and powering their operations and, over time, those systems have evolved to leverage customer data in the service of different outcomes: revenue (sales), customer satisfaction (service), direct purchase (commerce), and engagement (marketing).

Breaking down those silos requires companies to *resolve* customer data, and create *data portability* across applications. Let's talk about the first, and most important requirement: known customer resolution. How do you take data from a number of different sources (records) and create a single, unified profile for every customer? It's a daunting challenge. Joe Smith might have three different email addresses, several different phone numbers, and even multiple mailing addresses. What is the "source of truth" for Joe among that data, and how can Joe be resolved into one profile that serves as the "golden record"?

Moreover, when doing the actual "data munging" required to unify records, it quickly becomes apparent that each system stores data from fields in different ways (e.g. one system may identity Joe as belonging in the "FirstName" field, and another may call it "First_Name"). It's always a little bit different, and those small differences are what keeps the quest for a "golden record" a multiple billion dollar opportunity over the next 10 years. We will dig into this topic in depth in Chapter 4, but summarize it below.

CUSTOMER RESOLUTION

Customer resolution is the method by which companies create a data model to standardize those fields, and also build the ability to make those systems smarter by applying logic to map fields together accurately. For example, if Joe has a gmail address and an AOL address, which one takes priority? Or, if Joe has three postal addresses, which one is the most recent? These many individual conflicts need to be solved continually, at scale, across many databases.

It's not a trivial problem, but the reward for solving it unlocks incredible business value in terms of the ability to know and understand customers from an analytics perspective – and activate customers across many known customer touchpoints including sales, service, commerce, and marketing.

DATA PORTABILITY

Once a model is established for resolving customer data, the next step is to make different attributes available to other systems, or "data portability." Data portability is an incredibly broad area, but from a marketing perspective it's concerned with making sure customer data flows accurately from system to system in the service of a better understanding of a customer's status and intent. For example, if Joe bought the shoes (commerce data), his next email would be about socks or something else (marketing data). Each system is concerned with different attributes around the customer, but not necessarily relevant to the day-to-day operation of those systems.

It might be great to know that a customer has ten closed tickets over the last twelve months in the call center, but that's not mission critical data for the email marketer. However, if that fact was translated into a "satisfied recent customer" marketing attribute that could be segmented upon, then it turns into marketing gold. Deciding what data to port between applications (and ultimately store and persist in a single "golden record" system like a CDP) is one of the battlegrounds of marketing that will decide the winners and losers for years to come.

The CDP seems to be the technology *de jour* for solving the problem of unifying known customer data and provisioning a golden record that marketers can rely on to power the majority of their PII-based marketing efforts, largely centered around messaging. But what about the massive amounts of data created when customers are now known, but interacting anonymously with a brand's digital advertising, website, or mobile application?

UNKNOWN DATA

Joe Smith can look like 10 different Joes in the world of known data, but the problem really gets interesting in the digital world. All of a sudden, Joe looks like 100 different people based on his different identity keys. The typical customer owns 4.6 connected devices, has hundreds of active cookies, and different IDs for every platform she interacts with (an Apple ID, Google ID, unique device ID for Xbox, etc.). Every time we see an ad, visit a website, play a video game, or walk into a store with beacon technology, we are creating a unique identifier that lives in isolation from all of the other IDs we might have. This makes the customer journey technically difficult to deliver, given that up to 67% of online purchases are the culmination of a multi-device journey, and the fact that 66% of marketers say they fail to recognize the same customer when they switch devices during their path to purchase.

All of this disconnected data being created at high volumes and internet speed basically created the category of "data management platforms" (DMP) about 15 years ago – while creating a cottage industry for solving problems of "identity" for marketers that persists today. The challenges of known customer resolution discussed above look relatively tame in comparison to the thorny issues of resolving "unknown" customer identity. In addition to the massive scale of data, new data types generated for every unique device, proliferation of device types, and real-time nature of the data usage in things like programmatic media, there has been a tsunami of new data and privacy regulations making capturing and activating that data harder than ever.

When you consider the myriad issues brought on by privacy regulations like Europe's GDPR (General Data Protection Regulation) and California's CCPA (California Consumer Privacy Act), and the moves by Apple and Google to restrict the collection of cookie data, it's tempting to dismiss the value of capturing and unifying unknown consumer data. Is all of the compliance-related pain worth the cost associated with managing it? Marketers who don't fully understand the problem space are tempted to say that the "DMP era is over" and center their efforts around managing known first-party data. That would

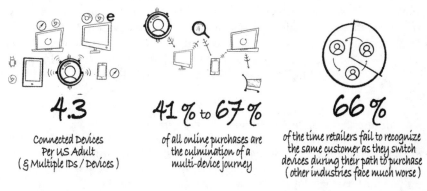

Journeys and Devices

4.3
Connected Devices
Per US Adult
(& Multiple IDs / Devices)

41% to 67%
of all online purchases are
the culmination of a
multi-device journey

66%
of the time retailers fail to recognize
the same customer as they switch
devices during their path to purchase
(other industries face much worse)

FIGURE 1.3 Statistics on identifying customers.
Source: Courtesy of Salesforce State of Marketing 2020 report.

certainly be tempting but, as the popular proverb goes, "If you bury your head in the sand, all people will see is an ass."

More specifically, marketers need to ask themselves some questions: Do you see the numbers of internet-connected devices growing or shrinking in the future? What percentage of customers interact with my brand anonymously versus in a known context? How important is it for my company to attract new customers?

In our previous book, *Data Driven* (McGraw-Hill, 2018), we talked about the problem of data richness and data scarcity, and how it was always amusing to see marketers who thought they had too much or too little consumer data. Marketers like Pandora know almost everything about the musical tastes and mobile consumption habits of millions of known customers, but had no idea who was in the market for a car or vacation. Marketers like Kellogg's had relatively few email addresses but had data on millions of consumers who interacted with their advertising on a daily basis. Even a marketer like Hotels.com with millions of known customers needs to optimize the way they interact with the millions of customers who simply visit their app or website without logging in.

Whether you are a data-rich or data-poor marketer, the consumer's mandate is for you to use their data responsibly to provision an experience across channels that acknowledges you know and understand their needs. Most of those interactions – especially at the top of the funnel – happen in the "unknown" or pseudonymous[1] identity space: website visits, mobile app experiences, video advertising, or display and mobile ads.

So, is the data management platform era over? In a word: No. Although we are not sure marketers will be buying a stand-alone piece of software called a "DMP" in five years, they will still need the ability to capture signals from devices, use data to personalize experiences customers have on websites and apps, activate data across touchpoints that include programmatic display, video, and mobile advertising – as well as apply pseudonymous "people data" for analytics. Perhaps most importantly, they will still need the ability to reconcile people and their various IDs and understand that Joe Smith is the single person behind hundreds of different connected devices.

---

[1]We will use the term "pseudonymous" to describe "unknown" data. Why? Most so-called anonymous marketing data like cookies and device IDs isn't really anonymous at all – if you really tried, you could identify somebody from their device, IP address, or a combination of those things (sometimes called "fingerprinting"). So, we use the term pseudonymous to describe the type of data that is anonymous for practical purposes, but technically not completely anonymous.

CROSS-DEVICE IDENTITY MANAGEMENT (CDIM)

Cross-device identity management (CDIM) is the discipline behind making sure Joe is recognized as a person, rather than a collection of IDs. With it, marketers can gather tons of contextual and behavioral data about Joe and his interests, create a rich profile of Joe, and add him to a scaled segment of like-minded consumers in the market for the next car, vacation, or smartphone. Without CDIM, marketers will blindly identify and activate hundreds of Joes across different devices, and spread their digital budgets randomly.

By unifying data from many different pseudonymous sources, we also get a very rich view of the pseudonymous version of a customer: a cookie reveals that Joe built a sports car on the dealer's website, has a self-declared credit score of over 740, lives within 10 miles of the dealership, has an Apple device, a higher than average household income (third-party data), and has a five-person household. Based on those signals, the dealership might target this customer with mobile ads for more expensive, sporty SUVs that are fun to drive but can haul the family to dinner. The applications for applying pseudonymous data for both analytics and activation are endless, and we will discuss them at length throughout the book.

Today's complicated data privacy landscape makes applying such data harder than ever, and that is another use of DMPs: managing consumer consent at highly granular levels, and applying it at scale to ensure advertising is compliant with consumer rights. DMPs were essentially built to manage the collection, unification, and activation of largely cookie-based data at scale. In order to "drop a cookie" (more properly, have the rights to place and refer to a browser cookie on someone's device), platforms needed a mechanism to track the status of consent for every individual device – and eliminate that ID from the system where users opted out of targeting or, later, chose the "right to be forgotten." Platforms were built on this capability over time, extending the notion of consumer rights to be more granular: consumers could opt in to different types of uses for their data, aligned to the privacy policy of individual apps and sites (Figure 1.4).

Different consent flags included data collection (capture your device or cookie ID), analytics (include your browsing behavior or other attributes in reporting), targeting (use your data to show you an ad or experience), cross-device (include your ID within a graph of other IDs representing different device types), data sharing (the consent to share your ID with another party), and reidentification (the ability to associate your pseudonymous ID with a PII-based ID to customize known messaging). Without such consent, marketers and media companies would be limited to a binary system: users would either be opted in to *everything*, or nothing at all. By managing such granular consent flags at scale, and in real time, DMPs unlock many different

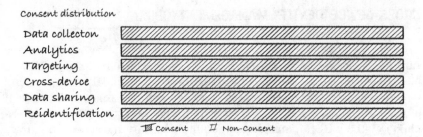

FIGURE 1.4   This representation of Salesforce's Audience Studio shows a segment of users that have opted in to all five consent flags.

use cases, all of which require user consent to operate. Later, we will go into the current privacy landscape, and how this type of infrastructure is being leveraged to manage even more complicated privacy policy schemes in the CDP era.

CONNECTING THE KNOWN AND UNKNOWN

Perhaps the biggest problem to solve in marketing over the last 15–20 years has been that of "identity." The problem includes what we just described above (known *customer resolution* and unknown *cross-device identity management*) and how you actually connect those two types of data together. Connecting pseudonymous and PII-based data together is the key to getting the "full funnel" view of customers you need to power a true customer journey (Figure 1.5). As above, if over two-thirds of journeys start on one device (website) and move to another (email), then without connecting your known and unknown data, you might as well be shooting in the dark from a marketing perspective.

Both data types are enormously important. Known data like postal addresses and email addresses power direct engagement with known customers. When consumers identify themselves and give marketers' permission to interact with them, they are "pulling" engagement from the brands and media companies they trust and want to be engaged with. On the other side, when marketers interact with unknown users through advertising or website visits, they "push" engagement toward consumers.

This action reflects the different dynamics at different parts of the traditional marketing funnel: building *awareness* and *interest* at the top of the funnel, and moving users to *desire* and *action* after they authenticate themselves. If we have both types of data for a user, and manage to connect them together, we can build a journey that starts with display advertising, goes into

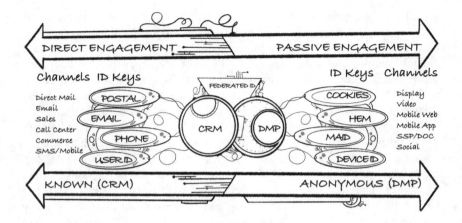

FIGURE 1.5 Connecting known and unknown user data.
Source: Courtesy of Salesforce Originally appeared in *Econsultancy*.

a web visit, where the user offers their email address, makes an offer, and watches the consumer convert on e-commerce. The virtuous cycle then begins, where the user dedicates more and more valuable data in their known state, so the marketer can more specifically target them when seen in their unknown state – casually browsing new products on the web or in an app.

DATA ONBOARDING

The ability to accurately match a person's pseudonymous cookie or device ID with their known postal or email address is so complicated and inefficient it has spawned an entire industry called "data onboarding" which offers the ability to put email addresses into a system and turn them into cookies or device IDs on the other end. LiveRamp is the most widely used of these companies, and it built a $3 billion business ($RAMP) by providing the identity infrastructure marketers and publishers can license to connect the known and unknown together.

A typical example of an onboarding use case would be as follows: A consumer packaged goods (CPG) company has collected millions of loyalty club members who have signed up with their email address to receive points and earn discounts on products. The CPG company wants to target users who do not open their rewards club emails on other channels, such as display advertising. The company goes to an onboarding company, uploads 100 million email addresses – and gets 40 million cookies in return.

The CPG got 40% of its known user data translated into unknown IDs (the "match rate"), which is fairly typical for a consumer goods company. Match rates vary depending on the company's data collection infrastructure and methodology, ranging between 30% to 90%. Companies like the *Wall Street Journal,* who require most users to log into the site to consume content have typically higher match rates, and CPG companies who collect comparatively little data directly from consumers tend to have much lower match rates. The higher the match rate, the richer the people data asset becomes. The auto dealer with only the unknown side of the coin may know you are looking at a black minivan on its website. But that fact, combined with your ownership status and lease maturity date from the known data side of the house, offers the ability to be multiple times more effective. With unknown data alone, the dealership could retarget users with generic offers for the minivan – but by combining the user's interest with known facts ("loyal Chevy customers get $1,000 incentive in June"), the auto dealer can match customers with the right offer, at the right time.

But connecting these two powerful data sets isn't just about optimizing targeting in advertising or email. It's also about enriching customer data for insights that drive results across the entire organization. First, the ability to connect and resolve known customer identity to map sales, service, marketing, and commerce data together unlocks massive value by unifying a profile of customers' total experience with a brand. Second, the ability to connect the diverse and rich landscape of connected devices and IDs to a person unlocks a wealth of enrichment data that reveals real-time intent and behavior.

Without the connection, brands struggle with *observational bias* – an understanding of a small number of known customers based on data they already have. With the connection, brands get richer insights that reveal customers' true intent and experience with the brand across touchpoints that go beyond marketing.

PEOPLE SILOS

The other problem with consumer data is that it creates more than just individual data silos – it actually stratifies the organizations inside a company, creating rifts that prevent transformation (Figure 1.6).

Many companies claim to be data-driven, but a look under the hood quickly reveals the insidious nature of siloed customer data. Although it's clear that customer data is most powerful when completely unified, it tends to organize itself around specific business functions, leading to more silos. It's a fundamental and thorny problem that has challenged most organizations.

Take the team responsible for customer service who runs the call center and responds to customer queries. Customer data is stored in a dedicated

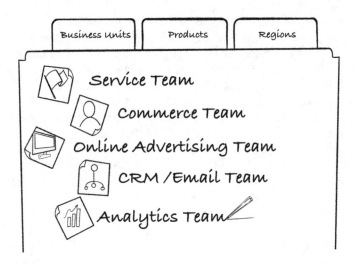

FIGURE 1.6 Business silos.
Source: Courtesy of Salesforce.

system, tracking customer "tickets" that come in, their resolution status, and notes from each interaction. Service managers are rated by key performance indicators like customer satisfaction from surveys or a "net promoter score" (NPS), and their compensation and goals are tied to closing cases faster, and increasing customer satisfaction. The email marketing team has another instance of customer data, centered around emails. They are concerned with open rates, engagement scores on email campaigns, and driving revenue on every campaign. The web analytics team has yet another set of customer data specific to website visits, and their compensation is tied to driving longer website visits, completing forms, and getting return visits.

In short, each team is working in service of the same customer, but is using a different application, dataset, and different ways of measuring success. This only gets further compounded at scale – think about global companies with multiples of these teams across regions, in support of different products or business units. Now, you have multiple copies of similar customer data, multiple teams, and many different KPIs driving success. But the customer is the same.

At its heart, the promise of the CDP is to go beyond solving for disparate data, and start to solve for unified business processes, putting customers at the center of every decision. A deep repository of connected customer data could do more than just connect a "customer journey" for marketers. It would be able to predict demand for products, sense trends in the market, adjust hiring based on data signals, and adjust capital investment. A connected dataset of rich profiles could also drive decisions through Artificial Intelligence, as machine learning runs across higher granular data, sensing deviations in customer sentiment and revealing trends (much more on that in Chapter 9).

But, before we get there, creating a "golden customer record" that all stakeholders can leverage is the right place to start, and has tremendously valuable marketing applications. What if a marketer at a large airline theorized that customers with a positive call center experience were more receptive to email marketing? In order to test that theory, the marketer would have to get access to the service database, map the call center customer data to the marketing database, schedule a data sync between the two systems, create a data extension that would make the service data useful to the marketer's email system, and schedule a specific campaign that targeted happy call center customers with an email campaign.

It sounds pretty complicated already, but now imagine the headwinds that gather in a large organization when the email marketer had to go through the process of requesting the data transfer with the IT department, getting the required permissions, and scheduling the transfer of data assets. The nature of this deep silo between marketing and service creates a perverse incentive to abandon that "no-brainer" idea and go back to blasting every prospect with a generic email.

> The only real way to break down the people silos that prevent cross-team collaboration is to unify the data completely, and start to build incentives for every stakeholder to enrich the core people data asset.

The call center team would benefit from understanding the customer's engagement with email marketing and website engagement. The marketing team would be able to test out satisfaction scores from the call center as a targetable attribute in campaigns. The digital team would be able to leverage the average order value from the commerce team, and the commerce team would be able to communicate the data needed to suppress online ads to people who had bought a specific product recently. Ultimately, having the core customer data asset in a single, unified system that enables broad access to all users across the business actually encourages the organization itself to work together in ways that are more customer-driven.

CUSTOMER-DRIVEN THINKER: KEVIN MANNION

As the President and Chief Strategy Officer of Advertiser Perceptions – a market intelligence firm delivering insights on the advertising, marketing, and ad technology industries since 2002 – Kevin Mannion has reported on the perceptions of advertising and marketing technology with the world's biggest brands and helped them predict the future. We asked Kevin about the rapidly evolving CDP space, how the world's biggest advertisers are looking at CDPs, and what they are looking for.

What inning are we in the CDP ballgame?

We are most certainly in the top of the first. Perhaps the first batter.

How are advertisers looking at the CDP category?

Advertisers see the potential of nirvana via CDPs. In fact, when we have polled both marketers and technologists, both groups point to advertising use cases as a primary benefit of CDPs. And the bright shiny future that advertisers, marketers, and C-level leadership want to believe is possible – a unified view of their clients at every step in their customer journey also known as "the golden record," is within reach.

Discuss your research results. Why is there so much confusion in the CDP category?

Marketers have expected that the companies they see as leaders in marketing clouds and enterprise customer data software have the capabilities of CDPs. In many ways, CDPs represent an evolution of DMPs. In many of our studies over the past few years, marketers and technologists have consistently stated that – not only do they expect firms like Adobe, Oracle, and Salesforce to be the eventual leaders in the CDP realm – but a majority of our respondents believe that *they already are* de facto CDP providers. As of our last survey, only Adobe had officially launched a CDP. Those who have been toiling in the vineyard, so to speak – pure CDP solution providers such as Segment, ARM Treasure Data, RedPoint Global, and mParticle – are not yet as recognizable as the marketing and data cloud leaders. Why are marketers and technologists so confused? I think that many are looking at the kinds of capabilities that they already see in Adobe, Oracle, and Salesforce, and, essentially, are saying, "They will continue to build what we need when we need it."

What are the main use cases marketers are exploring?

Marketers and technologists are clearly ready to embrace the promise of CDPs – enabling them to leverage their treasure troves of first-party data, marrying it safely with second- and third-party data, and enhancing the customer experience at every stage of the buying process. From our studies we see these use cases as priorities: Predictive marketing and advertising; customer profile management and expansion; customer segmentation; development or enhancement of marketing automation systems; and content delivery systems that reach the right person at the appropriate stage of their customer lifecycle.

How do agencies fit into the picture?

It would seem that among those agencies some that are involved with DMPs would want to step up their game, but our sense at this early stage is that agencies are not yet integral to CDP work.

SUMMARY: THE CUSTOMER DATA PROBLEM

- *Data silos:* Up to 65% of customer journeys start on one device and end on another, making it impossible for brands to deliver an end-to-end experience. This problem breaks into two specific components: stitching personally identifiable ("known") customer data together (*customer resolution*); and associating pseudonymous ("unknown") identifiers together through *cross-device identity management*, or CDIM. Both disciplines are critical to breaking down data silos and unifying customer data to improve targeting and analytics.
- *Known data:* Companies usually focus the majority of their marketing efforts on known data, but are often single-threaded to messaging campaigns with the primary identity key being a customer's email address. The opportunity is to connect powerful attributes from other known data sources such as sales, service, and commerce to build a richer customer profile and go "beyond marketing" to power other customer touchpoints. *Customer resolution* is the strategy for provisioning a single, unified ID or "golden record" that can power the new customer journey. *Data portability* is required for connected unified customer data across applications.
- *Unknown data:* Data management platforms (DMPs) have been the main technology for driving the capture, unification, and activation of pseudonymous ("unknown") data that includes cookies, mobile ID, device IDs, and second- and third-party data IDs, but they have been challenged by privacy legislation that limits cookie-based data collection. DMP's core infrastructure will continue to drive the capture, unification, and activation of pseudonymous data; use *cross-device identity management* to reconcile people and their devices; and power *consumer rights management* for data.

- *Connecting known and unknown data:* Matching known data to unknown IDs (data onboarding) and leveraging contextual and behavioral signals gathered pseudonymously to enrich known data (reidentification) are the two main methods for connecting these different sets of data. While every aspect of customer data is based on consent, the latter requires a highly granular consent flag in order to take place, and is not common to most systems. We believe the ability to provision a single data management application that can capture, manipulate, activate, and analyze customer profiles that contain both PII and pseudonymous data is the requirement for success in the emerging CDP era.
- *People data silos:* Functional departments within a single organization (marketing, sales, service, commerce) all use systems that put people data to work in the service of different applications and outcomes. Having separate applications that treat customer data differently has been the standard for years, but has steadily raised the walls of data silos – different departments all work to serve the same customer, but use different data systems, and are rewarded with different goals – and have little incentive to share customer data. These functional "people data silos" can only be eliminated when access to customer data is centralized, democratized, and placed in an application that is useful to the business user (not the exclusive domain of the IT department). We see the CDP category as a forcing function to drive alignment that impacts more than marketing, but creates the opportunity for real data transformation.

CHAPTER **2**

The Brief, Wondrous Life of Customer Data Management

Ours is not the first generation to struggle with customer data, nor are we the first to apply impressive computational power to the dilemmas of harmonization, identity, analytics, and engagement. Many of the problems faced in the first wave of customer data management technology remain today: how to unify disparate sources into a "single view" of the customer; how to deduplicate records and ensure they are clean and accurate; how to make data and decisions available to activation systems. This chapter shows how the modern CDP emerged as a natural evolution of customer relationship management (CRM) and relational databases, and what we can learn from the past.

CUSTOMER DATA ON CARDS AND TAPE?

Before any of us talked about personalization, one-to-one marketing, or even CRM, hard-working marketers toiled in an unglamorous but highly developed field known as Direct Marketing. First named in 1958 by legendary ad man Lester Wunderman, the discipline of Direct Marketing (DM) focused on offline channels such as direct mail and later email, but could also encompass such pre-digital methods as direct phone solicitation and door-to-door sales. It is the progenitor of modern customer marketing, and is older than you think.

How old? Well, interested readers who paged through the latest issue of *Business Automation* magazine back in December 1961 could have read about an operation called the "Society of the Divine Savior Data Processing Center."

Run out of a nondescript building in the middle of semirural Wisconsin, the Society housed a Catholic donor solicitation organization with remarkable success. Employing a cutting-edge IBM 650 magnetic tape system and an Addressograph Multigraph Series 900 data processing system (which cost them $12,000 per month to lease from IBM), they could read up to 750 punch cards per minute and output 60,000 mailing labels per hour. Meanwhile, a high-speed line printer could churn out up to 900 lines per minute of customized letter appeals to the flock.

The Society's operation enjoyed a stratospheric response rate of 80%, according to the center's director, Father Alfred Schmitt. He boasted that "by electronically sorting through our files, we can pick out a choice mailing list comprising names of donors whose past histories indicate that they will be receptive to the type of appeal we have in mind."

But wait a nanosecond. This is 1961 – just how did Father Schmitt make predictions based on "past histories"? Is this *Star Trek: Wisconsin*? In fact, he had a customer database, stored on IBM tape. This database encoded in 341 compact characters not only donor names and addresses but also key data such as solicitations, response times, types of appeals that worked, size of contribution, total donations, etc. In other words, predictive models and lifetime value calculations were business-as-usual for this charity.

Surprised? Many modern marketers assume they can learn little from the past – after all, they didn't have TikTok and influencers – but they're wrong. In many ways, most marketers today are trying to recreate the setup employed by the Society of the Divine Savior more than 50 years ago (Figure 2.1).

The key elements of this operation's martech "stack" are simple, and timeless. They can function as a prototype of our vision for a functioning customer data platform:

- *Data input:* Capture and ingest data from multiple sources.
- *Storage:* Persistent, available storage of relevant data.
- *Data processing:* Extract and transform the data in useful forms.
- *Activation:* Turn the output of processing into signals.
- *Engagement:* Send signals to multiple different channels.
- *Measurement:* Track and optimize results.

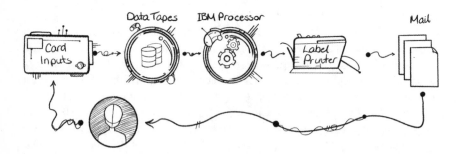

FIGURE 2.1   The marketecture of the Society of the Divine Savior.

So it's fair to say that marketing technology hasn't fundamentally changed since the dawn of electronics, and the principles of marketing go back much further. Many of the details have changed, as life moved on; the variety, velocity, and volume of data grow exponentially. Technology improves. But without knowing it, most marketers are trying to recreate the simplicity of the Society of the Divine Savior's tech stack, only on a much grander scale.

After all, that 80% response rate looks like a miracle today.

DIRECT MAIL AND EMAIL: THE PROTOTYPES OF MODERN MARKETING

Since the invention of parchment some 3,000 years ago, the most efficient way to say something to someone who wasn't standing in front of you was to send them a message. Before the advent of the printing press in the sixteenth century, written communication was by definition one-to-one. After Gutenberg's invention, marketers were quick to see potential in the magic of the printed word.

Early examples of direct mail marketing were catalogs and, yes, solicitations for various causes. For example, the Maule's Seed Company distributed gardening catalogs by mail before the Civil War. In the same era, abolitionists built mailing lists manually using city directories and names taken from newspaper correspondence. Direct mail circulars, generally lists of time-bound promotions, started to appear in the 1870s, around the time that retail pioneers Montgomery Ward and Fred Sears launched their visionary brands. The Sears catalog was an early example of the "endless aisle," the Amazon of its day, and it topped out at over 500 pages, selling everything from live chickens to prefabricated houses, and reaching almost half of all US households. Direct mail remains important to this day, and is currently a $41 billion industry. It is comparable in scale to paid search advertising. By some estimates, the return on investment (ROI) of the average direct mail campaign can be 10X, which explains why our mailboxes remain stuffed with campaigns, both wanted and not.

As we've seen already, direct mail is a prototype of the modern customer data-driven channel; we are still trying to reproduce it in the digital space. For example, direct mail requires a valid address (a "household ID," we might call it). This is personally identifiable information (PII). To work, it rewards careful segmentation using geo-demographic data, often obtained from third-party providers such as Acxiom and Epsilon, who curate validated repositories of household and consumer-level data. And it requires a feedback and measurement loop for optimization. Sound familiar?

The great ad man David Ogilvy, a model for *Mad Men*'s Don Draper, once said: "Nobody should be allowed to create general advertising until he has served his apprenticeship in direct-response."

Direct mail's online cousin, email, was invented in the late 1970s, but it took the coming of the consumer internet in the 1990s to make it a marketing workhorse. The first widely used consumer web browser, Netscape, enabled the development of email web applications. Meanwhile, networking software such as America Online – ironically enough – used hyperaggressive CD-ROM solicitations in direct mail to sign up millions of households to their online network and email channel. *You've Got Mail* became the plaintive bleat of an icon-watching generation.

Email remains a surprisingly effective way to reach customers and prospects. Despite regular reports of its imminent demise, email has a lot going for it as a customer engagement channel:

- *It is opt-in:* Generally, consumers provide their email to a brand in exchange for some value received.
- *It is controlled:* Thanks to consumer protection legislation such as CAN-SPAM in the US and GDPR in Europe, marketers are required to make "Unsubscribe" available, and spam filters are effective.
- *It is multichannel:* Unlike other channels such as websites and even display ads, email usually works at least partly on any browser or device.

Another feature in email's favor, often cited by hard-working CMOs, is that it is relatively inexpensive and easy to measure. Because it is addressable – that is, each message is tied to a known individual or household – email campaigns are much easier to tie to outcomes than other, more expensive channels, such as television or radio. For this reason, it remains a great channel to use to test messages, offers, and audiences in a low-risk environment.

A BRIEF HISTORY OF CUSTOMER DATA MANAGEMENT

Both direct mail and email are what we would call *customer engagement channels*. They are specific processes through which a message reaches a targeted person or household (or account or business – but you get the idea). As time marched on, other channels appeared; we'll address them directly later.

But it is worthwhile here to pause and ask a question: *Where is the customer data stored?* Where does it live? When the marketer wants to "pull a list" for her campaign, where does she go? When she wants to update a customer record with new information, what's the procedure? What is a customer *record,* anyway?

As we've seen, the Society of the Divine Savior stored customer information on magnetic tape. They were very organized about it, with each row storing a separate customer profile. But they had only a single channel: direct mail. Therein, we see the beginnings of a pattern that would be repeated – for better or worse – throughout our survey of the martech past. Customer data is very often tied directly to a particular application.

Originally, data was stored on punch cards (Figure 2.2), which were invented in the eighteenth century to guide mechanical looms. Although not electronic, they were a form of coded data storage and were used into the 1970s. The hard drive appeared in the late 1950s, and with the flexible floppy disk eventually displaced both magnetic tape and cards. Storage technology continued to improve during the 1980s with optical read-write, CD-ROMs, flash or "thumb" drives in the 1990s, and eventually today's virtually unlimited data storage "in the cloud."

Alongside improvements in storage media, the format of the data changed. When computer space was expensive, data had to be compressed, highly structured, and coded in machine language. Later, as storage became less scarce (and exponentially cheaper), data could be stored in what's known as "plaintext" format, or in a format people could read. The most convenient structure was the table, almost always with columns representing well-defined attributes (or features) of the data and rows representing individual records. These data tables were often stored on corporate mainframe

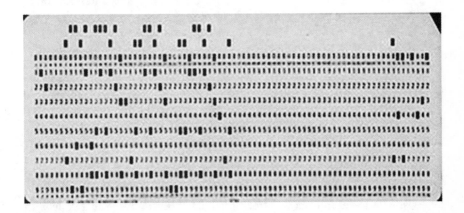

FIGURE 2.2   An example of a punch card for storing data.

computers, and were relatively difficult to access and edit using CRUD utilities (Create-Read-Update-Delete).

Relational Databases

All that changed in the 1990s with the invention of the *relational database* and the Structured Query Language (SQL). The challenge with storing data in tables is obvious to anyone who spends time thinking about it, and was obvious to data admins from the beginning: tables can get very, very large and complex very, very fast.

Try a quick thought experiment. Imagine you are a retailer and you want to build a database of customers. You could create a table with a row for each customer, including information such as their name, address, and email. Then you might want to keep track of their purchases, to determine their loyalty tier, which would require more columns with dates and amounts spent. But suppose you want to make offers tailored to their particular tastes – for example, featuring the kinds of products they buy, or might want to buy. That would require more columns with details about each of the products they bought, dates, and prices.

Think for a moment about the "products" column. Say you decided to put a number for each product, representing its shop-keeping unit (SKU), a standard designator for a product. That way you can keep track of all the SKUs each person bought. But imagine you want to run a sale for shoes, so you need a list of all the people who bought shoes in the past month. How would you create this list? All you have are SKUs, not item categories. So, you need to add many more columns for every single SKU that includes a description of the product, its size and color, etc.

Already you see how complicated this one table gets. In fact, it's clear that storing all the data in a single table, or even a few tables, is not practical. An answer to this problem was proposed by an IBM computer scientist named E. F. Codd in 1970 and was called the relational data model, which led to the invention of the relational database. The relational database is still widely used today, and was commercialized by Oracle. It still stores data in tables, with each row representing an entity (customer, item) and columns representing attributes (name, color). The innovation Codd proposed was to *relate* many smaller tables to one another in a structured way, using a common key or data point, so that complex information could be broken down into a series of much simpler, interwoven tables.

Using our example above, a relational database could create a table with *customer number* as the so-called primary key and a series of columns that list the SKUs purchased. Then a separate table could be created that uses *SKU* as the primary key (the row ID) and has a series of columns that provide a detailed description of each item. In this way, the complexity of the big table is spread across many more manageable ones.

A new challenge arises, however: how can the marketer do analyses on the multiple relational data tables? The answer is by using Structured Query Language (SQL), a query system designed to work directly on relational databases. In order to get a list of all the customers who bought shoes in a particular month, the marketer would simply need to write a query using SQL that specified the relevant tables and the attributes she wanted to find. The query would retrieve a list of the customer numbers associated with those attributes.

All this might seem like routine plumbing – and in a real sense, it is, – but the widespread adoption of relational databases and SQL made it possible for marketers to do more personalized marketing. In particular, they were able to pull better customer lists for batch email campaigns based on hypotheses that could be tested and improved over time. *Database marketing* became a profession, and it consisted primarily of writing SQL queries to produce customer lists based on criteria described manually to match a particular campaign.

THE RISE OF CRM AND MARKETING AUTOMATION

As marketers and sales professionals became more adept at handling databases, they naturally wanted to automate more of their day-to-day work. Automation describes the process of creating computer procedures that replicate usually mundane and often-repeated human tasks. Any task done by a human on a computer that is repetitive or can be described by a set of rules can – almost always – be automated.

Systems designed to automate business functions related to customers and accounts started to appear in the 1990s. These systems attempted to combine the workflow automation desired by sales and marketing teams with some of the more sophisticated statistical techniques developed by the database professionals into a package that could be used to improve efficiency. The umbrella term still used for such customer-facing automation systems is *customer relationship management (CRM)* software. The first CRM product, Siebel Systems, was launched in 1993, and by the late 1990s, there was something of a CRM-mania, driven in part by cheerleading from the influential analyst firm Gartner.

Salesforce was a pioneer in the CRM space with a then-revolutionary cloud-hosted subscription pricing model. Now the #1 CRM company globally, Salesforce describes CRM this way:

> Customer Relationship Management (CRM) is a technology for managing all your company's relationships and interactions with customers and potential customers. The goal is simple: Improve business relationships. A CRM system helps companies stay connected to customers, streamline processes, and improve profitability.

In the past two decades, CRM has expanded well beyond its origins as a way to automate database queries. Starting in sales and marketing, CRM expanded into customer service, and in the 2000s expanded further into e-commerce and field services, with some capabilities – such as analytics, voice-of-the-customer, and master data management (MDM) – spanning many domains. In fact, at last count, CRM encompassed 190 categories, with many large organizations employing hundreds or thousands of instances.

Marketing Automation

One key subset of CRM is *marketing automation*, which can be defined simply as CRM-like applications and services built for B2C and B2B marketers. Before the advent of marketing automation, the hard-working database marketer who wanted to run a campaign would generate a list by writing a manual SQL query against a relational database. The output of that query (i.e. the list of customer emails) would then be sent in batch to a separate email server, which would do its job of sending out the emails.

Starting in the mid-1990s, marketing automation systems such as IBM's Unica appeared that had a fundamentally different architecture (Figure 2.3). There was still a large relational database for storing the master customer

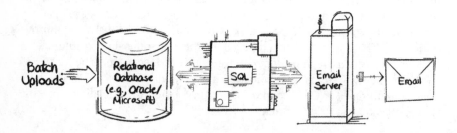

FIGURE 2.3 Marketing automation in its first iteration.

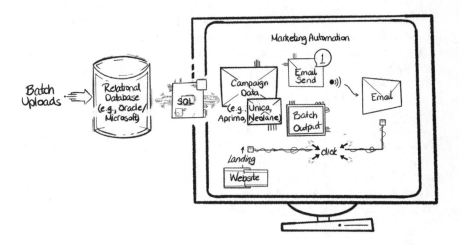

FIGURE 2.4   Marketing automation featuring a campaign database.

records, and this could still be accessed using SQL queries. However, these newer systems proceeded to offload some of the marketers' workload and improve her efficiency.

Marketing automation introduced a new database – specifically, for campaign-level data (Figure 2.4). This campaign data was still generated from the customer master database via SQL, but it took on a life of its own. In effect, customer lists were renamed *campaigns* and these campaigns could easily be automated. For example, the system could automate the updating of the customer lists and schedule a regular cadence of batch sending.

Improved User Interface (UI)

Perhaps the most important innovation of marketing automation applications, particularly those introduced in the 2000s such as Silverpop and ExactTarget, was the marketer-friendly UI. Manual SQL queries were no longer necessary, as users could drag-and-drop their instructions and visually lay out their desired "customer journeys." The result was a vastly expanded potential user base for the tools.

Some other new capabilities introduced by marketing automation systems in the 1990s and 2000s include:

- *Data beyond email* – with the ability to track and store data from landing pages and websites, to determine the outcome of email clicks and to register outcomes such as conversions. Later, data was collected from mobile apps and other sources as well.

- *Creating a feedback loop* – with the ability to measure conversions, rather than just count messages, the system can begin to generate reports, allowing marketers to improve performance over time.
- *Making A/B testing routine* – comparison of different marketing treatments, such as subject lines or offers, was built into these systems, accelerating the rate of learning for marketing teams.

But as we have noted, the most important impact in the long run was the creation of the campaign database. This separate database, refreshed with updates from the master (or "golden") record, allowed marketers to do their job – and do it more efficiently – operating as a shadow business, or a virtual island. What mattered to them was not *all* the data about customers but rather just the data they needed to execute and improve campaigns – that is, data relevant to marketing.

THE MULTICHANNEL MULTIVERSE OF THE THOROUGHLY MODERN MARKETER

As channels appeared, so did teams to support them – with the result that technology and teams proliferated, creating the near-chaos that surrounds us today. This proliferation of channels combined with a gradual expansion of the role and expectations of the marketing function, which had the effect of elevating the importance of the marketing customer database and paved the way for the current hype around the *customer data platform* (CDP).

To state the obvious, marketing automation automates *digital* marketing. In the 1990s, when digital marketing comprised a minute proportion of all marketing, its role was correspondingly minuscule. CEOs rarely cared what specific tools digital marketers used. Even in the early 2000s, as internet adoption soared, digital channels still made up only a small fraction of marketing effort and spend.

The Growth of Digital

Digital marketing started with email and exploded with the widespread penetration of the internet among households around the world. In 1995, only about one in ten US households had access to the internet. Ten years later, by 2005, penetration was at 70%, and it started to level off at just over 80% by 2009. That same year, smartphones appeared on the scene with the launch of Apple's iPhone, and within three years about 50% of the US population had an iPhone or other smartphone. Today that number is closer to 80%.

The growth of social networks was even more dramatic. When Facebook began making connections off campus in 2005, about one in twenty US adults used social media. In 2019, 80% of US adults use an increasingly diverse array of networks, from Facebook and Instagram to Twitter, LinkedIn and TikTok. As the leading network, Facebook (which also owns Instagram), reaches approximately one in three people on the planet today.

Obviously, the marketer has had to incorporate a host of new digital consumer touchpoints into their arsenal over the past two decades. These volatile consumer-driven requirements put unprecedented strain on already stressed marketing teams, forcing them to adapt to new modes of communication and consumer preferences, even as they try to evolve their data collection, analytics, and creative management functions.

Take a luxury automotive brand in the Midwest, an iconic brand one of us worked with for years. Their experience is typical. In the 2000s, they were doing sophisticated CRM programs using email channels in a batch-and-blast form, and employing a relational database and SQL queries to pull lists from a store of customer profiles. A separate team was created to manage and run the brand website. When smartphone use grew, in the 2010s, a separate team was created to manage the "mobile strategy," and this team acquired mobile analytics software. Then social networks became important, and a separate "social team" was created, which in turn acquired its own social management and listening tools.

The result was a natural process of accumulation, both of tools and teams, and the brand ended up with what its Chief Digital Officer not-so-lovingly described as "a train wreck." There were at least four uncoordinated teams, and three different agencies (creative, media planning, and CRM), each aligned around a different channel. They did not share information because their channels were fiefdoms. Even more critically, each team had its own martech and ad-tech systems, each of which had its own customer profile. So, by the time the brand did a data audit, they discovered that a *single customer could have data sitting in up to twelve different databases, which were not connected.*

The result? Obviously, the marketing processes and tech budget were not optimized or particularly efficient. Tasks were duplicated, and simple updates – such as changing a customer's last name when they got married, or updating their address when they moved – took too long. But the worst business impact was on experience. To put it kindly, the customer's experience was not coordinated. They might enter information on a website and have to repeat it on the phone; take an action on a mobile app that was not reflected when they logged into the website; follow one of the brands on social media and have that preference not reflected anywhere else.

Bear in mind that this brand was successful; its digital marketing had won prizes. All of its team members were competent professionals, and its agencies were highly respected. It was not lack of intelligence that led to the "mess" they were in. It was simply the rapid rate of change – "internet time" – they endured, and the nature of ad hoc adaptation.

It is precisely this disconnected data problem that the modern customer data platform aims to solve.

Today's Landscape

We've seen how the internet technology landscape of a typical brand became overcomplicated and inefficient, as channels piled on channels and teams spun up next to other teams. Outside the marketers' own walls, there was a similar proliferation of technology. Seeing an opportunity to sell to a new buying center – the CMO – with no shortage of problems to solve, hundreds and then thousands of smart ad-tech and martech startups found plenty of willing venture capital (VC) funding and began to multiply at a rapid clip in the 2010s.

ChiefMarTech, aka Scott Brinker, is a well-known blogger and pundit in the marketing technology industry. He released his first "Marketing Technology Landscape" logo map in 2011. It featured about 150 different vendors in categories ranging from email service providers to mobile management and social listening platforms. Each year since then, his updated Landscape graphics have had to expand their margins and shrink the size of logos to microscopic proportions in order to accommodate the flood of new vendors, each with their own "unique" value proposition to marketers. Eight years after his 150-logo inaugural graphic, the Landscape featured more than 7,000 vendors in 2019 and a whopping 8,000+ in 2020 (Figure 2.5).

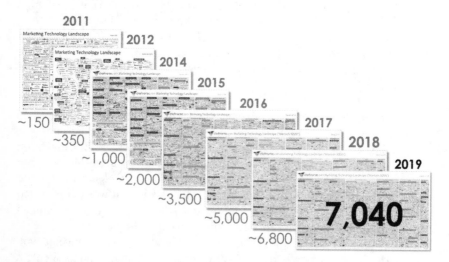

FIGURE 2.5   Growth in the "Marketing Technology Landscape."
Source: Courtesy of Scott Brinker, Chief Martech.

Today's Martech Frankenstack

The results of inner fragmentation and outer proliferation, combined with the pressure on marketing to deliver, resulted in the most common phenomenon today: the martech "Frankenstack."

Frankenstacks come in all shapes and sizes – in fact, that's what makes them Frankenstacks. They have in common an ad hoc design-in-flight structure, where a need to connect and reconnect systems that were not designed to work with one another struggles to serve the ever-changing needs of impatient business users. The result is a hodgepodge of technologies, each with their own particular purpose, the sum total of which can obscure the actual customer it is ultimately trying to serve. Customer-centric, it ain't.

There is a way out of the Frankenstack syndrome. In recent years, more advanced teams have begun to rethink their customer data architectures in fundamental ways, leading to the current customer data platform revolution. Often in concert with broader enterprise business transformation efforts, marketing technologists and their IT colleagues have put time into conceptual exercises or pseudo-marketectures pointing the way toward a more efficient future.

One such marketer is a major big box retailer, which decided a few years ago to do a gut rehab of its marketing systems. Starting from the ground up, the team sketched out a working system that would allow it to house customer data in a perpetual, updated store at scale, and meanwhile execute engagement with its customers (called "guests") in real time based on triggers and contextual signals.

What was interesting about their initial hypothesis was that it provided a two-layer architectural approach that we discovered – in a separate analysis that we'll describe in Chapter 3 – to be a key component of a true enterprise customer data platform. The team decided that there needed to be both a place to store customer data and do analytics and *another layer* that takes an abstract of the customer data and combines it with real-time systems to do tasks like real-time interaction management, decision, and content assembly. In other words, the customer data platform isn't just a customer information database to rule them all – it's *also* a real-time engagement system that makes split-second decisions.

What would an idealized marketing architecture look like, anyway? Well, it would differ by industry and requirements, of course, but its (very) high-level components would probably look something like Figure 2.6. It would require:

- *Unified user profile:* A unified customer profile that included data from all the various systems built up over the years, matched by ID and harmonized for use.

- *Smart segments:* The ability to perform segmentation, machine learning, and AI on this data.
- *Plan and react capability:* A campaign management and decision capability, where the marketer could set up preplanned journeys for customers and prospects, as well as develop rules (including machine learning-driven decisions) to handle in bound events, such as an unknown customer arriving on a website or mobile app.
- *Engagement:* The ability either to directly engage with the customer (e.g. by sending an email or SMS message) or interact with engagement systems that reach the customer on their channel of choice, often via application programming interfaces (APIs).
- *Optimization:* Finally, the ability to close the loop by capturing conversion and other signals, reporting results, and enabling or even recommending ways to improve outcomes.

That may seem clean and simple, but it's a very long drive from the marketing architecture used by the typical marketer. Given that the Frankenstack's architecture is likely closer to yours than the utopian diagram in Figure 2.6, how can a marketer get from point A to point B in the customer data management quest? That's what the rest of this book is about.

Ideal Marketecture

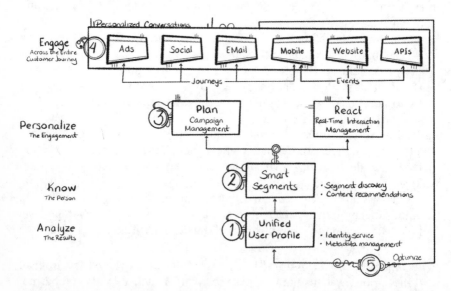

FIGURE 2.6   The ideal marketecture.
Source: Courtesy of Salesforce.

CUSTOMER-DRIVEN THINKER: SCOTT BRINKER

Scott Brinker is known to thousands of martech enthusiasts across the globe as @chiefmartec – author of a widely read and well-respected blog and newsletter on marketing technology, co-founder and CTO of ion interactive, chair of the MarTech conference series, and author of *Hacking Marketing*. Currently, Brinker is VP of Platform Ecosystems at Hubspot and the mastermind behind that ever-proliferating Marketing Technology Landscape logo map that becomes more inscrutable each year. As he told us, don't expect the number of logos to decline anytime soon – and that's not necessarily a bad thing.

Why do you think interest in the CDP category exploded in recent years?

It's the story of the martech space in general. It was growing steadily until about 2014 and then took a hockey-stick leap in the number of vendors and categories. It's the dynamics of how software development changed, how digital marketing started to change. For the CDP in particular, I can relate it to the landscape explosion. A big problem that people have across the landscape is that the [stuff] doesn't integrate. You have systems spewing data and you've got to orchestrate that ... CDP was an evolution. Marketers really wanted to be able to pull data, somehow make sense of it, rationalize identities, do analysis in context, segmentation, push data out into other services. The CDP emerged to [help] with that problem – things spewing out data.

Do you think the CDP is a new category or a natural evolution of CRM?

In my worldview, CRM has been the system of record for the martech stack. At the end of the day, everything has to come down to a single identity – not limited to marketing. The challenge is that most CRMs were classic relational databases. They have well-defined data structures to some extent you can customize. But as you customize, the database model can start to get complicated fast. What CDPs try to do is create an environment where there is a more flexible data model you don't have to define in advance. There is a dynamic structure to the CDP.

Where do you think the CDP category is going?

I know I write about categories, but I kind of hate them too. There are lots of products now that push the boundaries. It's more about what the customer wants to do rather than a predefined competitive set.

But putting aside the label of CDP, it's hard not to see a data platform as the bedrock of the martech stack. Everyone needs a flexible model for data around the customer. They need to rationalize and act on it. Maybe these capabilities get absorbed into things we call CRMs.

More broadly, I have a theory that there is going to be more diversification in software. This is counter to what others are saying. Look at how AWS and Google allow people to create highly specialized apps. It's wild and going to get more so. But I believe that having a common platform at the center of the martech stack makes the proliferation workable. Platforms such as CRMs and CDPs bring coherence to a diverse universe of apps by unifying the underlying data. Platforms turn the app explosion into a major benefit, not a headache. How many times do you go to a party and hear people rant that there are too many apps in the AppExchange? Never. Look at WordPress. It has 60,000 plug-ins ... Those platforms provide a stable foundation for blossoming ecosystems. But you need guardrails, the platforms, so all these apps are working from the same underlying source of truth.

SUMMARY: THE BRIEF, WONDROUS LIFE OF CUSTOMER DATA MANAGEMENT

- *Marketing heroes' journey:* In their ongoing quest to deliver the right message to the right person at the right moment, marketers have used the technology available. Starting with direct mail and statistical techniques, marketers harnessed computers in the 1960s to deliver targeted campaigns to households and track results.
- *Rise of automation:* As digital channels such as email and websites began to appear in the 1990s, enterprises began to rely first on relational databases and SQL queries, and then on increasingly sophisticated CRM and marketing automation systems, with their own customer data storage. The result was a multilayered stack, built up over years, that made the original vision of relevant one-to-one messaging very difficult.
- *Common themes:* It's always good to remember that the basic requirements of marketers don't really change, and that complexity itself doesn't change intentions. Marketers still need updated profiles with relevant information, gathered with consent; they still need to group customers into cohorts (segments) with similar traits; and they still need to know what message to deliver, when, and how to measure results. History grounds us in the present mission.
- *The ideal marketecture:* Companies may not be able to rip and replace their Frankenstack of legacy systems, but they can strive to re-architect their

systems within a framework that focuses on: a unified customer profile, intelligent segmentation, rules-based journey management that leverages AI for decisions, API-driven engagement to every endpoint the consumer interacts with, and optimization that works within a closed loop where historical data feeds go-forward recommendations. This is the recipe for success.

CHAPTER 3

What Is a CDP, Anyway?

Now that we understand the dynamics in data-driven marketing that have motivated the need for a solution like the CDP, we start defining the category. What is a CDP? What do marketers expect from them in terms of functionality? Are there different types of CDPs, based on different use cases? In this chapter, we define terms, organize CDPs into useful categories based on capability, define the essential "must haves" for CDPs, and discuss the emergence of a new category: the "enterprise" CDP.

RISE OF THE CUSTOMER DATA PLATFORM

We remember working for and analyzing the hottest data management technology of the last 20 years: the DMP, or "data management platform." We watched as this advertising technology went from an internal publisher tool for yield management only used by the most savvy of online publishers, to the data backbone powering programmatic advertising for the world's biggest brands, to a software category that fell out of favor, despite its continued usefulness. You could actually witness the evolution of the category through the volume of requests for proposals (RFPs) coming through software vendors. At the height of the market three or four years ago, Salesforce Audience Studio (formerly Krux) was receiving thousands of requests a year as companies who weren't even sure they needed a DMP suddenly were in the market, performing evaluations.

Watching the nascent CDP category is *déjà vu* all over again. Every company wants a CDP, but for slightly different reasons. The category is new, largely undefined, and confusing. As an example, in 2019, research firm Advertiser Perceptions asked hundreds of senior-level brand marketers and agencies, "What CDP have you used in the past 12 months?" The top three answers were Salesforce (62%), Adobe (49%), and Oracle (42%) (Figure 3.1).

The problem? None of those companies had an actual customer data platform in the market at that time! Clearly, marketers were using different types

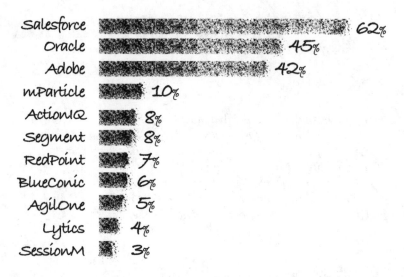

Customer Data Platforms Used in Past 12 Months.

FIGURE 3.1   Who are marketers using as a CDP?
Source: Courtesy of Advertiser Perceptions.

of data management tools, sometimes in combination, to achieve things like data unification, segmentation, activation, and insights. They probably didn't care what category of software the tools they were using were in. Yet, in software, businesses and analysts like to lump things into grouping (see Brinker's Martech Landscape Map in Chapter 2), and the CDP category has become a convenient catch all for all kinds of advertising and marketing software.

Many of the "CDPs" in the market today were built from the ground up to modernize older categories like "master data management" and have tried to create a very specific niche – some companies, like older tag management or personalization technologies, pivoted into the hot CDP category to chase venture capital dollars and revive flagging business fortunes.

"What is this thing called a CDP, anyway?"

In 2018, we wrote a column for the industry publication *AdExchanger* with that title. It was based on the past few years one of us (Kihn) spent as an industry analyst covering the customer data and analytics industries. Our firm kept track of client inquiry requests, which are the questions most commonly asked by marketing clients, and the top request, month after month, was the one in the title: *What is a CDP?*

The reason for the interest is that the CDP category seemingly appeared "out of nowhere" around 2016 and shot up the virtual "hype cycle," peaking sometime in late 2019. A hype cycle is a pattern seen among all tech categories (and celebrities, by the way): they appear, catch on, become buzzed and talked-about at industry conferences and webinars, startups and pivots jump into the space, and – of course – disillusion sets in, doubts are raised, and as fast as the category rose, it seems to fall to earth. It's a natural cycle, and smart marketers basically ignore it, focusing on fundamental problems and existing solutions. Hype is for PR pros, not data doyennes.

Like all fast-moving categories, the CDP at first suffered from confused definitions, blurred boundaries, and a lot of vendor hype. This situation is settling down, as we expect when a category matures. Our concern is not to dissect the "CDP" phenomenon, but rather to excavate the real problems marketers are trying to solve, and how this new flavor of CRM can help.

CDP as a martech category was born in 2013, in a series of blog posts and a report written by an independent martech analyst based in Philadelphia, named David Raab. In his report, Raab pointed out, "Marketers face a growing gap between what they need from their customer databases and what those databases actually do." He identified the specific problem as "the integration gap," and said, "reasons for the integration gap include lack of technology, missing marketer skills and organizational fiefdoms."

We agree. Although Raab, who later went on to found the Customer Data Platform Institute, has been teased for drawing too capacious boundaries around the category, letting too many vendors "in," he deserves credit for putting his mouse-finger on the fundamental problem of data *and* organizational lack of integration. Over the next few years, very few people talked about CDPs *per se,* but virtually all marketers tried to address the problem of data disconnection. Most of these efforts involved a combination of in-house IT-led initiatives – often involving data lakes and marts built on open source frameworks such as Hadoop, Cassandra, and Spark – and external vendors. Systems integration consultants such as Deloitte and Accenture reported growing numbers of "data integration" engagements.

Gradually, a set of capabilities loosely coupled under the label "Customer Data Platform" emerged. This happened as a theoretical exercise, since no single vendor yet existed who was capable of delivering this vision (no matter what they said). The idealized CDP feature set looked like Figure 3.2.

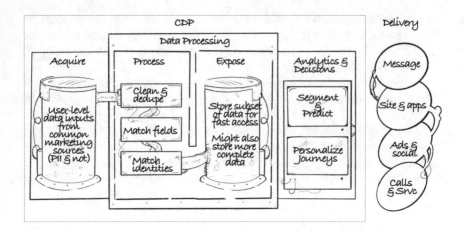

FIGURE 3.2 Depiction of the idealized CDP feature set.
Source: Courtesy of Salesforce.

The key components are:

- *Acquire:* The ability to natively collect and extract data from a wide variety of common sources.
- *Process:* Built-in tools to cleanse and manage both attributes (fields) and identity markers (IDs).
- *Expose:* Make the normalized, ID-mapped data available in a persistent data store.
- *Analytics and decisions:* Execute decisions and perform predictive analytics on the data.
- *Delivery:* Once decisions are made, send the signals to the engagement systems that actually deliver the message.

A couple of things to note about this wide-ranging construct. First, end-to-end, it encompasses pretty much all of marketing technology – so it's clearly an overambitious agenda to fold it all under one product category, let alone a single logo. Second, the "Expose" portion early on encompassed both a real-time or in-memory component and a more batch-mode, persistent, long-term data store. The reason is simple: some data would have to be available for rapid response (such as segment membership or key attributes, like "High Value Customer"), but most would not. And third, "Analytics and Decisions" were originally seen as optional, present (or partly present) in some purpose-built systems but not in most.

From the beginning, CDPs were more about data management than built-in analytics. They are not a business intelligence (BI) tool or an analytics workbench. Their role is to organize customer data and make it available to the systems that needed it, including BI tools and analytics workbenches. Like its close cousin, the DMP, the CDP lives in the unglamorous but absolutely essential world of plumbing and day-to-day data management.

As we followed the CDP conversation, we began to notice something else. It looked a lot like CRM, as originally conceived. Recall that in the 1990s, CRM for marketing promised a single view of the customer, the ability to harmonize and deduplicate data records, and persistent storage. Later, marketing automation systems added the ability to apply rules and even statistical algorithms to the data and send decisions to external systems, such as websites, to deliver more personalized marketing (Figure 3.3).

In other words, the promises made by CRM for marketing systems in the past are almost identical to those made by CDP for marketing systems today. And this makes sense: the problems faced by marketers, though more complex, are no different in kind. They still just want to deliver the right message to the right person in the moments that matter. So, the CDP category is not new; it is not an invention *de novo*. Rather it represents the latest evolution of the CRM category, applied to B2C and then to B2B contexts, and expanding (as CRM did) well beyond marketing into service, commerce, sales, and beyond.

What Marketers Really Want from the CDP

It became clear by late 2018 that we could learn very little about what marketers really needed by studying the CDP vendor space. The Customer Data Platform Institute boasts 90-plus members, and counting. Every vendor calling itself a "CDP" was different from every other, and in some cases their capabilities did not even overlap. No wonder so many analyst clients were asking, "What is this thing called a CDP?" No two vendors agreed, and marketers

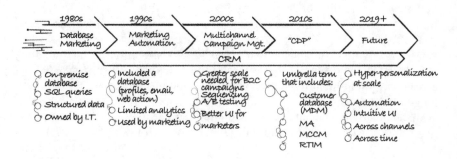

FIGURE 3.3 The history of customer relationship management.
Source: Courtesy of Salesforce.

were growing frustrated. It became clear that the answer lay, as always, with the actual users.

THE GREAT RFP ADVENTURE

We decided to take a bottom-up approach to figuring out what a CDP was by reading through hundreds of the requests for proposals (RFPs) we were getting at Salesforce. What problems were marketers trying to solve? What types of buyers were asking for this technology – digital marketers, email marketers, analysts? What were the requirements to win a "CDP" deal? We sat down and read through a dense collection of these requests.

Quickly, we began to discover the reason that the "CDP" category was so difficult to define – basically, it could be almost anything the user wanted it to be. Unlike DMPs – known for capturing, unifying, and activating pseudonymous user data – requests for CDP functionality were all over the map. We looked at over 300 highly detailed requests from the world's biggest companies: major global retailers, banks, fashion houses, pharmaceutical companies, energy companies, and technology companies. The requests for functionality ranged from getting "a single view of the customer" to "personalizing every touchpoint across channels," to building "a new data-driven multitouch attribution engine."

Some customers wanted to fix a very specific problem, such as unifying data sitting in dozens of different legacy systems. Some were looking to solve highly specific use cases, such as utilizing e-commerce purchase data to personalize visits on a website. Still others were looking to find a wider variety of customer data to improve their segmentation for advertising use cases. Some companies wanted it all.

While the RFPs read at times like wish lists for Santa, they were done in good faith and reflected genuine pain on the part of real marketers. In terms of use cases, a number of distinct themes emerged. A healthy cross-section of marketers told us they wanted a tool to help them with the following issues:

- *Cross-channel campaign management:* Manage the frequency and sequence of messages across the website, app, email, and ads, e.g. do not promote a product in an email that a person just bought on the website or in the store.
- *Segmentation:* The ability to build better segments from more complete profiles. Also, for better up-selling and cross-selling, by recommending items in an app based on what a person looked at on a website, as an example. And to have more accurate lifetime value (LTV) and value-based segments so they could send better offers to high-value customers who were dormant.

- *Loyalty:* Offer management and loyalty (despite the fact that many vendors already offer loyalty management solutions).
- *Measurement:* Calculate more accurate ROI for marketing tactics, so they could know what works and what doesn't, based on real outcomes, such as in-store sales, clicks, or form-fills.

Most of these requirements are generally within the realm of more traditional CRM and marketing automation solutions. What is different is the scale and the scope of the requirements: more channels, greater speed, faster and smarter decisions.

We also kept track of more detailed product features requested by these marketers and pulled out salient themes. In order to achieve the outcomes above, marketers told us they wanted a tool to help them do the following key tasks:

- *Profile building:* The ability to build and store a profile of a user who is known (PII) or unknown (pseudonymous).
- *Data ingestion:* The ability to receive data from common systems – the most often cited were email, website (tag management, content management systems), mobile apps, e-commerce, analytics (Adobe and Google), point-of-sale (stores, event venues), and enterprise data warehouses.
- *Identity management:* The ability to tie records from ingested data to a unique individual or account, including probabilistic (fuzzy) matching, cleansing, deduplication, and householding (mapping associated profiles together).
- *Normalization:* Provide manual and automated ways to normalize the attributes in data tables, e.g., so the same attributes from different sources share a label.
- *Marketer-friendly UI:* Of course, users wanted the ability to democratize customer data beyond SQL power users, with drag-and-drop segmentation and point-and-click rule building.

"We Want a Platform, Not a Product"

While we found a fairly simple way to bucket the marketers' overall requests into two broad categories (see below), what really struck us was that all of these companies were looking for an operating system they could use to organize the technology investments that had been made – and were continuing to be made – in marketing and advertising technology. In simple terms, how could a company leverage a platform that could sit underneath a "Lumascape" or "Martech Technology Landscape" and help them plug into all of the cool innovation thousands of vendors were building?

Building a Platform Solution

Ultimately, we see the CDP game as a *platform* challenge. Companies are living in a world of ever-changing technology, cool new innovative tools are coming out all of the time, but every new addition sparks a nightmarish integration challenge. Marketers want to be on the cutting edge and license new tech, but find themselves struggling to integrate every new system into their "stack," get adoption throughout the organization, and create value. Could the CDP be the underlying tool that serves as the operating system that marketing and advertising tech plugs into?

According to the Mulesoft Connectivity Benchmark Report in 2019, 53% of organizations reported having 800 or more applications in use, with 43% having 1,000 or more – but only slightly more than a quarter of them are integrated. If the logo growth in both the advertising and marketing technology landscapes represents an application for every problem, then CDP represents the desire for enterprises to unify and integrate the landscape. The glue? Customer data.

CDP CAPABILITIES

In order to empower customer data to be the single thread connecting thousands of different marketing, advertising, and customer-centric applications, CDPs have to do a few things well. We discovered five broad categories of capabilities, which we think of as minimum-level functionality. Every CDP will do some things better than others, but every offering that wants to claim membership in the category will need these basic capabilities: data collection, data management, profile unification, segmentation and activation, and insights (Figure 3.4).

For example, an auto dealer would expect the CDP to capture a user's data when they fill out the "take a test drive" form on a website, align that data so it fits into their database, create a new customer record (or update an existing one), place the user into the right segment of "auto intenders," send them an email offer, and be able to see whether or not the offer was accepted. It's the same basic functionality we've had in marketing systems for decades – but the difference is in the CDP's ability to perform those functions in a world where the variety, scale, and velocity of that data have increased exponentially – alongside the amount of channels and expectation of real-time interaction. Let's define the five minimum requirements in more detail.

Data Collection

CDPs need a way to collect a wide variety of customer data, both natively and through batch-oriented processes (manually uploading records). They must

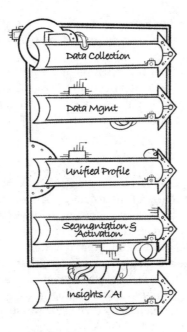

FIGURE 3.4   Five categories of
CDP capability.
Source: Courtesy of Salesforce.

also offer the ability to capture data through APIs (application programming interfaces) SDKs (software development kits), or JavaScript tags. A good CDP will have data connectors built in, to enable inbound data partners to plug in, and also be able to capture data from both known (PII-based) and unknown (pseudonymous) sources. To manage today's customer journey, the modern data platform must account for the wide variety of customer data available for collection across websites, forms, mobile applications, loyalty systems, data warehouses, second- and third-party data stores, and traditional databases. Getting just a few of these right doesn't count if the goal is to capture the data required to provision the true "golden record" of customers.

Data Management

This capability category sounds a bit confusing at first – isn't the whole thing about managing data? Yes, but when we think of "data management" specific to CDP, we are talking about the classification of data within the system, how it is defined, and the overall schema the data is organized into. At its simplest, it's the ability to reconcile the difference between "FirstName" and

"First_Name" fields in two different databases – but it's also at the heart of holistic data unification, and setting up the ability to provision that mystical "golden record."

We will delve into a nerdy discussion of the nuts and bolts of things like "fuzzy name matching" in greater detail in Chapter 4, but think of "data management" as the manipulation of disparate customer data into a common format so it can be queried and accessed at scale.

Profile Unification

Marketers who send a lot of emails tend to think in terms of "contacts," and the molecular structure of their data centers on this (name plus email address plus some attributes). This tends to work well in isolation, but falls apart when people have more than one email address they use, or interact with a brand across another channel that doesn't depend on an email as the primary identifier (like a website) – in other words, everyone. The basic idea of profile unification is to move from static, singular "contacts" to rich profiles of people that not only unify multiple contact records for the same person, but also include the other identifiers they use (browser cookies, device IDs, a company's first-party ID, etc.).

The most useful profile should not only align people data stored in multiple records across multiple data stores, but also records that include someone's loyalty profile, call center activity, marketing interaction data, advertising engagement data, and even third-party data like a credit score. Profile unification depends on the two capabilities above (the ability to capture data from different sources, and the ability to "manage" it into a common taxonomy). Profile unification lies at the very center of CDP. You cannot do it well without data collection and management. Moreover, segmentation, activation, and insights are only as effective as the fidelity of the profile allows.

Segmentation and Activation

Once all the relevant data has been associated into a unified profile, marketers need a way to organize customer data into scalable segments to get reach. Although marketers have always dreamed of perfect "one-to-one" engagement – and it is quite possible in theory – the world is not quite operating at the scale to allow every individual to receive perfectly tailored cross-channel experiences in real time. Brands need to organize their customer data into segments that align with their ability to match creative executions. The biggest problem with customer audience segmentation over the years has been the sheer number of places that it happens. The email team builds lists of known contacts in their ESP, the digital team builds segments of pseudonymous

IDs in their DMP, and the brand and their agencies are constantly building audiences in platforms like Facebook and Google.

The promise of CDPs is not only aligning customer data – but unifying the place where marketers do the work of segmentation. The right tool should enable a business user to put together a broad set of attributes (media engagement, web analytics data, purchase data, third-party data, and even things like call center interaction data) using a declarative, easy-to-use interface. Marketers should be able to dream up the most granular of segments (middle-aged suburban men who love sports, but drink wine instead of beer) and see how many of them there are in the data store.

Once segmentation is complete, activation is the next priority. Where can I find these consumers? DMPs typically activate data on the open web, for programmatic media. CDPs need to think beyond advertising use cases and activate customer data wherever it's needed: email campaigns, display advertising, social media networks, website personalization platforms, and platforms that drive dynamic optimization. Going further, the enterprise CDP should be able to serve as the "source of truth" for decision-making in other systems that have a consumer endpoint: e-commerce systems that might decide what to show a user based on their last purchases, or call center employees who might read a different script based on the segment a customer falls into (new, return customer, highly engaged, or high probability of churning).

Insights/AI

CDPs are creating an interesting dynamic, as many different channel-specific platforms will start to see more intelligence built into the place where the customer data is stored rather than the endpoint. What do we mean? Take all of the amazing intelligence built into the DMP over the last decade, such as the ability to use artificial intelligence to build segments, or the capability to overlap audience data to create scaled lookalike models. As the CDP takes over as a more robust central data store featuring richer attributes, it makes more sense for those capabilities to live alongside the customer data. Same with email systems that can predict the right content to send, the best time of data to trigger a message, or the engagement score for a particular user.

Because CDPs will cut across multiple channels, and be the core source of truth for customer data, it makes sense that they should be the main source of detailed data for AI to run across. As a result, over time we will start to see channel-specific systems (DMPs, ESPs, social media plug-ins, web personalization tools, and the like) focused more on real-time delivery at each endpoint, rather than the source of AI-driven insights. A good CDP will initially focus on data-specific analytics, looking at things like consent across the data set, migration of users in and out of segments, broad cross-channel

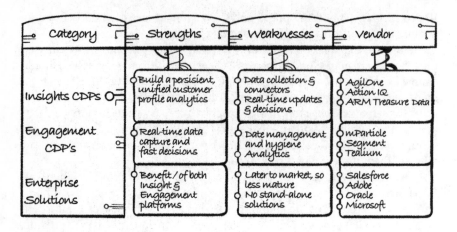

Category	Strengths	Weaknesses	Vendor
Insights CDPs	Build a persistent, unified customer profile analytics	Data collection & connectors Real-time updates & decisions	AgilOne Action IQ ARM Treasure Data
Engagement CDP's	Real-time data capture and fast decisions	Date management and hygiene Analytics	mParticle Segment Tealium
Enterprise Solutions	Benefit / of both Insight & Engagement platforms	Later to market, so less mature No stand-alone solutions	Salesforce Adobe Oracle Microsoft

FIGURE 3.5 The three types of CDPs.
Source: Courtesy of Salesforce.

engagement, lifetime value (LTV), and propensity scoring. In the future, CDPs might start to concern themselves with multitouch attribution (more on this in Chapter 11), and delivering models that get a truer sense of how customers experience interactions across channels that go well beyond marketing touchpoints.

The Two (Actually Three) Types of CDPs

What became clear after reading 400 proposal requests was that there were two very distinct uber-trends that cut across the many different capabilities that companies were asking for (Figure 3.5).

A SYSTEM OF INSIGHTS

Some marketers wanted a system focused on sorting out data silo problems, as discussed above. They had lots of customer data in lots of different systems, many different identifiers, and lots of error and duplication. These companies wanted a "golden record" of the customer – a profile that would serve as the single source of truth for customer data that every stakeholder across the enterprise could refer to. They needed the ability to query the data easily, enrich it with different attributes (service, commerce, and sales engagement), and also make it smarter by adding things like propensity scores to a profile to sort out customers more (or less) receptive to marketing. We started to think about this system of data organization as a *"system of insight"* – more concerned with what one could learn about a customer than how one could interact with them.

Customers looking for this type of CDP wanted any number of these capabilities (lifted directly from those RFPs):

- data unification
- data cleansing
- deduplication of customer records
- federated ID across my systems
- "golden record" of my customers
- "single source of truth" for customer data
- lead scoring
- master data management
- manage creation, deletion of customer data in a central store
- stitching different IDs together in a single profile
- enriching customer records with second- and third-party data
- managing consumer consent for GDPR
- building customer segments
- add computed attributes to a customer profile
- unifying customer data between clienteling application and marketing data
- single place to query user data for analysis

These types of proposal requests were all centered around getting a better understanding of customer data by making it more unified, easier to connect, and easier to query. As discussed in Chapter 2, companies have been evaluating and buying this type of software since the early days of direct mail. Today's challenge is that – instead of the nice, computerized list of donors the Society of the Divine Savior had – now companies have customer data in dozens if not hundreds of different systems, and different types of customer data, from email addresses, to postal, to online cookies, to mobile advertising IDs. If we only had a system that could unify all of this disparate data, we could actually learn something new about our customers, and make our marketing better!

These "systems of insight" would serve as the single source of customer truth, the aggregation point for the many different sources of organizational data, and offer a way to stitch different data attributes together to get smarter about the people interacting with your brand. Ultimately, such a system would be able to bring different first-party data attributes together from the company (marketing engagement, advertising engagement, what people previously purchased, call center interactions, et al.) and add in second-party data and third-party data (credit score, purchase intent, etc.) to get a really rich profile.

SYSTEM OF ENGAGEMENT

Other proposal requests featured quite different use cases, centered around using data to personalize interactions customers have across the typical customer journey: creative executions in online advertising, offers in emails, products featured on e-commerce sites, or what homepage a consumer might see when visiting a company's website for the first time. Unlike systems of insight, slower moving systems where data is meant to be queried and manipulated by an end user, these systems were required to have data in a real-time customer profile store, red hot, and ready to be accessed by other applications to make decisions in milliseconds.

Customers looking for this type of CDP cited the following needs in their requests:

- serve first-time website visitors the right page based on their profile
- decide which offer to deliver to a customer on email
- up-sell/cross-sell by matching existing customers with next best offer
- decide, based on last brand interaction, what next message/offer is on another channel
- centralized and predictive segmentation
- predictive real-time offer management
- deliver the right mobile offer
- manage "next best action" (NBA) on different endpoints
- power dynamic creative optimization (DCO), or the ability to deliver creative advertising executions based on data
- automatically update customer propensity score in real time
- use rules to move streaming profiles from one segment to another

For these use cases, the CDP needed to be fast-moving, and capture and activate people data in near real time. Unlike the "Insights" CDP, these systems favor actionability over the manipulation of customer data for segmentation. Many of the CDPs in this category started as tag management systems, or real-time interaction management tools (RTIM), and pivoted to become "CDPs" to chase the generous amount of venture capital money – and customers – entering the category. Most can lay claim to very important aspects of CDP – namely, managing a real-time profile store of customer data and activating them – but these systems are hard to use for traditional "data management" use cases, like data cleansing, unification, and deep segmentation.

We visualized the different requirements ("They Want to …") and the ultimate dualistic solution set like this (Figure 3.6).

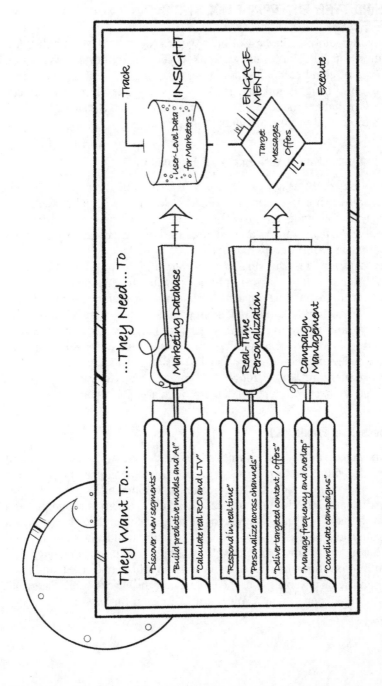

FIGURE 3.6 Results of the "great RFP adventure."
Source: Courtesy of Salesforce.

THE THIRD TYPE: ENTERPRISE HOLISTIC CDP

What if you could put the best of both worlds together? Peanut butter and chocolate, if you will. That's what we think will occupy the developers working for the biggest cloud companies for some time to come: efforts to combine the strengths of insights and engagement CDPs into one, enterprise-strength offering. So, what are the requirements for building such a system? We think there are three, and they set a high bar for success.

Known and Unknown (CDMP) Data Must Be Unified

We like to joke that the successful CDP will have to be the best of CDP and DMP combined, but the term we coined, "CDMP," is actually resonating with analysts following the space. As discussed in the Introduction, it's not possible to truly understand customers without accounting for their interactions across PII and pseudonymous data modalities. Customers tend to weave between "known" channels like email and "unknown" channels like a website at will, and it's simply not possible to construct a customer journey without reconciling the identity data produced along the way. Today, marketers spend lots of time and money "onboarding" data from known to unknown and trying to re-identify it back. The hops required to match the data and heavy consent requirements needed for doing so are highly inefficient today and require two expensive systems. This leads to two places for segmentation and lots of room for error. We see a future in which the "pipes" that connect both types of data reside in a single system.

A Business-User Friendly UI

One of the biggest missed opportunities over the decades in data management has been designing data systems for technical people. Today, even though we live in a world of "clicks, not code" development, "drag-and-drop" functionality, and intuitive user interface design, marketers must go through their counterparts in IT to get access to valuable customer data. As the saying goes, "Data is the new oil." Yet, just like petroleum, it must be extracted and refined before it can power anything. Why should the curious marketer who wants to find out how many customers have bought between $50 and $200 of merchandise on a website over the last six months have to submit a formal request to the IT department? You find this in even the most sophisticated of companies: customer data, centralized in a data warehouse or data lake, and just a few power users who know how to query the data using SQL or R. Unlocking the value of unified customer data requires an interface that enables business users to query, analyze, and segment customer data on the fly. This will enable a lot of hidden business value to be unlocked as the best marketers spend their time querying their data asset and testing new theories quickly, rather than acting as interdepartmental diplomats seeking the release of business critical data from gatekeepers.

A Platform Ecosystem

The third, and arguably most important, aspect is the way in which tomorrow's enterprise CDP will be built. We talked about the hundreds of companies in the Lumascape and 8,000+ companies in the Martech Landscape Map. How can you take advantage of the cool new applications you need at scale? How do you future-proof your technology strategy in a world where the hottest new software offerings seem to pop up out of nowhere and command attention? What is the substrate upon which you can lay these expanding capabilities and make them instantly useful to your organization? As discussed above, there is a requirement for an operating system to organize today's wildly disconnected ecosystem – a platform-based approach.

By their very nature, platforms spur innovation by giving developers a canvas for creating new business ideas – alongside an active marketplace of buyers. In a world with almost 10,000 innovative marketing and advertising technologies – and new ones popping up seemingly every day – the only way to organize such chaos is through a common code base and application exchange. This will be a heavy lift for CDP players building solutions on proprietary technology, and also challenging for players (Oracle, Microsoft) looking to build upon legacy infrastructure. That said, this approach will be a requirement for "enterprise" strength CDPs.

In a recent interview with *Ad Age*, Scott Brinker said:

> The barrier for entry [in marketing technology] has really changed in the last five years. It's much easier now and anyone can make a specialty app. Now, anyone in their basement can make a specialty app ... In such an environment, the value of any individual app as a monolith diminishes. What becomes more important all the time is the platform environment, the foundational services and capabilities that support the blooming of a thriving app ecosystem.

THE FUTURE IS HERE

This platform theory aligns with what our friend Scott Brinker has been calling the "second golden age of martech," an era in which platform dynamics will shape the winners and losers in the space (Figure 3.7).

In other words, the marketing world is moving from "suites" with lots of loosely connected applications to "platform ecosystems" which can be provisioned on a "common core" infrastructure. When they adopt a common platform to plug into, marketers can finally stop having to choose between best-of-breed applications for different types of channel marketing based on their integration capabilities – and finally get the assurance that most of the technology they end up acquiring can "plug into" their platform. It's a highly disruptive notion, but anyone familiar with the way Microsoft or Salesforce has built their platforms understands the power of thousands of developers working on a common platform, and the power that application marketplaces and APIs bring to the table.

We think that the future of CDPs will follow the same trends we have seen in cloud platforms: a race to gain market share among the world's biggest companies who are looking to centralize their customer data asset, and will pick a horse to bet on. Following the dynamics of CRM software, once customer data becomes centralized in a single platform that becomes the "source of truth," it becomes challenging, if not downright painful, to move to another provider.

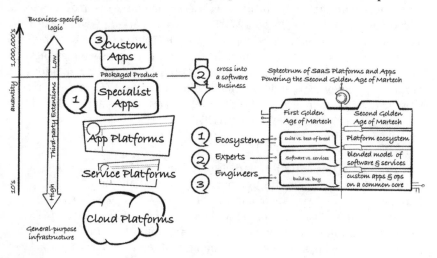

FIGURE 3.7   Platform ecosystem.
Source: Courtesy of Scott Brinker, Chiefmartech.

CUSTOMER-DRIVEN THINKER: DAVID RAAB

In some enlightened quarters, David Raab is known as the "Godfather" of the CDP. Why? Because he's the guy who first identified, wrote about and – yes – named the category back in 2013. Raab has been principal of his own analyst shop since the 1980s, after enjoying a Harvard MBA and a stint as a marketer. In 2016, he started the Customer Data Platform Institute, a vendor-neutral clearinghouse for industry information and standards-setting, and he's an advisor, speaker, and writer on martech topics – especially the CDP.

Is it true that you invented the Customer Data Platform category?

> Well, I'm the person who named it. The first time I used the term "Customer Data Platform" was in a blog post I wrote in April 2013. It was titled "I've Discovered a New Class of System: the Customer Data Platform." I came up with the term in a very scientific way: I made sure the acronym [CDP] was available. After that, I kept on talking about it, and eventually people started paying attention to it.

What was so different about this system?

> What was new was that there was packaged software that was doing things that used to be more custom-built. Until the CDP, you would have a marketing application, such as campaign management, that connected to a custom-built database. For the first time, I was seeing an application [the CDP] that built its own database. Originally, I said the CDP was the application plus that database, but later I decided the core was the database itself. The different types of CDPs I originally identified were campaign engines, audience management, customer retention, and B2B data enhancement.

When did the category really start to get noticed?

> It took a while for the term to catch on. The whole thing really exploded in 2016. Why? I don't know. No one thing happened. I guess the time was just right … I started the Customer Data Platform Institute in 2016, right when it took off. I didn't want any single vendor to own it, so I made the Institute vendor-neutral. The vendors themselves were enthusiastic. Pretty soon, it became a full-time job.

What do you predict for the future of the CDP category?

In the future, everybody's architectural diagram is going to have to have a box labeled CDP. The box will fit between all the data sources on the left side and all the data consumers on the right. We sometimes call this the "squashed spider diagram." My main achievement will be that the label on that box will be "CDP." I'm not sure if in future that box will be a standalone system from an indie vendor or a component of another system, like an email or e-commerce platform. But the box will be in every architecture.

SUMMARY: WHAT IS A CDP?

- *Rise of the CDP:* CDP as a software category was born in 2013 to address "the integration gap" in data that created silos between marketing channels, and the groups in the organization that managed them. The category exploded in 2017, earning a spot on the Gartner "hype cycle." The category is still broad and largely undefined, with many different vendors addressing integration problems across multiple data types, and solving many different activation and analytics use cases. There is still no broad industry consensus on an accepted definition of "CDP."
- *CDP core requirements:* We analyzed over 400 requests for proposal, performing a bottom-up analysis of what marketers wanted from the CDP technology category. They boiled down to five areas of capability: data collection, data management, data unification, segmentation/activation, and insights. These capabilities were exactly like those in the data management platform (DMP) for managing pseudonymous, but inclusive of known (PII-based) customer data.
- *CDP advanced requirements:* More advanced marketers are looking for capabilities for identity management across known and unknown data (both customer resolution and cross-device identity), maintaining a real-time profile store for activating data for personalization, machine-learning to drive propensity modeling, and advanced consent management to address consumer privacy requirements.
- *Systems of insight and engagement:* Our analysis revealed two highly distinct "buckets" of use-case based functionality. "*Insights*" CDPs, primarily needed to deliver a "single source of truth" across customer data by unifying customer records into unified profiles, and making them available for segmentation, activation, and analysis. This type of CDP delivered functionality similar to traditional CRMs or master data management (MDM)

solutions. *"Engagement"* CDPs were primarily concerned with leveraging real-time profile store of customer data to manage personalization across channels including messaging offers, website content, and advertising creatives. This type of CDP delivered functionality akin to DMPs, tag managers, or marketing personalization vendors. No vendors covered both capabilities fully.

- *The "enterprise" CDP:* Given the binary nature of the CDP landscape (vendors falling into the "insights" or "engagement" category), we see the opportunity to define a category for "enterprise" CDP that encompasses both and represents a best-of-breed offering. There are three requirements to be successful. First, the ability to unify both "known" (PII-based) and "unknown" (pseudonymous) data, and produce a rich customer profile based on consent. Second, the ability to provision a declarative and easy-to-use user interface that enables business users (not technical users) to import, query, manipulate, and enrich customer data. Finally, enterprise CDPs must be built on a platform that provides a code base for outside development and an ecosystem (or marketplace) for applications, such that companies can take advantage of innovation.
- *Platform dynamics in CDP:* In a world with almost 10,000 innovative marketing and advertising technologies – and new ones popping up every day – the only way to organize such chaos is through a common code base and application exchange. Only a CDP built upon a platform can facilitate this type of flexibility and future-proofing.

CHAPTER 4

Organizing Customer Data

In Chapter 3, we discussed the different kinds of customer data platforms (CDPs), including their core requirements. In this chapter, we describe the industry standard and other definitions of the components of the CDP. As we'll see, this definition isn't as definite and baked as we might expect, and is characteristic of a relatively nascent, developing category. We also look at what it actually takes to start stitching together data silos to create a single view, and take a deeper dive into the five specific parts of the solution in more depth. Key capabilities and processes, such as identity management, harmonization, segmentation, and activation are described.

MUNGING DATA IN THE MIDWEST

Nestled in the heart of Midwestern dairy country, Land O' Lakes is a cherished American institution. This Fortune 500 food business has $13 billion in sales, 10,000 employees, and is the third-largest US farmer-owned cooperative, with a presence in all fifty states and more than fifty countries. Four business units span the agribusiness model from crop and animal feed to a well-known consumer dairy business, anchored by its Land O' Lakes Butter, slathered on pancakes and toast more often than any other spread in the heartland middle states.

Yet in 2016, Land O' Lakes faced a data dilemma. Its Minnesota-based data practice leads, Dwayne Beberg and Chakra Sankaraiah, realized the company's farm-to-fork business model presented both promise and peril as they attempted to revolutionize their legacy marketing engine. In particular, Land O' Lakes' different business units were siloed, with different data stores, and its channels were likewise managing customer data in isolation from one another. Sound familiar?

Luckily for the company's growth mandate, the marketing and IT teams had a deep bench of practitioners with experience in data management and large-scale integration projects. They set up a data center of excellence with expertise in data architecture, Big Data, visualization, and data engineering. Their bias was toward home-grown solutions, and in particular they experimented widely with open source architectures ranging from Apache Kafka and Spark for data streaming to Hadoop for storage and Elastic Search and R for data mining.

From the beginning, the team looked to external best practices. They realized that data management would allow them to do better analytics, which would yield direct business benefits in three key areas:

- *Make better-informed decisions:* Like a competitive agribusiness that had been able to cut inventory levels by 81% by configuring farm machinery better.
- *Discover new insights:* Like an insurance company (Infinity), which reduced fraudulent claims by 75% using historical text analytics.
- *Automate business processes:* Like McDonald's, which claimed to eliminate thousands of pounds of bun waste through photo analysis of their buns in production.

To serve these and other business goals, the team built a Digital Command Center (DCC), which presented real-time visualizations of social media streams, website click streams, internet search results, and various business metrics. Although the DCC dashboards were intuitive and easy to use, they disguised an enormous amount of planning and work behind the scenes.

For example, Beberg and Sankaraiah summarized their data management solution in four pillars:

- *Ingestion:* Used Apache Nifi to consolidate data flows from clickstream, social media, search, and other sources.
- *Store & analyze:* Used Hadoop for raw storage, and Hive and other internal tables to build a "cleaner data model" for power users.
- *Discovery & API access:* This was enabled with ElasticSearch and Kibana, and through integration with Hive (above).
- *Engagement layer:* In the case of the DCC, engagement was a crowd-sourced dashboard which was implemented using APIs and D3 for JavaScript visualization.

The result was a powerful analytics suite that was based on a solid data management pipeline. With the pipeline in place, business users could make better decisions based on fresh, consolidated data. Meanwhile, data analysts could dig into cross-business unit data sets to uncover new ideas for cross-sell, up-sell, supply chain efficiencies, and even new products.

ELEMENTS OF A DATA PIPELINE

As the example of Land O' Lakes shows, managing data is a complex task. We should point out that the team didn't spend lots of time writing code because they had nothing better to do; in fact, they couldn't find tools to do what they wanted. Midproject, Beberg was delighted to learn about a startup called Datorama, which could automate some of the marketing campaign data integration steps, and he quickly signed them up.

Today, there are more tools available to help marketers and others manage all the myriad tendrils of their customer data requirements. (Impressed by its success integrating data at companies like Land O' Lakes, Salesforce acquired Datorama in 2018.) Fewer and fewer teams today choose to do-it-yourself using open source tools. Regardless of the specific process or vendors employed, data management encompasses a number of steps that must be executed in turn for success.

At the highest level, the key steps for successful data management are, as shown in Figure 4.1:

- *Acquire:* Data collection (often in real time) from existing channels, such as websites and mobile apps; and data ingestion from other data stores, including CRM (customer relationship management) and point-of-sale (POS) systems, email providers, and more.
- *Organize:* The process of transforming data from disparate original sources into a common data model to allow analysis; includes also identity management, which links IDs together.
- *Analyze:* Analytical processes, such as segmentation, machine learning, and Artificial Intelligence.

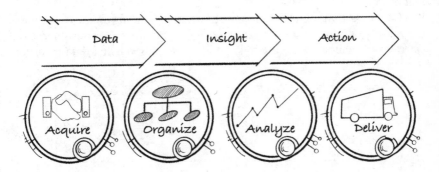

FIGURE 4.1 High-level data management model.
Source: Courtesy of Salesforce.

- *Deliver:* Sending signals to systems of engagement with instructions and content, based on embedded decisions; visualizing data; includes exporting data for more persistent use elsewhere.

This generic data management model can easily be mapped to the CDP requirements outlined in Chapter 3, as follows.

DATA MANAGEMENT STEPS

For the rest of this chapter, we'll use the consolidated requirements in the third column in Figure 4.2, as providing a more descriptive and tactical set of labels for the key categories of work. But you can see how they align with the generic industry component model cleanly.

1 Data Ingestion

Data ingestion is the customer data management phase where all the disparate, far-flung data about your customers (or accounts, or whatever) that you'd like to unlock is identified and pointed toward a centralized architecture. There are a lot of ways to "point" and store data – including physical and virtual methodologies – but for the sake of clarity we will focus here simply on the ways in which customer data is collected for use.

The purpose of the data ingestion or acquisition step is to identify data sources, ensure that the needed data is collected, and produce it in such a way that it is available for the next steps, i.e. harmonization and identity management.

Data ingestion requires different strategies depending on the data source, the velocity of information, and the type of information to be consumed. Considerations include the ability to support high-volume batch data ingestion,

Generic	CPD Capability (Chapter)	Consolidated Req's
Acquire	Data Collection	Data Ingestion
Oragnize	Data Management	Data Harmonization
	Unified Profile	Identity Management
Analyze	Segmentation, Insights & AI	Segmentation
Deliver	Activation	Activastion

FIGURE 4.2 High-level model, mapped to CDP requirements.
Source: Courtesy of Salesforce.

real-time stream data processing, messaging subscription-publication, highly volatile or unstructured data (e.g. call center transcripts), and others.

The two main patterns for data collection are:

- *Batch processing:* An asynchronous method for ingesting and storing data in bounded intervals. This method is effective for processing high volumes of data for specific time periods (e.g. daily point-of-sale purchase data) and allows for automated analysis, which in turn, can be output in batches.
- *Stream processing:* A synchronous method of ingesting a data stream, often including unordered datasets produced at high velocity. These include web logs, mobile events, sensor data, etc.

It should be noted that collection does not imply availability for use – it is simply a description of the timeline for ingestion. For example, data may be ingested in real time from website clickstream logs, but if it is not promptly harmonized, etc., it will not be available for use. Likewise, data collected in batches may be available immediately.

Salesforce's State of Marketing Report regularly surfaced marketers' desire to deliver messages "in real time." The 2019 report revealed that the marketers' *number one* goal was to communicate in real time. And their number one challenge? You may have seen this one coming: It's to communicate in real time. We suspect part of their frustration comes from a misunderstanding of the meaning and importance of real-time data collected vs. availability, and the value of insights vs. raw data. Maybe real-time *everything* is not the right goal? (We address this point more fully in Chapter 11 on analytics.)

Back to data ingestion. Following on the two major data collection patterns, there are three ways data can be ingested for use. It can be:

- *Extracted from an existing source:* Often a database, either in the cloud or on-premise, or an application of some kind that stores customer data, such as an email system.
- *Collected in real time:* Literally pulled from a data stream in progress, such as a website clickstream or a stream of Twitter posts.
- *Collected in a batch process:* Conceptually the same as the above method, but parsed into larger chunks of data to be ingested, often based on a preset schedule.

In practice, most customer data will be collected using the following methods:

- *Behavioral data:* Usually collected via JavaScript tags on websites, placed either manually or using a tag management system; or by software development kits (SDKs) placed within mobile applications. Can also be collected from sensors (e.g. Internet-of-Things [IoT]) and via Application Protocol Interfaces (APIs) from streaming sources.

- *Demographic and other attributes:* Usually imported in batch and appended to a customer data record using a file transfer protocol (FTP) on the internet, or another server-to-server or batch file transfer method.
- *Campaign and product data:* Information about campaigns and products, which is generally not collected at the customer level, can also be useful for customer data platforms. This data is often ingested via a batch process or via APIs.

2 Data Harmonization

Once data is created or ingested, it usually requires some processing or transformation before it can be used, either for analytics, decisions, or some kind of business process. In this and the following step, the data is prepared, cleaned, modified, and/or enriched so that it will be fit for the specific business use case.

Data harmonization is a broad category that includes all the practices, architectural techniques, and tools for collecting data from disparate sources and combining that data into a unified view to meet the data consumption requirements of applications, business processes, and users. It tends to be more complex for marketing than other departments. The reason for this sad reality is that marketing data – as we have seen – is sourced from many more, and more disparate locations, including usually external partners (e.g. customer data vendors and agencies); regularly uses continuous data streams with unpredictable or unknown structures and schema; and needs to support self-service business users who may not be data engineers. These challenges require an agile, flexible harmonization strategy.

What is harmonization in practice? The best way to think about it is as a way of mapping fields in different customer data sources to one another, when those fields are supposed to represent the same type of data. To take a simple example, suppose you are a marketer, and you have three different data sources. In one source there is a field (usually a column header) labeled "First_Name," in another, there is one called "FName," and in the third, it's called "firstName."

Without any harmonization, the process of "integrating" these three data sources would result in the creation of three different columns with three different labels. However, it's clear that these columns all represent the same common data field: a customer's first name. A simple harmonization would map these three similar fields onto a single entity, called (say) "FirstName."

The final form of the database would include only one column with that name, containing the data from the three different sources – now, in a more useful and certainly efficient form.

Integration can be accomplished using solutions that are:

- embedded in databases, operational software, or analytics software;
- stand-alone integration middleware, either as a service of through federation and virtualization.

However, increasingly marketers and other business users are turning to customer data platforms (Figure 4.3) to provide the tooling necessary to map data fields from different sources in an intuitive, drag-and-drop way.

Using an Information Model

One best practice for data harmonization is to start with a standard data model, customize it for your particular requirements, and use that as a canonical model or template for your final format. Standard data models

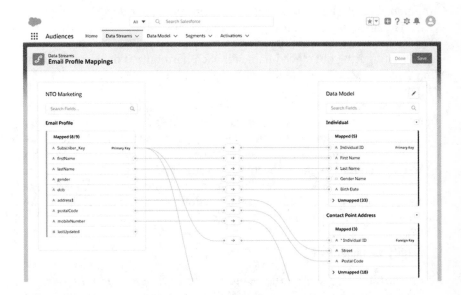

FIGURE 4.3 The "profile mapping" screen within Customer 360 Audiences, the Salesforce customer data platform.
Source: Courtesy of Salesforce.

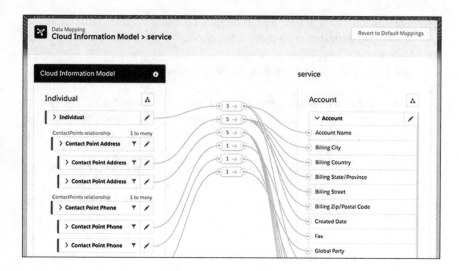

FIGURE 4.4 Mapping fields into a common data information model.
Source: Courtesy of Salesforce.

include common fields already, such as "FirstName," as well as other common data designations such as favorite product categories or loyalty tiers. The advantage of starting with a standard model and adapting it is that the marketer does not have to go through the tedious (and error-prone) activity of figuring out a good name for each harmonized field and ensuring they have a MECE (mutually exclusive and collectively exhaustive) list of fields.

For example, Salesforce uses a standard model called the Cloud Information Model (CIM) across its various clouds, and the CIM has proved to be a highly effective way to build consistency into the system and improve efficiency across applications. A customer information model is a subset of the CIM, and it simply codifies data commonly attached to customer records into a standard taxonomy. Salesforce's Customer 360 Audiences CDP makes use of a highly configurable and customizable version of the CIM out of the box for data harmonization (Figure 4.4).

3 Identity Management

Identity management is to harmonization what yin is to yang in Taoism, or chocolate to peanut butter in less enlightened circles: the perfect complement. Whereas customer data harmonization attempts to reconcile

*fields within different data sources, or map them to a common data
model, identity management seeks to do the same thing for customer
IDs – that is, identifiers such as names and addresses, mobile phone
numbers, emails, anonymous browser cookies, etc.*

Managing identity can power more effective multichannel engagement, improve targeting and creative tactics, and make measurement more accurate. Good identity resolution and management enable a marketer to approach the people-based experience advantage held by platforms like Facebook, Google, and Amazon. Such platforms have a user base that identifies themselves by logging in across devices and browsers, allowing a consistent experience. Consumers are increasingly primed to expect the same experience from every marketer, so identity management is not optional.

The average US adult has four digital devices and spends five hours a day using them, according to Nielsen. Sixty-seven percent of these adults use mobile devices to research products and services, according to the Consumer Technology Association. Meanwhile, 60% of consumers who research a product on a mobile device end up making the purchase on a different device or browser. Leading marketers try to link devices and browsers to individuals – pseudonymous or known – and to layer on additional information from campaign management and other systems. Forty-three percent of marketers said cross-channel audience identification and matching were a top concern in a study by the Interactive Advertising Bureau.

In addition to linking individuals to their various devices, identity management also seeks to link together all their various offline IDs. In the offline world, of course, this practice is not new. Starting in the pre-digital era, marketers were challenged to match different forms of names and addresses, keep up with moves, and associate people with demographic and other data. Statistical techniques such as record linkage were developed to determine whether different records likely belonged to the same person. Marketing service providers such as Acxiom, Experian, Epsilon, and KBM Group continue to maintain authenticated identities for almost every consumer and business in developed countries.

Benefits of Identity Management

Ensuring that data collected in different contexts and channels can be resolved to the right identity (whether person or account) offers benefits that extend well beyond improving marketing efficiency. Increasingly, disciplined identity management is a requirement for doing business.

Specific benefits of identity management are:

- *Improved media effectiveness:* Better efficiency (e.g., frequency caps), targeting, audience extension.
- *More relevant content:* More personalized messages and offers, and enhanced ability to sequence across channels and devices.
- *Better analytics and insights:* More accurate profiles for better segmentation, predictive models, recommendations, and measurement.
- *More informed governance:* The ability to meet consumer and regulatory requirements for opt-outs, preference management, etc.

The latter point is critical. If customers expect a coherent experience across channels and devices, they also expect (and have a right to expect) that their privacy preferences and settings are consistent. Identity management is required for both. (We discuss privacy and consent management in more depth in Chapter 5.)

Spectrum of Identity

Marketing identity is not just binary: known or unknown. It is also not synonymous with cross-device identification or "device matching." It is best seen as existing on a spectrum (Figure 4.5) that develops in detail from generalized

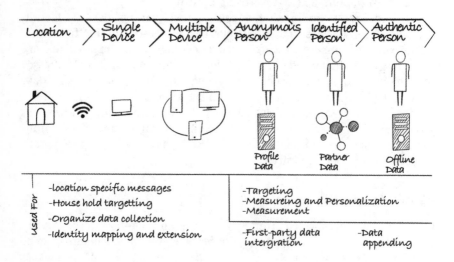

FIGURE 4.5   The spectrum of "Identity."
Source: Courtesy of Salesforce.

anonymous data to authenticated personal information, with many shades in between.

As Figure 4.5 shows, there are many degrees of identity resolution, from the most general (or pseudonymous) to the most specific. Pseudonymous identifiers are those that don't point directly to a known person but rather to locations, devices, or other extensions that function as a proxy for the person. (For more on the different types of identity data, see Chapter 2.) Known identifiers, on the other hand, can usually be resolved to a person in the real world, and include common IDs such as email addresses, phone numbers, names, and addresses.

Identity management is built around what are known as *keys*. These are the ID handles that represent the specific proxy or known individual (or account). Common keys include browser cookies, hashed emails (HEMs), IP addresses, plaintext emails, and customer IDs. Identity management is the process of matching one ID with another ID as pointing to the same individual (or account). As we described in Chapter 2, these matches can be done to some degree of statistical certainty (i.e. probabilistic) or can be exact one-to-one matches (i.e. deterministic).

Identity Management in Practice

Since identity management is so critical to so many marketing use cases, important subdisciplines have arisen over the past decade or so. Each serves a specific requirement. The most common identity use cases are summarized in Figure 4.6.

4 Segmentation

Segmentation is the practice of grouping customers or accounts together based on similar characteristics. There are a number of different ways to form such groups, based on the end use of the segments and the data available. Segmentation is a mainstay of data-driven marketing and, when done well, can be a source of competitive differentiation.

Segmentation is used for a variety of purposes, including product development, pricing, targeting, messaging, and measurement. Smart segmentation is a key step toward meeting consumers' demands for more relevant experiences. Some 97% of marketers say customer analytics, including segmentation, are either essential or important to their business, according to analyst firm Gartner. Not surprisingly, 42% of marketers surveyed said they planned to increase investment in their customer analysis efforts.

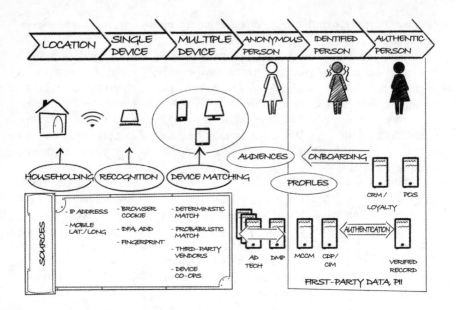

FIGURE 4.6 How different types of "identity" work within the spectrum, such as householding, device matching, and onboarding.
Source: Courtesy of Salesforce.

A segment is a group of people or other entities, such as companies or stores, that share quantifiable attributes that matter to the marketer's business. Most marketers don't use a single approach to segmentation for all their efforts, but rather apply a number of different approaches for different business reasons. For example, a national health-and-wellness retailer we know uses five different schemas:

- *Psychographic:* Lifestyles and attitudes toward managing family health, for brand and other awareness campaigns.
- *Behavioral:* Frequency of shopping by category and engagement with marketing tactics for couponing and promotions.
- *Benefits:* Functional or emotional benefits (e.g. whiter teeth) for product advertising.
- *Geography:* Region and density for product mix and pricing.
- *Occasion:* Special occasions (e.g. birthdays) or purchase intervals for reminders and recognition.

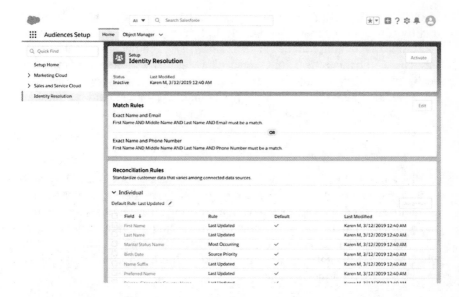

FIGURE 4.7   Screenshot of the Identity Resolution setup screen in Salesforce Customer 360 Audiences, showing the match rules the customer is using to get to the source of truth of customer records. *Source:* Courtesy of Salesforce.

Segments can be based on almost any type of attribute. In practice, they tend to draw on a handful of basic approaches. They can be formed manually, based on attributes selected by the marketer; or they can be built using statistical procedures and software that discover groups with similar attributes called *clusters*. Based on the evidence of our customers, Salesforce surveys, and our experience, we believe the most common segmentation models among marketers tend to be based on:

- *Customer value:* Simple tiering by value (or potential value) to the company.
- *Product preferences:* Types of products or services bought.
- *Loyalty:* Share of wallet and stickiness, which is correlated with (but not the same as) value.
- *Price sensitivity:* Often tied to product margin (e.g. business vs. personal buyer).
- *Use:* Depth of engagement, frequency of use.

What is the "right" number of segments? There is a popular perception that five to eight segments are ideal. In fact, there are statistical methods to determine the optimal number, such as latent class and two-step cluster analysis. There is no theoretical limit: You can have as many segments as are statistically different and useful. The key term here is *useful*. It is always a good idea to go into a segmentation exercise with a rough idea of a maximum number your organization can actually use, based on available resources.

The Importance of Attributes

Attributes are at the heart of any segmentation exercise. Therefore, a clean and updated repository of customer profiles that has been identity-matched and harmonized – as discussed above – is a prerequisite for accurate segmentation, and one of its main motivating use cases. Attributes come in three basic types: they describe what a person (or account) *is* (*demographics/firmographics*), what they *do* (*behaviors*), or what they *think* (*attitudes*). Examples of each of these types are presented in Table 4.1.

TABLE 4.1 Examples of common data attributes.

Type	Uses	Data Types	Common Sources
Are	▪ Media targeting ▪ High-level filters (e.g., women only) ▪ Offline media buying ▪ Predictors for attitudes	▪ Demographic ▪ Filmographic ▪ Income and credit ▪ Family size	▪ CRM systems ▪ Marketing service providers ▪ Public sources ▪ Third-party sources
Do	▪ Product preferences ▪ Channel preferences ▪ Locations visited ▪ Price sensitivity ▪ Content interests ▪ Likelihood to respond	▪ Online behavior ▪ Purchases ▪ Location data ▪ Devices used ▪ Social media use ▪ Content and media consumption	▪ Multichannel campaign management systems ▪ Point-of-sale systems ▪ Digital analytics ▪ Email services ▪ Media platforms
Think	▪ Messages ▪ Advertising campaigns ▪ Competitive positioning ▪ Call scripts	▪ Psychographic ▪ Affiliations ▪ Sentiment and valence ▪ Responses to content	▪ Inference models ▪ Surveys ▪ Social analytics ▪ Voice of customer

Source: Courtesy of Salesforce.

FIGURE 4.8 Screenshot showing the segment building tool inside of Customer 360 Audiences, showing different data attributes on the left, and the workspace where attributes are combined on the right. In this example, a segment is being constructed of female shoppers who have purchased shoes costing more than $100.
Source: Courtesy of Salesforce.

Interestingly, when we were combing through requests for proposals (RFPs) in the CDP category (see Chapter 3), we were surprised to find that the most common use case was some form of "business user-friendly segmentation." If the primary requirement for the CDP is to be able to ingest and manage data, one of the most desired uses is simply allowing the business to have access to the profiles – not necessarily (or even ever) to the actual user-level data, but rather to the ability to explore and query it, test hypotheses, run and rerun segment ideas, and get fast results. Fast, accurate segmentation based on real-time profiles may turn out to be the "killer app" of the category.

5 Activation

The final step in organizing customer data for use is to use it. Activation means taking all the collected, identified, harmonized, and segmented customer data and putting it to work. Without activation, the best customer data management operation is in the business of admiring itself: It needs to drive operational marketing systems and results. This is the moment where things get real – for better or worse.

Customer data activation is a broad discipline that could be seen as encompassing pretty much everything a marketer needs to do. For our purposes, we're going to focus on the building blocks of customer-driven data activation, based on feedback from our customers and Salesforce survey research. We've outlined the most basic prerequisites for activation above, including data ingestion, harmonization, identity management, and segmentation. Recognizing that data has no real value until it's put to work, what comes next?

GETTING IT DONE

Consider a customer-driven marketer at a retailer we know, which we'll call Northern Trail Outfitters (NTO). When we ask them what they'd like to do with their customer data, they describe some general activations, including:

- *Selecting* a message or offer to send to the customer, including brand messages, special promotions, discount offers, and item recommendations.
- *Communicating* this selection decision to the right channel, including email, mobile messaging and apps, websites, social networks, and ads.
- *Monitoring and measuring* what's happening in their marketing channels via dashboards and command centers.

NTO runs campaigns that are prescheduled and handled by their campaign-management tool, Journey Builder. For these campaigns, the marketing department would like to use the customer data platform to provide segments (audiences) and perhaps to suggest messages or content, if there isn't a preplanned campaign that preempts it. In the case of visitors to their websites and mobile properties, NTO would like the customer data platform to act as an instant (sub-millisecond) source of data, such as segment membership or lifetime value – in other words, as a real-time data source. And finally, NTO would like to be able to access the customer data to track changes and measure results.

DIFFERENT SPHERES OF INFLUENCE

As you can see, the activation stage of customer data management intersects with engagement channel technology and campaign management tools, such as multichannel campaign management, email, mobile, and social platforms. This intersection is to be expected, as the latter systems are in charge of executing decisions that are developed, managed, and tracked based on the data and profiles sitting within the customer data platform. There is overlap among vendors in various categories, as well as among definitions used by practitioners. In the case of Salesforce, selection of messages and offers is handled by our *multichannel campaign management* solutions, Salesforce Marketing Cloud and Journey Builder, and by our *real-time interaction management* system, Salesforce Interaction Studio. So, in our case, the Customer 360 Audiences enterprise CDP stores and organizes customer data, and the Salesforce Marketing Cloud components manage journeys and deliver customer engagements.

Whatever the configuration of your particular marketing technology stack, the activation stage of customer-driven marketing includes the following key activities:

- Engagement activation:
  - send segments to engagement systems (email, SMS, push, mobile, website, display ads, OTT, IoT)
  - personalization of websites, dynamic creative optimization
  - support for sequenced and multistep journeys
  - support for testing (a/b/n)
- Real-time event-based marketing:
  - triggered messages and other treatments
  - predictive sending and scoring
- Predictive analytics
  - product recommendations
  - content recommendations
- Reporting and insights
  - dashboards/reporting
  - AI consumer insights

Engagement activation encompasses all the ways that the platform communicates with engagement systems. These systems include the channels that customers and prospects use to engage with your brand. The most common are email, mobile messaging and apps, websites and landing pages, display and social ads, over-the-top and connected TV, and connected devices (IoT). The platform needs to be able to send segments to these channels, as well as support multichannel campaign management (MCCM) and journey tools, testing, and optimization. *Real-time event-based marketing* use cases for the customer data platform require it to provide sub-millisecond query response for data such as segment membership, loyalty tier, and next-best-offer or -product recommendations. *Predictive analytics* and *reporting and insights* are either integrated within the CDP or make use of data feeds from the CDP, e.g. into a dashboarding tool.

Since system-to-system communication and data queries are critical to this stage, the platform should support a wide range of data transport and access methods. These include, at least:

- *File transfer:* Batch file transfer (FTP, file transfer protocol, secure file transfer protocol, SFTP), server-to-server and automated transfer; streaming data export.
- *Queries:* Ability to explore, analyze, and retrieve data using common query methods, such as SQL (structured query language) and Hive/Presto.
- *APIs:* Published APIs for both batch and real-time data retrieval; prebuilt connectors to common marketing and other systems are often provided out of the box.

CUSTOMER-DRIVEN THINKER: BRAD FEINBERG

An eleven-year veteran of global beverage behemoth Molson Coors, Brad Feinberg has a front-row seat at the first-party data tailgate that's raving within most consumer packaged goods (CPG) companies we know. The company's North America V.P. of Media & Consumer Engagement, Feinberg is an outspoken advocate for the role of digital customer data in the ongoing transformation of his and other industries.

What lessons have you learned in your time at Molson Coors and what is your customer-driven strategic plan?

CPG has been lagging in first-party data, maybe because we haven't had a means to access it. The world has changed so much recently, and the future of marketing depends on any company's ability to collect and scale consumer data, primarily through first-party and second-party sources. Everything will be digitally-enabled. I think some CPG companies are doing a great job, like Kraft Heinz or Conagra. They've built a robust first-party data practice. My attraction to it is all-around precision marketing at scale and understanding the consumer journey, and closed-loop creative and media optimization.

A couple of years ago, we worked on a consumer journey mapping project. And basically, a lot of journeys were closed to us because the information was not available. We couldn't see the path to purchase. And the big [third-party] data aggregators we work with didn't have enough granular data to really help us in the work.

There was not enough consumer touchpoints available to make a meaningful impact in precision media and marketing to the right person, at the right time with the right message. By relying entirely on third-party data, we know we are chasing information sources everybody else is using.

We have some special challenges as Molson Coors. We aren't doing robust recipes sites like Kraft Heinz. We don't have direct relationships with retailers, because legally we can't work with them. There's Prohibition Era legislation that means we can't work with Walmart or Target [to share data]. So, in many ways, we have had to fly blind. On the other hand, due to the local nature of our products and the alliances with sports, entertainment, fairs, and festival properties, we recognized we had hundreds of points of direct inter-section with consumers where we were not collecting data. We also had built e-commerce merchandise shop.com destinations where we give away or sell custom branded apparel, Miller Lite holiday knit apparel, or Coors Light at-home "Chillware." Those direct consumer experiences become the ground floor in data available to build out a consumer profile for those that opt in to our brand world.

With thirty-plus local sports partnerships across the country, across all major sports, we interact with consumers with dozens of localized events/programming. Like in Chicago, where we have run in-person ticket giveaways in key on-premise bar accounts to support our Chicago Bears Alliance. A typical bar activation was a low tech and low complexity approach where we deployed our sales activation representatives to execute a bar-top name drawing. We would pull names out of a bowl to win tickets on the spot for an upcoming game where legal. We asked our activation team what they were doing with the names after the winner was selected, and not to our surprise, they would innocently dispose of all of the participant information because there was no planned use for that information at the time. For those consumers that give us permission with precision market-ing, we now have a use. In addition to sports franchises, we sponsor major music festivals such as Jazzfest and have built out custom temporary and permanent branded destinations – all of which where we have direct customer interactions with our brands. That was my "aha moment." We just needed the back-end technology to support our ability to build meaningful customer relationships.

A lot of retailers find cross-sell within the category and beyond [based on customer data] very attractive. A lot of times, our con-sumer will go into a retailer to buy multiple brands for a party or to have in the refrigerator. They can sell bundled brands together for a particular occasion ... Or we have brands that launch a line extension in order to expand their consumer base and/or keep their loyal audience inside their franchise more often. Like the recent successful launch of Blue Moon Light Sky, which expanded our ability reach beyond our Blue Moon Belgium White loyal consumer base. By using our data, we can better understand the interaction rates between brands as well as identify new ways to drive growth. With a portfolio of over thirty different products on the shelf at one time and a robust innovation pipeline, by having a centralized way to harness consumer data, it will allow us to meet the needs of all consumers along their individual journey and hopefully become the brands our consumers want to hang out with more often.

SUMMARY: ORGANIZING CUSTOMER DATA

- *Customer data management:* Customer data management is the discipline of collecting, organizing, and making your valuable customer data available to power your customer-driven dreams. It's the essence of the customer data platform – not glamorous, but absolutely fundamental for success. In this chapter, we described the five key steps required for successful customer data handling:
- *Data ingestion:* First is data ingestion, which is the collection or import of data from various marketing and other systems, both inside and outside the company's sphere. Ingestion can be handled in many ways, including batch file transfers and streaming-data ingestion. Data collection can be done by tags, SDKs, or ingestion via APIs.
- *Harmonization:* This step is about harmonizing the attribute fields that exist in the different data sources. If you're like most marketers, different sources have different ways of organizing and describing data. Fields that refer to the same entity may be named slightly differently (or very differently). In order to build a usable single customer view, these fields have to be reconciled to one other, mapped, and harmonized.
- *Identity management:* Identity management is the process of reconciling customer (or prospect, or account, etc.) identity handles, when they refer to the same entity, and mapping them to one another. This step is important in order to combine data about the same customer that is in different systems, or within the same system under different IDs. A complex art and science, identity management includes both statistical and rules-based methods.
- *Segmentation:* The first step a marketer enjoys after building a harmonized and ID-matched customer database is often segmentation. This

is the process of separating customers into discrete groups based on important commonalities or descriptive states. For example, marketers will often group high-value customers together, or build more sophisticated clusters using machine-learning models. Segments are needed for more personalized marketing.

- *Activation:* The final step in the customer data management process is to send or otherwise communicate customer data, decisions, and/or metadata to engagement systems that need it to execute marketing campaigns. In a typical scenario, the MCCM tool will pull segments from the customer platform, as well as other data (such as product recommendations); and a RTIM tool will ping the platform for key data such as segment membership. All digital channels and common query methods should be supported.

CHAPTER 5

Build a First-Party Data Asset with Consent

Everyone is talking about first-party data these days, but why? What is it? We explain the different types of data, how roles have changed in recent years, and how they're likely to change in future. A large part of this conversation is about consent, privacy, and data collection under regulatory regimes. The key success factor for customer-driven organizations is to build a flexible data collection mechanism that isn't purpose-built for a single regime but is able to adapt. Ultimately, consent and compliance are just components of a larger exercise of developing a transparent, trusted data-value exchange with customers.

PRIVACY-FIRST IS CUSTOMER-DRIVEN

By any measure, it was a disaster. In the summer of 2020, for reasons that are still murky, two servers were left unprotected and were easily breached by hackers. They contained a trove of customer data collected, used, and sold to marketers by Oracle's BlueKai data management platform and data cloud service. While breaches aren't rare, what caught widespread attention was the scale and scope of the data collected by the platform: as a headline in *TechCrunch* said, "Billions of records exposed."

What was in these records? There was location data tied to mobile device IDs, which are anonymous, and a great deal of website behavior tied to cookie IDs, also anonymous. There was some purchase data, e.g., that a person who lived in Istanbul ordered $899 worth of furniture online. One record included a German man's (unencrypted) address, phone number, email address, and the fact that he used a debit card to place a bet on a betting website.

As *TechCrunch*, which broke the story, noted in the piece, Oracle's BlueKai does not sell personally identifiable information, which would not have left the server if it hadn't been hacked. But the incident unleashed a torrent of journalistic paranoia familiar to ad tech observers: BlueKai "uses ... covert tactics like allowing websites to embed invisible pixel-sized images to collect information about you as soon as you open the page." Also raised were the inevitable specters of "tracking you around the web" and "fingerprinting."

Of course, web browser cookies have been around for a long time. They were invented by a 24-year-old Netscape engineer named Lou Montulli in 1994, so the data in the BlueKai servers should not have shocked the journalist. What has changed was the level of mistrust and paranoia prevalent in the media and among consumers – both of which have accelerated in recent years.

The truth is that the internet was not designed for advertising. It was intended as a tool for academic links and was purposely "stateless" – each message between browser and server is self-contained, thus, the cookie and the infrastructure exposed in the Oracle breach. As written by Montulli, the original spec describes what we would call a first-party cookie that stored information for a shopping cart. Expanded a few years later, the standard guaranteed users "control" over data collection but left the details up to the browsers. And in fact, the whole ethos of the cookie – the fact that it's an anonymous ID and the user could delete it – was to provide a better internet without invading privacy.

Over the years, a $100 billion-plus business developed on top of techniques such as the "pixel" and "piggybacking" – but these are basically workarounds. Think about it: The "pixel" is an image that is purposely invisible, requested solely so that a third party can establish a connection and retrieve a cookie in the browser. "Piggybacking," where tags call other tags and so on (and so on), is even more confusing.

We've entered an era of avoidant consumers, who are increasingly resistant to data collection and use by companies and their marketing departments. More than half of US online adults say they consciously avoid advertising, if they can, according to Forrester. Approximately one in four are using ad blocking technology on their browsers to minimize targeted advertising. And data from the Advertising Research Foundation shows that the cohort of consumers who have "low receptivity" to marketing messages rose steadily over the past decade, to more than one in three.

What if we could get a do-over? In a way, that's what impending browser changes and global regulations – aligned with the customer data platform approach – can grant us. We now have a chance to reinvent the web in a way that is more customer-focused and privacy-first, for advertisers, marketers, and consumers alike.

PRIVACY POLICE: BROWSERS AND REGULATORS

Digital data privacy is maintained by four parties with (at times) different agendas. These are:

- *Web browsers and standards bodies* – that want to protect themselves from legal exposure, and provide a product (the browser) that meets the needs of its users (consumers).
- *Government regulators* – who presumably act on behalf of legal principles to serve the people they govern.
- *Consumers* – who want to protect their data, while providing enough to get the experiences and services they want.
- *Companies* – that want to maintain productive and delightful relationships with customers, while obeying all relevant regulations.

We'll take a brief look at recent trends within the first two groups now, saving consumers and companies (including marketers) for longer subsequent views.

WEB BROWSERS AND STANDARDS BODIES

Most consumers access the internet via browsers or applications, such as those downloaded onto their mobile devices. Browsers themselves adhere to protocols that are developed through a process of peer review and adoption managed by the World Wide Web Consortium (known as the W3C), which has overseen internet standards such as HTML from the beginning. Browsers also adopt their own standards and methods, both as competitive differentiation and to meet the needs of their users, as they perceive them. Both browsers and standards bodies are therefore big players in the digital customer data conversation.

The browser market is highly concentrated, with Google's Chrome browser commanding more than 60% global share and Apple's Safari a distant number two, with less than 20% share (Figure 5.1). Mozilla's Firefox and Microsoft's Edge, which uses Google's open-source Chromium technology, each command less than 5% share.

Apple's Safari has always maintained a more privacy-focused posture with respect to data collection, particularly by advertisers, publishers, and advertising technology vendors. Since 2017, the Safari browser has blocked most third-party tracking cookies by default.

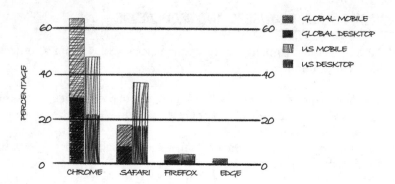

FIGURE 5.1 Google's Chrome dominates desktop and mobile browser share globally, with Apple's Safari a distant second. Alternatives like Firefox, Microsoft's Edge, and Brave have not found scale.

Intelligent Tracking Prevention

Safari privacy protections took a more stringent turn in 2017 with the launch of Intelligent Tracking Prevention (ITP), which sought to suppress various techniques ad tech companies used to identify users. Recent versions of the protocol clamp down on techniques such as redirects and link decoration used to fill gaps left by third-party cookie deprecation. In the summer of 2020, Apple announced a mandatory opt-in for its Identifier for Advertisers (IDFA), used by mobile application publishers, signaling their reluctance to allow any user-level tracking in future.

Enhanced Tracking Prevention and Brave

In 2018, Mozilla announced a similar policy to Apple's with the launch of its Enhanced Tracking Prevention (ETP). While Mozilla's stance is not as stringent by default as Apple's, the Brave browser takes a privacy-first position as a competitive differentiator, blocking ads by default and allowing only "Brave" ads, which are enabled by the user.

Google's Chrome and AdID

In January 2020, Google announced that the third-party cookie would expire in 2022, to be replaced by something to be worked out among privacy engineers and advertisers through a collaborative process in part facilitated by the W3C. At the time of writing, this process was ongoing. Although no announcement was made concerning its mobile AdID, similar to Apple's IDFA, the year 2020 marked the beginning of the end for user-level browser and app targeting as it was done in the past.

While the exact contours of the browser solutions aren't clear, it's safe to say that the future of ad targeting and measurement will be driven by first-party data (where it's available); consumers who explicitly opt in to collection and use of their data; and the use of aggregate – rather than user-level – information.

GOVERNMENT REGULATORS

Legislatures around the world are also eager to enact regulations related to digital data collection and use. The European Union's ePrivacy-related General Data Protection Regulation (GDPR) was enacted in May 2018 and has resulted in some high-profile fines and widespread opt-in requirements for European internet browsers. Other regions followed suit, e.g., the Australian Competition and Consumer Commission, which recently firmed up that country's protections, and the Brazilian General Data Privacy Law (LGPD), enacted in January 2020. In the US, the California Consumer Protection Act (CCPA) was rolled out after some squabbling in mid-2020.

While the ultimate impact and details of such legislation continue to be discovered, the principles laid out by the European regulators show its ultimate intent. As described in Article 5 of the legislation, the so-called "Seven Principles" of GDPR are:

- *Transparency* – the consumer should know what data is being collected, by whom.
- *Purpose limitation* – data can only be used for the explicit purpose granted by the consumer.
- *Data minimization* – only as much (and no more) data can be collected to serve the purpose above.
- *Accuracy* – self-explanatory.
- *Storage limitation* – there are limits to how long data can be retained.
- *Security* – must be stored in a way that it cannot be accessed by unauthorized parties.
- *Accountability* – the data "controller" (legally defined) must provide ability to audit and edit data.

While reasonable enough, these principles in practice place a tremendous burden on the marketer not only to collect consent alongside data, but also to provide the necessary technical infrastructure to support compliance. Such infrastructure is already becoming simply the cost of doing business online.

At a practical level, we approach privacy and compliance as a three-tiered practice. The tiers are:

- *Classify data:* Assign data ownership, field usage, field status, and meta-data, such as data sensitivity level.
- *Determine user entitlements:* Role-based entitlements and governance to data, internal and external (i.e. customer-facing).
- *Ensure compliance:* Audit and persistence; ability to analyze compliance.

Ultimately, privacy is about building a trusted relationship with customers. As we have seen, customers have shown that they *will* share data with *trusted partners*. The key phrase here is "trusted partners." According to Salesforce's State of the Connected Customer report, 83% of customers say they are either comfortable or neutral (not averse) to relevant personal information being used in a transparent and beneficial manner by companies they trust. Data-sharing relationships are not all created equal.

Building trust has elements that can be built into a martech architecture. Its components (quite similar to the GDPR principles outlined above, not coincidentally) are:

- *Consent:* "Get my permission."
- *Restriction of processing:* "Stop processing my data."
- *Right to be forgotten:* "Delete my data."
- *Data subject requests:* "What information do you have about me?"
- *Security:* "Prevent unauthorized access to my data."
- *Data use preferences:* "This is what I am okay with."

THE MISTRUSTFUL CONSUMER

The Oracle data breach was the latest in a string of high-profile incidents that caused consumers to question how and why companies are collecting and using their data. Some of these incidents, like the Facebook-Cambridge Analytica imbroglio, end up in the hearing rooms of the US Senate. Others, such as Equifax's major breach in 2017, result in civil litigation and fines. Still others, such as when Target inadvertently alerted a father to his daughter's pregnancy through marketing based on her shopping habits, become the stuff of oft-repeated legend through the years.

As a result of these incidents and broader social changes, consumers are growing more distrustful of institutions and more wary of sharing their data. These institutions include governments and corporations. Mistrust is the new attitudinal default, and it shows up repeatedly in consumer surveys. For example, a Pew Research Center survey of adults in the US revealed the following sobering findings:

- *Lack of control:* 81% think they have little to no control over companies collecting their data.
- *No benefit:* 81% think the risks with data being collected about them outweigh the benefits.
- *Confusion:* 59% say they have little to no understanding of how their data is being used; and only 6% say they have a "good understanding" of this important flow.
- *Paranoia:* 72% think nearly everything they do online is being tracked by advertisers/vendors.

Against such a backdrop, it's easy for some marketers to lose hope or feel it's too late to recapture lost trust. However, consumer behavior and our own surveys show clearly that consumers are willing to share data comfortably as long as certain conditions are met. These conditions include (1) transparency; (2) clear value exchange; and (3) consumer control. In other words, if a marketer takes steps to counteract the attitudes unearthed by the Pew Research Center data – meeting "lack of control" with controls, and "confusion" with transparency – it is possible to provide personalization with trust.

Our research repeatedly shows that customers report positive feelings and behaviors toward companies that collect and use data openly and with consent. Almost 80% say they are more loyal to companies that are transparent about how their data is used, while almost half say they have stopped doing business with a company due to concerns about data privacy.

To build – or rebuild – trust with a consumer is critical to collecting and using their data for personalization. And we've seen that consumers will share data happily with brands they trust. In fact, the data advantage of certain brands is their competitive edge, the very thing that keeps their customers coming back. People regularly share the most intimate data with Facebook (family photos), Amazon (purchases), LinkedIn (job searches), Google (search history), Stitch Fix (waist sizes) – and many more – because the personalization and responsive experience they receive make it worthwhile. They trust these brands.

How Can a Marketer Gain Trust?

As our grandmothers said (or should have said, if they forgot), trust is something that is earned and not bought. Building trust is a multipronged effort that includes:

- *Reliability:* Data security and uptime; patching and maintenance
- *Legality:* Legal compliance and the flexibility to adapt to regulatory changes
- *Transparency:* Transparent collection and use of customer data
- *Value:* Sufficient benefits received for exchange

An additional requirement is more existential: corporate ethics. Part of a customer's comfort with data sharing resides in their feelings about a company's general trustworthiness, which includes perceptions about the company's behavior in the world and corporate ethics. Our research shows that 73% of consumers say that ethics matter more than they did a year ago, and fully 80% said they are more loyal to companies they believe have strong ethics. Of course, the reverse is also true, and 68% tell us they just won't do business with companies they believe to have shifty eyes and tendencies.

For their part, corporations are taking steps to improve their privacy posture with customers. The change has been dramatic, in recent years. Between 2018 and 2020, the proportion of marketers who told us they were "more mindful of balancing personalization with customer comfort levels than we were two years ago" rocketed from just over half to 81%. And the number who said they exceeded regulatory requirements for privacy controls shot up from 44% to 57%. Meanwhile, companies increasing demands from consumers and regulatory regimes have sapped marketers' confidence, as the number who told us they felt "completely satisfied" with their ability to balance personalization and "customer comfort levels" actually fell from 30% to 28%, a small and diminishing cohort.

Even the largest brands are affected. In 2019, Facebook's Chief Financial Officer, David Wehner, admitted in an earnings call:

> Privacy [concerns] are a headwind for [Facebook] in 2019. It's one of the factors that is contributing to our expected deceleration of revenue growth throughout the year ... Platforms like iOS are making bigger pushes in privacy and that has the potential impact ... than changes that we're making ourselves ...

So, it's clear we're at a pivotal moment, when consumers are inherently mistrustful, governments are taking action, and companies are on the hook to deliver personalization while maintaining a trusted, transparent relationship with customers. It's the new reality for customer data, and it's the key to success in the future.

ATTITUDES AROUND THE WORLD

Mistrust in institutions and consumer privacy concerns are growing across the globe. It is not a local phenomenon, although its contours differ by region. What is different, of course, are local variations in statutes and regulations, which force multiregion marketers to maintain more regulatory vigilance than they did in the past.

A Harris Poll conducted in 2019 revealed some variation in privacy concerns around the world. Residents of China and Taiwan were the most concerned about privacy, with 91–92% of respondents admitting as much. Meanwhile, respondents in Italy, Germany, and the Netherlands were less concerned (66–78%). However, more than half of respondents in all regions said they were willing to "accept certain risks" in exchange for convenience and value from companies with which they do business. Globally, an average of 61% of consumers were willing to accept such risks.

To date, European regulators have been the most willing to enact consumer privacy legislation that directly impacts the collection and use of consumer data. The European ePrivacy directive and GDPR have affected both consumer attitudes and marketers' practices, of course. In the US, the California Consumer Privacy Act heralded a wave of potential legislation from other states. And marketers in particular industries have had to contend with privacy regulation for some time, for example, HIPAA and HITECH for the healthcare market, Payment Card Industry Data Security Standards (PCI-DSS) for credit-card processes, and the Child Online Privacy Protection Act (COPPA) for those marketing to minors.

There is evidence that having regulations in place can make both chief marketing officers (CMOs) and consumers less anxious, presumably because they feel more "in control" of the consumer-corporate data exchange. For example, in 2018, the global advertising holding company Dentsu Aegis Network conducted a survey of 10,000 CMOs and found that US CMOs are even more wary of potential data protection legislation than their non-US counterparts (Figure 5.2). While only 35% of non-US CMOs said regulations such as GDPR would be a top barrier to consumer relationships, 44% of US CMOs said as much. Similarly, two-thirds of US CMOs agreed that such regulation makes consumer relationships more difficult, compared to 60% of non-US CMOs.

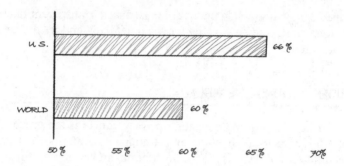

FIGURE 5.2 Dentsu Aegis Network Global CMO Survey, 2018 (n = 1,000).

And research conducted by the European Interactive Digital Advertising Alliance (EIDAA) recently showed that GDPR has gone some way to restoring consumer comfort with data collection. While 76% of European consumers expressed some awareness of GDPR, about 40% of all respondents said the regulations helped them to "feel more knowledgeable about the way in which information about me is collected and used online."

So, there is ample reason to welcome reasonable regulatory regimes as a way to restore trust. Even more poignantly, for those of us interested in the future of customer data, the EIDAA's research found that the appeal of greater personalization *increased* for those who expressed a greater level of awareness and understanding of how their data is used. The difference was dramatic, with a majority (63%) of Europeans with the greatest professed understanding saying they found online behavioral advertising "appealing" – with a paltry 15% of those with no awareness of data controls finding such personalized messaging appealing.

The message is clear: a healthy majority of consumers are willing to share data in return for relevance – as long as it is collected and used in a way, and under structural controls, that makes them comfortable.

The question is: How can a marketer make their customers more comfortable sharing their data?

THE PRIVACY PARADOX

The summer of 2020 was a long, hot one for marketers. In addition to everything else, the CCPA was unleashed on a bewildered public. Plus, Apple announced a major change to its Identifier for Advertisers (IDFA), forcing users to opt in to ad tracking in apps starting this fall and raising the specter of a flurry of GDPR-like consent screens tripping gamers on their way into Animal Crossing.

At the heart of this orgy of opt ins lies a dark secret: people are not good at making decisions about privacy trade-offs. We just aren't. Why? Because of a strange phenomenon called the "privacy paradox."

What Exactly Is the Privacy Paradox?

Here's the pickle: when we're asked if we value our personal data, almost all of us say "yes." Yet our behaviors show otherwise. For example, in 2018, Facebook confronted a flush of bad PR after a public data scandal, yet its revenue grew 30%. As we've already pointed out, we regularly surrender intimate information to platforms such as Google (searches), Facebook, Amazon, Stitch Fix, and so on, all without a squeak.

There is ample evidence that we appreciate relevant content: Amazon and Netflix both built a business on trenchant recommendations. After GDPR appeared in Europe, the cost of advertising to consumers who had opted in to targeting actually rose. And anecdotal evidence suggests that prices for comparable ads are about 50–60% lower on Apple's Safari (which blocks most user-level targeting) than on Google's Chrome browser (which does not, for now). What's a marketer to do? It turns out, there are a lot of theories about the privacy paradox – including one that it doesn't exist. A detailed overview of the academic literature found 35 explanations packed into 32 studies. These and other briefs can help to point the way.

How Do You Solve the Paradox?

Imagine the following: you arrive on a website or download an app and a pop-up appears saying something like, "We'd like to track you so we can make your experience better – yes or no?" At that moment, you haven't experienced anything, you just got there. You can't value a "good experience" because you haven't had any experience yet.

So, the trouble with "rational choice theory," as it's called, is that we're usually forced to make decisions without enough information. Our ability to do continual "privacy calculus" is constrained. Common biases that plague privacy decisions include time constraints, lack of information or interest, immediate gratification, and a tendency to think we're "giving up" more data than we are.

FOUR PRIVACY TACTICS TO TRY

Marketers and advertisers are going to have to master the art of gaining consumer trust. How? Some general guidelines from the research include:

1. *Don't talk about people behind their backs.*

     It turns out that we don't like this behavior online any more than we do at work or school. Our attitudes toward information sharing depend both on the type of information and the way it's shared, what social scientists call the "information flows." One study found we are much more comfortable with open, direct, so-called "first-person sharing" than we are with covert "third-party sharing." The latter, when disclosed, actually drove down purchase interest by 24%. Conversely, using "overt data collection" can restore interest and rebuild trust. *Bottom line: tell people directly how you are gathering their data.*

2. *Give a sense of control.*

     Like Janet Jackson, we really want "control." When consumers in the US and the EU were asked if they would opt out of data collection in future, US consumers were 1.5 times more likely to say "yes." Why? One likely explanation is that, for all its fits and starts, GDPR provides a sense of control. In America, our hodgepodge of legislation and tools does not. People have been shown to share data much more willingly when they believe they can control what they share, even if that control is an illusion. *Bottom line: make customers believe they control the data.*

3. *Explain the benefits in concrete, positive terms.*

     It's up to the marketer to describe the privacy value exchange as concretely and positively as they can. The insight here is that concrete benefits might often dominate abstract risks – and that privacy "threats" are usually abstract. But stay positive and benefit-focused, since there's evidence that mentioning risks makes people nervous. The idea is to give the consumer a sense of the awesomeness of your personalized experience, either in words or pictures. In one study, for example, an ad for a rental company using a person's physical location performed better when it was explained that location data was used specifically to mention services not available elsewhere. *Bottom line: paint a happy picture of tangible benefits for sharing data.*

4. *Remember, people are different.*

     It is often assumed that attitudes to online privacy and ad targeting are demographically determined. Millennials and Gen Z are the cultural paranoids, while Boomers and GenX are more relaxed. It turns out these attitudes are more a function of our personalities than our demos: they're a state of mind. A few years ago, the Advertising Research Foundation released a report on "ad receptivity" that concluded that the anti-ad crowd were more likely to be "suspicious" and "headstrong." And a different study, published earlier this year, identified about one-third of the online population as "privacy actives," more informed and aware. Rather than retreating from data sharing, these "actives" were twice as likely to share their purchase history in exchange for better recommendations. So, the privacy conversation will be different with different groups, and these groups are likely not segmented by age, gender, or income. The "actives" just need more information, and the more the better. The "rejecters" need their suspicions allayed. It's up to the marketer to figure out which psychographic segment each consumer inhabits. *Bottom line: throw your customer insights and data science teams at the problem.*

And remember, you can always try something new. Ask people to share data after you've given them something of value. Be explicit. Ask them how they feel. Give them the remote. The human rules still apply: trust is something that is earned, not just given.

CUSTOMER-DRIVEN THINKER: SEBASTIAN BALTRUSZEWICZ

Sebastian Baltruszewicz is the CPG Product Owner for Consumer Data & eCRM at Reckitt Benckiser (RB). RB is a company operating in the consumer health and hygiene sector, with dozens of well-known health, hygiene, and home care brands around the world, such as Enfamil, Air Wick, Calgon, Clearasil, Lysol, Durex, etc. Many of the brands were brought into the company through acquisitions, making unifying and reconciling customer data across regions really important. This task was a priority for Senior Product Owner Sebastian Baltruszewicz when he joined RB's automation and testing IT team in 2016. Given the company's global footprint and numerous brands, Baltruszewicz discovered that customer data was a challenge he had to address one brand at a time.

How did you address the customer data challenge?

> At RB, we have a lot of brands, but our customers don't necessarily know us as "RB." They know the product names. As I started to move more toward the consumer side of the business, collaborating more with the brand teams, I realized that a lot of the brands work independently and don't have the bigger picture. This is also because we

have so many brands with their management teams across different time zones, different teams, different priorities. Each brand has its own marketing team and its own budget. Most of the brands rely on a global IT team, so when the demand is heavy, planning and scheduling are essential.

Sometimes, our data needs to have limited access for reasons of consent. For example, we might have a customer who gave us consent to engage with them for the Enfamil brand – but not for Durex. So we can't send them a communication from Durex. If we did, they might think something went wrong. It makes communicating the whole portfolio to consumers complicated. And then, of course, there is regulation – the brands that are heavily used in Europe, for example, absolutely need to comply with GDPR. That is just one example of how regulation matters. A lot of the time we do have a detailed view of the customer, but it's for a single brand. Across different brands, the view could be different. The structure of the company can determine where the data sits. Currently two different brands might have their own IT infrastructure, so even when we know their customers are correlated, we don't make the connection. For example, in the US, families using Enfamil have babies, and we know that when people have babies they often use Lysol because they want to clean everything. We don't have a connection, but we're working toward building a profile that we can query. Our goal is to have a consumer-centric "360 view" across all of RB's products so that we can get the consumers relevant information when they need it.

SUMMARY: BUILD A FIRST-PARTY DATA ASSET WITH CONSENT

- *Growing tension:* No matter what your industry or geography, you are most likely experiencing a growing tension between your customers' desire for a personalized and relevant experience and their desire to maintain data privacy. Our research shows that while 73% of consumers say they want personalized experiences, 65% have already stopped doing business with a company because of data mistrust.
- *Web browsers and standards bodies:* Web browsers controlled by Google and Apple, most significantly, are adopting changes that make it harder for marketers to collect data without consent. Even with such consent, online advertising will likely never have access to detailed user-level data in future – just aggregate info. First-party data becomes more important.

- *Government regulators:* Global regulators are increasingly enacting privacy-related legislation that significantly impacts digital advertising and marketing. Europe's GDPR and California's CCPA are the most visible example of regulations giving consumers broad and enforced rights to control how their data is collected and used.
- *Mistrustful consumers:* Consumers in all regions are growing more distrustful of institutions, especially marketing-reliant enterprises. Ad blocking and marketing-avoidance are on the rise, and it's clear marketers are in a defensive position of having to earn back trust, over time. The good news is that data show consumers will share information with companies they trust.
- *The privacy paradox:* Sadly, consumers are not good at making trade-off decisions regarding privacy, often because they lack enough information. How can they opt in to a "personalized" experience if they haven't even used an app yet – and don't know what such an experience is like? Luckily, academic research reveals how marketers can help consumers make more informed decisions and accept a data value exchange with brands.
- *Privacy tactics to try:* Permission-based marketing works when you institute these four impactful tactics: Use overt data collection to directly ask customers for information that will give them value; give people control over the data they share, and consumers will offer it; explain the benefits of data collection and draw explicit one-to-one correlation between data given and personalization and service received; and segment your personalization efforts by understanding who your consumers are.

CHAPTER **6**

Building a Customer-Driven Marketing Machine

In this chapter, we move beyond customer data and into the organizational dimension of the problem: How can you build a more effective organization? We describe the things you need to be able to do in marketing around the framework of "know, personalize, engage, and measure." We also talk about how you construct the right "stack" of people through a Center of Excellence (COE) model that any company can implement, and offer ideas on how your company can scale a maturity model to transform around data.

KNOW, PERSONALIZE, ENGAGE, AND MEASURE

As marketing technologists, we love a good framework and there is no shortage of them in *Customer Data Platforms*. However, there is one that has matured over the years, and really stood the test of time: we call it "Know, Personalize, and Engage" and it's as simple as it sounds. *Know* your customer as much as you can through collecting data; *personalize* every interaction where the customer encounters your brand; and *engage* across at the channels and surfaces they touch. Later, we added a piece: *measure* everything and use that data to get better every time you start a new journey.

Several years ago, we wrote about this as the "martech layer cake," which is the same thing, but from a technical capabilities perspective (Figure 6.1).

The "know" was data management, writ broadly, for capturing and unifying people data. The "personalize" was Artificial Intelligence for discovering segments, predicting propensity, and recommending creative executions. And the "engage" was journey management, where you orchestrated a customer's interaction with your brand across touchpoints and measured their effectiveness. These represent the technical backbone of "know, personalize, and

107

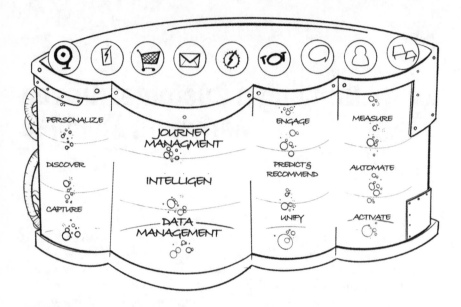

FIGURE 6.1   An early version of the "know, personalize, and engage" framework – represented by capability.
Source: Courtesy of Salesforce.

engage." Let's put them together, and define the requirements for building this simplified stack of capabilities:

Know ("the Right Person")

Can you ever really "know" someone? If it's hard in life, it's just as hard in marketing. Fortunately, as marketers, we don't need to peer into people's immortal souls, just sell them the next box of cereal or minivan. "Knowing," however, has several dimensions, as we discussed at length above. First, it's the technical ability to capture data across the known (personally identifiable information, PII) and unknown (pseudonymous) data modalities. Marketers must capture all of the information customers decide to reveal (name, address, email address, preferences, purchases, store visits, surveys, etc.) and all of the things they are able to infer about their intent (clicks, video views, website visits, PlayStation sessions, beacon pings, and the like).

"Know" not only requires tremendous technical capability to capture and store those data, but the development of a point of view regarding data's organization into a common taxonomy and "source of truth." Knowing is about deploying data management, not as a technology *per se*, but as a company imperative – a thirst for capturing and building a wholly owned first-party data asset based on people and their attributes. Knowing cannot be done properly by buying data management platforms (DMPs), customer data platforms (CDPs), or data warehouses (although they are required) – "knowing" must be an organizational philosophy that requires a company to make as many decisions as possible through the light of people data.

Today, to successfully know as much as you can about people also requires a whole new way of thinking about customer consent and data privacy. It's easy (somewhat *too* easy) to capture tons of "people data," but harder to capture just the amount of data customers want to volunteer. As we discussed in Chapter 5, it's not the amount of customer data that's important – just the amount that's *consented into*. Collecting data without consent is like filling your refrigerator with expired meat: caring for and storing lots of valuable looking, but useless, produce. It's just a bad idea and, like a bad pork chop, bad data can be as deadly in a world where the penalty for using it can equate to $23 million or 4% of annual turnover.

The "Know" layer is also fundamental to the rest of the framework. As a saying, "garbage in, garbage out" is a hoary old chestnut, but there's no better way to describe the importance of building the right dataset. What does the right data asset require? First, *consent*. Every attribute connected to customer data must be consented into – and offer the ability to be forgotten in the database. That means having a flexible infrastructure that enables customers to opt in and out of specific types of targeting and experience, based on their preference rather than a binary, "opt in/out" framework where choosing one thing (weekly email) means you opt in to everything (daily, continual retargeting).

It also requires "*truth*," or the ability to resolve customer identity across known (customer resolution) and unknown data (cross-device identity). With that, you are marketing to multiple versions of people, creating massive inefficiencies, and introducing doubt into the truth set. It also requires *scale* to power artificial intelligence. The bigger and richer the dataset, the greater the ability of AI to find the small deviations in the data that lead to valuable insights.

Personalize ("the Right Message")

If you look at the Martech Landscape Map, it seems as though there are entire industries dedicated to making people's interaction with brands just a little more personalized. Systems for choosing the right webpage for every visit ("site-side personalization"), delivering the exact right creative in a banner ad in real-time ("dynamic creative optimization"), or figuring out the right message based on someone's previous interactions through messaging ("next best offer"). Why? As with Casey's personalized pizza example, personalization just works. Let's take an example from the most popular and predictable channel for marketers since the time everyone had an AOL address: email marketing.

Say you are a clothing retailer trying to market a new line of winter clothes to your customer list. You have data on the last 1,000 email campaigns you ran, and the numbers look something like this:

Customer list: 2,000,000

Open rate: 20% (400,000)

Average click-through rate: 5% (20,000)

Average conversion rate: 5% (1,000)

Average shopping cart value: $100

Revenue: $100,000

Obviously, we are working with a super-simplified example (sophisticated email marketers use many more variables and dynamic models to predict campaign performance and revenue), but this isn't far off the course. In this example, 400,000 customers open the email, 20,000 come to the website to browse, and 1,000 people buy an average of $100 in stuff during that visit. That's $100,000 in revenue, directly attributable to that campaign. Not bad for sending an email, right? Especially considering the relatively low cost for assembling the creative and sending the message through an email service provider.

It kind of explains why, as soon as you buy something from an online retailer, you get daily emails until you opt out of them. Email is like a marketing ATM machine. The problem is that, thanks to how well it works, people are getting far too many emails, and it's harder than ever to break through the noise and be one of the few emails a customer will pay attention to with any frequency.

But what if, like Casey's, I could tweak my open rate by showing people the right product, my click-through rate by having the right offer, and pump up my conversion rate by having the right experience waiting for people the minute they hit my website? Let's imagine that personalization could increase my performance by a measly 10%. Things would look like this:

Customer list: 2,000,000

Open rate: 22% (440,000)

Average click-through rate: 5.5% (24,200)

Average conversion rate: 5.5% (1,331)

Average shopping cart value: $100

Revenue: $133,100

So, just by increasing performance by an average of 10% through personalization, every campaign is 33% more effective. Over 100 similar email campaigns, my revenue goes up by over $3.3 million. Wow. We've been working with many online retailers who are seeing increases of up to 50% per campaign with the right personalization, so there is real money to be made building the pipes to get the "right message" aspect of marketing right. Email marketers have been getting this down to a science for years, and having highly predictable models helps them make the "invest X in technology, get Y in uplift" argument to the chief finance officer.

Over the last several years, their counterparts in display advertising have started to aggressively invest in dynamic creative optimization tools to wring performance increases out of programmatic campaigns. Social advertising teams have been heavily investing in A/B testing in popular new social commerce channels like Instagram, where there seems to be a 100% correlation between creative video ad execution and e-commerce revenue. The "right message" aspect of personalization has been around since the Society of the Divine Savior. What has changed is the sheer number of channels that require personalization, and the real-time nature of engagement.

But, to really get the personalization layer correct means going beyond messaging, and permeating personalization throughout every touchpoint. That means putting it wherever the customer encounters your brand – not just email and display advertising, but also e-commerce, sales, and the call center. That's all about the engagement layer.

Engage ("the Right Channel")

When we consider the state of the art in cross-channel engagement, we think about Delta Air Lines. As frequent travelers, we enjoy some of the most high-touch marketing any consumer can get, and we are constantly impressed with how seamless our experience is across the entire journey, from the initial booking to the postflight customer survey. We tend to book our flights on the website, engage with the call center to change our itinerary or try and get a coveted seat upgrade, check in via the mobile app, visit the Sky Club when at the airport, and engage Delta on social media – sometimes *during the flight* to arrange connections or ask questions.

We always seem to get offers for the right routes on the website; we update our flight on the mobile app, and the website updates automatically; we make changes on the phone, and see our boarding pass updated on our phone; we are greeted personally at the Sky Club and even when boarding the plane. Delta seems to have managed to connect every single touchpoint, from marketing to e-commerce to call center to in-person, "real-life" experiences.

How impactful is this delivery of total experience? A few years ago, prior to the global pandemic of 2020 (a simpler time), we were about to miss a connection between Atlanta and St. Thomas, putting the entire family vacation at risk. Even though the entire trip was purchased with loyalty points, we tweeted to @Delta and told them our status (very late!) and that we were worried we would miss the connection (a very long walk and train ride between gates). Delta met us at the gate, took us down the stairs to the tarmac, and whisked us from Concourse A to F in a Porsche Macan, saving our entire vacation. What was that small gesture worth? We may never book a flight on another airline again!

Delta runs on experience – whether you are a Silver Medallion loyalty customer, or a "Delta 360" super elite flyer, Delta's goal is to make your loyalty count through better and more personalized experiences. As you build points and (hopefully) satisfaction along the way, Delta nurtures a customer relationship that makes you more likely to pay a premium for staying loyal, and it pays off in travel awards. In order to make that equation work, Delta has to be extremely close to its loyal customers, and make sure each touchpoint (website, social, mobile app, call center, and e-commerce) is perfectly aligned, and operate in as close to real-time as possible.

Of course, not every marketer has the operational pressure of an airline that requires such tight connectivity between website, app, and call center. But the value of connecting those touchpoints is very real, and compels marketers to consider the lift in lifetime value when customers are recognized across channels. It can start with connecting advertising and e-commerce at the people data level, so you can stop showing your customers ads for products they have already purchased. It can extend into the call center, so your interactions on the phone with a company proceed from a place of knowledge ("I see you just returned the blender you purchased").

We think of the engage layer as the ability to provision an experience across channels in two distinct modalities. First, the ability to manage "customer journeys" in a prescriptive way. Second, the ability to provision a real-time customer journey "in the moment" as the engagement is happening. Marketers require both skills.

Journey management is the ability to orchestrate the way a customer engages with a brand across a number of channels over time. Email service providers often feature capabilities that manage what a new customer journey looks like, right after an initial purchase is made. This might start with an introductory email ("Welcome!"), send an offer to sign up for a loyalty program ("Join and Save!"), and have intelligence built in to manage interactions based on what customers do. Didn't open the email? Nurture the customer with social media advertising until they sign up. Finally signed up for the loyalty program? Great – send them a weekly email with offers based on their purchase history. Journey orchestration is a huge part of the Engage layer, especially for wringing maximum value out of known customers through personalization.

Real-time Interaction Management (RTIM). RTIM is the "in the moment" version of orchestration, requiring different tools and more real-time data capabilities. Whereas traditional journey orchestration takes place largely over known channels (email, SMS, push, social media) and moves over hours, days, and weeks, RTIM requires personalization that occurs over seconds and minutes over channels like websites, mobile apps, SMS messages, and push notifications. The customer data an RTIM must reference to be effective has to be kept in a real-time profile store, which is updated every time a customer undertakes an action relevant to the next step in a real-time journey. (We go into depth on both of these critical capabilities in Chapter 10.)

As an example, a customer browsing travel content on a general interest site may encounter "recommended articles" about travel on the very next web-page. A customer who clicked on a specific offer for a product in email could immediately see that product on the e-commerce site seconds later. In a world where consumers move from channel to channel in near real time, RTIM is the way to connect and relate fast-moving experiences, driving relevance and delivering lift.

Marketers need to be able to provision both types of personalization, but how to unpack the thousands of different combinations of interactions across multiple channels and guess what the next-best offer or action should be? In traditional journey management, setting up an "If-This-Then-That" (ITTT) type of rules-based approach is possible, but not optimal, as the marketer must anticipate every possible combination of interaction and guess what the right offer or action is. In the case of real-time engagement, that becomes impossible. Increasingly, marketers are moving away from a rigid rules-based approach, and toward using artificial intelligence to make those decisions.

Measure (and Optimize)

All of this knowing, personalizing, and engaging must lead to some insights about who your customers are and what they want. This has been called "analytics," "measurement," and "attribution" over the years. In some companies, the three things are different; in others, they mean exactly the same thing (see Chapter 11 for a deep dive). Over time, different ways of measuring marketing performance have taken hold, and there has been no shortage of technology platforms to supply a "source of truth" around which a marketing department can see whether or not they are hitting their goals. Like customer data, most sources of measurement live in silos, and rarely inform each other. With marketing and customer analytics converging, marketers are moving to a measurement nirvana state of being able to optimize both the customer experience and the value of every dollar spent.

ORGANIZATIONAL TRANSFORMATION

We've worked through technology evaluations over the years, either as an impartial analyst or (biased) software salesperson. Companies looking for the latest data management software, personalization platform, or media analytics dashboard all have the same thing in common: they want to get better at understanding and engaging with their customers. At first glance, investing in the latest "shiny object" platform checks a lot of boxes. The world is constantly changing, and consumers with it.

Things are moving faster, and people have more demands on their time and attention. How do you solve a technology problem? More technology! Also, businesses are always looking for an edge and, when they rush into a software category, your company can't be the one rushing to catch up. We watched the DMP category evolve from a specialty technology for large, enterprise publishers to a "but of course" software investment for smallish marketers. The one thing that is true about any investment in a hot software category is that the software itself cannot solve the problem alone.

We've all heard the software meme about the company that spends millions of dollars in technology and complains that "they bought the Ferrari, but can't take it out of the garage" because they cannot operate it. CDP is much the same. Because it sits at the heart of understanding and acting on customer needs, and it touches every part of an organization, selecting and implementing a customer data platform require a strategy unto itself.

THE CDP WORKING MODEL

We think there is a fairly simple working model, or philosophy, which can help structure a CDP project (Figure 6.2).

Team

Every transformation comes together around "people, process, and technology" and we argue that, while you need all three, the people are probably the most important aspect. There is no partial credit for getting one or two of the three right. In this section, we will describe who you need on the team, but the key is alignment. Marketing has been frustrated with their inability to get valuable customer data from the IT department – they "hold the keys"

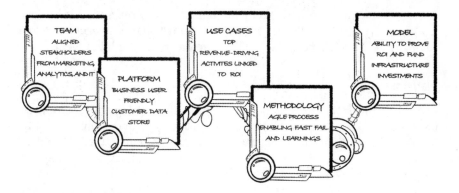

FIGURE 6.2   CDP working model.
Source: Courtesy of Salesforce.

to the data kingdom, "move too slowly" on projects, and put up roadblocks to innovation due to worries around data security and compliance. But the IT department feels as though they are constantly burdened with ad hoc projects to query data for the marketing team. They often feel like requests for data don't align with overall strategy, the marketing team doesn't understand the nuances and potential liability involved in moving customer data around, and treats them "like a vendor," rather than a partner. If that sounds familiar, it should. Most companies unwillingly build these walls over time.

This process is so natural that in 1967, computer programmer Melvin Conway unintentionally created "Conway's Law" to describe the process by which companies operate based on the structure of their organizational chart:

> Conway's Law: Any organization that designs a system (defined broadly) will produce a design whose structure is a copy of the organization's communication structure.

But what if a few renegades decided that there was a better way? A technology that could confer access to customer data for marketers without making it an IT project, and help IT through streamlining and unifying customer data into a repository that made it easier to manage? What if the analytics team – another stakeholder stymied by the constant need for diverse data, but lack of access to them – jumped in and offered their time and energy into helping marketing and IT structure the data and build success metrics around the project?

This group of aligned stakeholders are what is required to get a successful CDP project off the ground. In every successful implementation we have witnessed, a least one senior executive from these departments have worked to form a "center of excellence" approach that made data management a top company priority, and helped to build the financial case for investment.

Platform

The "platform" is the investment, but it is also an operating philosophy. Platforms work because they work on a common language, and enable creativity by allowing an extensible model that lets people develop on them. At Salesforce, our co-founder Parker Harris took a huge gamble by developing our core platform the "hard way" by opening it up to developers and creating a common data object model and codebase, rather than building it on a closed system. That vision was richly rewarded when we built our second big product, Service Cloud, to manage customer service. We didn't have to start from scratch – the codebase from our original product and all of the tools were there to leverage. Today, we have thousands of companies that develop applications on our codebase and nearly 8,000 connected applications available in our marketplace, the AppExchange. If we don't have the app you need, some other super smart company has probably already developed it.

This "platform" approach is essential to unleashing the value of CDP. Customer data, once the provenance of wonky "data geeks" who know how to write structured query language (SQL) and "munge" together datasets using technical tools, must be made highly available to every stakeholder who needs it. Data cannot be "the new oil" if everyone who needs a quart has to have the ability to dig a hole 6,000 feet deep. We believe that the right CDP features a "business-friendly" approach that enables nontechnical users to dive into the data, query it, test out new assumptions, and quickly put the data to work.

If CDP is the tool at the core of "transformation," it must democratize data across the organization, and enable access to them across roles. Rather than displacing the IT team, this platform-based approach partners with IT more closely, and unlocks more and more value as all kinds of diverse customer data comes into the system.

Use Cases

This may seem beyond obvious, but data unification for its own sake doesn't produce value. Yes, a "single view" or "single source of truth" around customer data is highly valuable, but it's akin to writing an encyclopedia that no one has read. Broad and aspirational CDP use cases are needed to start the project ("we want to transform our entire company around data") but companies need to pay the bills too. What does the marketing department want from data transformation? The analytics team? Defining the initial use cases is crucial to getting the company aligned around creating near-term success, and showing the executive suite that the juice is worth the squeeze. Every use case needs refinement that drives highly specific outcomes.

As an example, if a business goal for the company is "reduce the cost of new customer acquisition," then that should be aligned to a specific *data transformation use case* such as "refine customer segmentation to increase conversion rates on targeted campaigns." Initial data-driven use cases must have a compelling and measurable outcome. "Know more about my in-store customer" is an important, but squishy, goal. "Combine point-of-sale data with digital display campaign data to better understand video media investment in key segments to increase conversion rates by product," in contrast, is a measurable, achievable goal.

You cannot track the effectiveness of your data transformation without a clear performance framework, and having KPIs to align with is paramount. Many companies start with simple KPIs that show platform adoption. For example, a company with fairly rudimentary segmentation around gender, age, and income might want to add some behavioral characteristics ("sports lovers," etc.) to start to make creative executions more personal. So the initial goal might be "go from 20 to 200 segments" but the advanced goal, tied to ROI, might be "use advanced segmentation to increase conversion rates on online purchase by 5%." This helps align data and business goals together, such that executive alignment can be achieved more quickly.

Methodology

A lot has been written about the wisdom of Silicon Valley firms that have the "permission to fail fast and fail often," and much more has been written about why that might be a terrible idea. We won't weigh into the debate, but when it comes to totally transforming your company with customer data at the center, there will be plenty of failings along the road to total success. When we say "failure" we're not talking about adding questionably collected customer data into your store and running afoul of GDPR laws. We're talking about supporting a culture that allows for inquiry ("I have an idea that customers who have had success resolving problems with our call center would be more receptive to this new offer"), allows for fast results through testing ("it turns out that campaign performed less well than the same campaign targeted at customers with zero call center interactions"), and rewards data-driven insights ("it turns out that the untargeted campaign consisted largely of middle-aged women, and *that* was the key differentiator"). Having this type of agility within the organization requires a cultural shift which we will delve into more deeply below.

Operating Model

Finally, the CDP project needs its own operating model to fund ongoing executive support and investment. With CMO tenure continuing to fall year-over-year (Spencer Stuart recently announced that the average tenure for chief marketing officers of leading US consumer brand companies decreased to 43 months from 44 months), it's more important than ever for marketers to align their data transformation goals with the CEO and CFO. A common complaint in marketing departments is the way companies tend to view technology investments. But is CDP a "capital" or "operating" expense?

By its very definition, CDP investment should be considered as "capex" or a capital expense: "funds used by a company to acquire, upgrade, and maintain physical assets such as property, buildings, an industrial plant, technology, or equipment." Companies are investing in CDPs as the core infrastructure powering customer engagement and upgrading old systems. Although the physical nature of its infrastructure may live on servers rented from Amazon, the CDP forms the core piece of technology no company can live without: the system of record for customer data.

On the other hand, CDP is also "opex" or an operating expense by definition: "An operating expense, operating expenditure, operational expense ... an ongoing cost for running a product, business, or system." This is largely due to the way most software is sold today: as-a-service (SAAS). The beauty of software-as-a-service for companies is twofold: companies don't have to buy and maintain loads of expensive hardware; and they get the ability to deduct the equipment immediately as a direct expense, rather than over the life of the product – saving net income.

There are few software categories that can be as transformative to a company as a new factory, as an example, but benefit from the ability to be deducted as an everyday business expense. CFOs can learn to love CDPs, as long as the ROI statement is in line with the level of investment. DMPs thrived over the last 15 years as SAAS businesses which promised massive increases in media efficiency for relatively minor, monthly cost. Some large CPG advertisers we worked with spent $1 million over three years, and saved $20 million or more through media efficiency.

So, the question is: what is the entry point that gains executive support? The first and most compelling is to replace vintage data management components with the CDP. This is tricky, as CDP is an as-yet-unproven technology, and there are still a lot of data warehouses, brand new data lake environments, and MDM solutions embedded in companies – and many store critical enterprise data unrelated to marketing (an individual's product usage log, or clickstream data as an example). But there are several vectors: cost savings ("we can shave x% off our annual media budget through efficiency, since we will get better at hitting our target customer"), security ("we can avoid penalties of $X by aligning our customer data to comply with new privacy requirements"), or operations ("we can eliminate $X in expensive consulting costs by making our data easier to analyze and action"). A combination of all three will make any CEO and CFO happy to fund an investment.

THE PEOPLE AT THE CENTER (THE CENTER OF EXCELLENCE MODEL)

Many CDP projects start out from the perspective of the software pieces needed to build the right tech stack, but what about the "people stack" required to achieve success? As we said, doing CDP right is a matter of "people, process, and technology" and not necessarily in that order. We think the "people" part is probably the most critical. There are three primary stakeholders needed to get CDP off the ground the right way, and many more in supporting roles. The primary three are Marketing, IT, and Analytics (Figure 6.3).

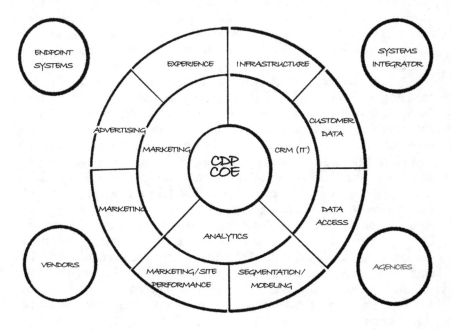

FIGURE 6.3 CDP Center of Excellence model.
Source: Courtesy of Salesforce.

Marketing

In the future, customer data platforms will expand their use case libraries and have an impact beyond marketing but, for now, most systems are aiming at the CMO organization in their go-to-market approach. Marketers have budgets, and they own the problem of integrating the many siloed martech and adtech systems they have licensed over the years. Today's CMO is challenged to deliver top-line growth, and has more P&L responsibility than ever before, and we are seeing the marketing team lead, rather than follow, key technology decisions.

In a CDP center of excellence, marketing should be thought of as responsible for the delivery of experiences that can be optimized through the use of customer data: website and app experience; display, mobile, social, and video advertising; and traditional messaging including email, SMS, and push. At small to midsize companies, these functions might be overseen by a small team, or a single department and are mostly vendor-driven.

At larger companies, there are individual teams managing online advertising, email marketing, and websites and apps. However, to be successful, "marketing" must be heard as one voice inside the CDP center of excellence, and represent the need for customer data as the unifying thread that connects advertising, messaging, and website and app experiences across the organization. That's why the CMO must own CDP; she is the executive that has purview across the many disconnected teams, vendors, and agencies across the portfolio.

This means that the CMO or her representative must be seated at the table, or aligned stakeholders from each marketing department must formulate a center of excellence team that speaks with one voice. This is easier than it sounds, because better access to unified customer data gets everyone more of what they want. The email team wants to re-engage customers who didn't respond to messaging campaigns through display advertising, and "nurture" them as they move into the funnel. The display advertising team wants to better understand website and app engagement to drive personalization and retargeting. The web team wants to build first-page site experience with interaction data from messaging and ads to deliver more targeted creative and offers. What should they ask for from the IT/CRM team? A single source of rich customer data that is easy to access (from IT/CRM). And from the Analytics team? Well-defined customer segmentation, data models that enrich customer data such that they predict and score customers' engagement across marketing channels, and an agreed set of KPIs to work toward.

IT/CRM

Ever since the dawn of database marketing, there has been an awkward relationship between marketing, analytics, and IT departments. The marketing and analytics teams are consumers of customer data, and the "tech guys" are the stewards who store it, manage it, and control access to it. Last year, we were at one of the country's largest telecommunications companies and discussed how they might leverage customer data from cable television subscribers to drive more "triple-play" subscriptions that included mobile and home phone services. But 100% of their customer data was stored in a data warehouse which contained everything the marketing team would need to create highly bespoke segments and match them with the right channels and offers. The problem? The IT department would not allow the marketing team to have access to the data. This seemed shocking to us, but was just one of many "WTF?" moments we experienced trying to help marketers corral and marshal customer data in their everyday roles.

As we discussed earlier, the evolution of CRM over the years has moved customer data closer to the marketing consumer as systems become less technical and more accessible to business users. But if CDP is really to become the natural successor to CRM, it must be the single source of truth for more than just marketing data. The IT team must bless the CDP as the system of record for capturing, storing, and unifying customer data. This means migrating data traditionally stored in data server farms, data warehouses, and data lakes into a central store (referring to Figure 6.3, the *infrastructure* component); owning the process by which the data are enriched through second- and third-party sources and the stewardship of customer data including compliance with data privacy (*customer data*); and going from being data gatekeepers to data retailers, as they provide more open access to customer data to end users (the *data access* component).

The latter concept is interesting. Notice we didn't say "free" access to data, rather that the technology team be "storekeepers" of customer data, which implies the consumer of that data pays a price. What does IT want in return for access? The ability to further enrich the data with attributes that make it valuable. The marketing team may take customer data out of the store for use in campaigns, but can also return highly granular attributes from messaging, advertising, and site and app engagement that can be used to create propensity scores. The analytics team can further enrich customer profiles and segments with second- and third-party data, attribution data, and campaign performance data. Companies that want to survive the Fourth Industrial Revolution need to manage customer data well, but the companies that will thrive will find a way to build an underlying data asset as something that may be valued on the company's balance sheet.

The IT team that manages the customer data store also has a huge incentive to give business users seamless access to it: the ability to go from a client-vendor relationship dynamic, working on many ad hoc and project-based requests, to a strategic partner that can add value quickly. In the center of excellence, the IT/CRM team's "give" is faster and better access to customer data. Its "ask" is for marketing and analytics to commit to streaming attribute data back into the datastore to enrich it.

Analytics

While the IT/CRM team may be the stewards of customer data, and the marketing team the prime activator of them, the analytics team must own the segmentation strategy, and set the metrics for success by building models that can measure the value that customer data brings to the organization.

In recent years, the explosion in the amount and variety of customer data, the inexpensive access to them at scale through data lakes, and the ability of sophisticated algorithms to plumb their depth for insights have created a sea change in marketing. Historically, the digital media analytics function was owned by the "geeks" who knew how to write an SQL query and find outliers in campaign performance, using the data to optimize vendor selection or tweak programmatic bidding approaches.

Data was stored in slow-moving on-premise Oracle databases, and insights were gleaned daily, after days-long processing times. Today, campaign data moves at real-time speed, algorithms scour the data constantly, and AI makes granular changes while the digital campaign is in motion. This new world has taken the power of analytics from the hands of technicians who can access data, and into the hands of data scientists who build algorithms to study data that is highly available and "always-on."

We saw this first hand at Salesforce (big marketers ourselves) when we tried to normalize campaigns across digital media, social networks like Facebook, direct buys from publishers, ad networks, and Google search. Just getting the data into a single spreadsheet required the efforts of multiple people to produce a monthly performance report. Later, we licensed software from a company called Datorama, who built hundreds of API connections and a clever ETL engine to do that work for us. (Note: Salesforce acquired the company in 2018.) This freed up several people from doing manual data "munging" and gave us reporting that ran hourly and daily, giving us continual access to insights for campaign optimization. This is software in a nutshell: moving from manual process to automation, and having AI doing work that frees up humans for higher-order activities.

Just as the world has shifted from manual to automated data munging through software tools, we have quickly moved from broad-based campaign analytics delivered in aggregate, to what we can call "people data analytics" which looks at highly granular, contact-level data and "scores" people based on the entirety of their interactions. In the COE, the analyst team will need to go beyond typical marketing and advertising analytics, and start to focus efforts around creating customer segmentation that is as rich (based on newly acquired access to people data) as it is dynamic (based on the ability to migrate people from one channel to the next as they traverse a highly liquid funnel).

In the modern data center of excellence, the entire organization is concerned with putting the customer at the center of every decision, and those decisions are only as good as the customer data they have and – more critically – how they are structured. The analytics team must have the ability to consume the unified people data asset at will, structure the data into broadly scaled segments, and enrich the underlying customer profiles with modeled data (e.g., propensity and lifetime value scores) that are easily consumable by the marketing organization. This not only involves the use of data science to construct models out of obvious interaction signals (e.g. clicking on an online ad, buying a specific stock keeping unit in e-commerce, or getting a "ticket" resolved with the call center around a specific issue), but also to bring survey-based, declared data to the profile to include attributes unavailable through addressable channels (ad recall, brand affinity, radio and television consumption, etc.).

The analytics team must also be responsible for helping create marketing's overall ROI model, and work to establish individual KPIs that can determine the value of data-driven marketing. This helps the COE determine how much value, by channel, can be extracted by adding additional segments and targetable attributes – and when precision-based methods start to yield negative results through diminished scale and added complexity.

HOW THE COE WORKS

When executed well, the center of excellence produces a cyclical, flywheel effect (Figure 6.4). The IT/CRM team gives analysts access to a unified set of people data that is highly enriched. The analytics team builds customer segmentation that includes AI-driven scoring, and sets the framework for success. Marketing activates the segments across addressable channels, based on where people interact and propensities to engage. Campaigns create more data (clicks, views, opens, content consumption, purchases, etc.) that are consumed by the CRM team and further enrich the people data asset.

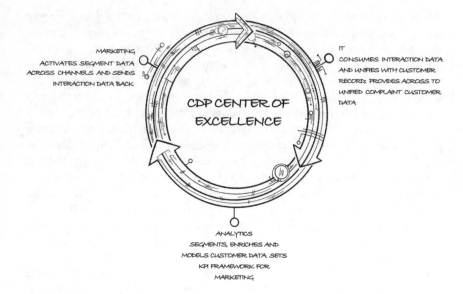

FIGURE 6.4 Center of excellence core responsibilities.
Source: Courtesy of Salesforce.

Put more simply: Better data leads to better segmentation. Better segmentation leads to better engagement. Better engagement leads to better data. Rinse and repeat. The real function of the center of excellence is to remove the barriers from that flow, and continue to improve results so more funding can increase the variety and amount of data put into the system, and increase the number of "channels" the data can optimize. Getting it right will eventually mean a lot more than deciding which type of cereal to advertise to which segment of consumer for a CPG company – the right people data asset may help a beauty company decide what food to manufacture in the first place. Imagine if Kellogg's had caught onto the entire Greek yogurt trend 12 months earlier and bought Chobani before they became a competitor!

HOW TO GET THERE FROM HERE: A WORKING MATURITY MODEL

Building the muscles to succeed at omnichannel marketing is an endeavor that not only takes the right philosophy and people at the helm, but also years of iterative development. In its simplest form, it's about going from being really good at delivering experience in a single channel (email), to connecting several channels together (email and display), to provisioning experiences across multiple channels in near real time (website, email, and display), all the way to an "always-on" 1:1 engagement where a brand is continually delivering contextually relevant experiences to customers in true real time.

Most brands get stuck after they manage to connect just a few channels, and we can't say we've seen a marketer truly achieve "connected omnichannel" excellence – but not for lack of trying. First of all, true 1:1 engagement may not be worth the expense and effort required to deliver it, and we are certainly a few years away from the technical capabilities to execute omnichannel well. But we need stretch goals, and the logical evolution of more connected customer data, more real-time capabilities, and orchestration across an increasing number of channels is what is depicted as "level 5" in Figure 6.5.

According to findings from the Mobile Marketing Association's "MOSST" study, 99% of marketing organizations have reorganized in the last two years, and 47% of those companies say it's due to the technology investments they have made. In other words, new marketing tech creates new processes, which require new skill sets, which require companies to completely shuffle the way they go to market. It makes sense. The email marketing team and the display advertising team both want the same things, but they work in very different ways. When the CMO forces the teams to work together to coordinate efforts,

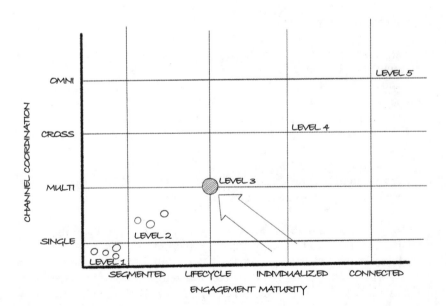

FIGURE 6.5 Where marketers get stuck on the engagement maturity curve. *Source:* Courtesy of Salesforce.

"work fast and break things" isn't just a neat-sounding tech mantra, it's what actually needs to happen to achieve success.

At the risk of oversimplification, the maturity scale progresses along two distinct axes: the ability to coordinate different marketing channels, and the ability to personalize interactions and deliver relevance. Each level of achievement requires exponential gains in competence and technology capability. Let's define the terms of success:

Channel Coordination Stages

- *Single:* Delivering marketing messages through a single channel, like email.
- *Multichannel:* Coordinating a campaign across two or more advertising channels (email, display, mobile).
- *Cross-channel:* Delivering customer journeys that cut across multiple customer touchpoints, including nonadvertising channels like the call center.
- *Omnichannel:* Delivering personalized experiences on all channels, including marketing, commerce, sales, and service.

Engagement Maturity Stages

- *Segmented:* Customer data is organized by broad segments, and campaigns are personalized based on an individual's segment membership ("travel intenders").
- *Lifecycle:* Customers are organized by segment, and funnel stage ("new travel intenders").
- *Individualized:* Customers are activated at the contact level, based on their funnel stage and status.
- *Connected:* Customers are activated at the profile level (multiple contacts from different systems creating a rich profile that enables personalization based on interactions across sales, service, marketing, and commerce).

We see many marketers who get extremely good at building broad customer segments and building customer journeys that tie together email campaigns and social media campaigns, for example. But we also see the vast majority of companies fail to deliver individual customer journeys that leverage multiple data attributes for personalization. It's just plain hard to do, especially at scale and at the speed in which the modern customer operates. Yet this is where the puck is going, as it were, so we must skate towards it. Here's a simpler way to think about it (Figure 6.6).

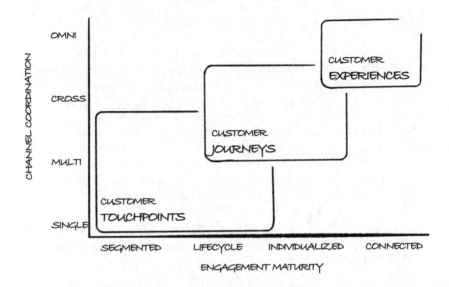

FIGURE 6.6 The three major phases of engagement maturity.
Source: Courtesy of Salesforce.

Touchpoints: That Was Then

All marketers start by engaging customers on various touchpoints: email, Instagram, banner advertising. Even brands without any of their own customer data can go into Facebook and build targeting segments around age, gender, and interest. This first stage of maturity – "touchpoint" marketing – evolves as companies start to capture and own their own first-party data asset, build broad segments of customers, and start thinking about aligning different creative executions to people at different stages of the purchase funnel.

Touchpoint marketing is oriented around specific campaigns ("Book Today and Save!"), planned in an ad hoc fashion (weekly, monthly, or quarterly), and is executed in an episodic fashion (one campaign idea at a time). This is the way marketing has worked forever, and brands can be highly successful in this phase, and never progress to the second phase of maturity: Journey-based marketing.

Journeys: This Is Now

Building customer journeys not only requires orchestrating two or more channels, but starts to require better identity capabilities. For example, it's no big deal to connect someone's email address and browser cookie when they are logged into a website. It's much harder to identify a person browsing a site anonymously and the fact that they are actually an existing customer. In addition to stitching together rich profiles of customers (their various IDs across CRM records, cookies, mobile IDs, etc.), the marketer must have the capability to determine what part of the funnel customers are in, and match them with the right creative, offer, or message. This is "lifecycle" marketing that can coordinate across channels.

Journey-based marketers are those who have "crossed the chasm" from touchpoint marketing, and have moved from a campaign-oriented approach to a multichannel methodology. Rather than planning new campaigns monthly or quarterly, journey marketers try to tie channel engagement together in sequences ("if you liked this product, try that one") and they execute across multiple channels (email, website, social media). The key from moving from touchpoints to journeys has everything to do with a company's data management capabilities (tie people data together) and technical ability to orchestrate (tie channels together).

Experiences: This Is the Future

The natural evolution beyond journeys is to move to "experiences." What does that mean? It requires moving the marketing department's orientation from channel-based interactions to being able to deliver the right message, creative, or offer in real time – "in the moment." The campaign planning cycle goes from plotting out rules-based sequential journeys to delivering iterative experiences that build upon each other over time. And execution goes beyond merely stitching various channels together, and requires an "always-on" real-time capability.

More broadly, evolution is a move from *systems of engagement* to *systems of intelligence*. This is an exponential leap into AI-based marketing. AI requires lots of customer data, highly organized into rich profiles, the means to continually gather behavioral and contextual data, update profiles in real time, and deliver experiences across any number of channels – also in real time. Sound familiar, right? The requirement for executing the future state of marketing is owning a CDP. We will evolve to experience marketing over time, and succeed to the extent that customer data platforms enable the required capabilities.

SUMMARY: BUILD A CUSTOMER-DRIVEN MARKETING MACHINE

- *The KPE model: Know, Personalize, Engage, and Measure* is a valuable model for framing CDP goals. "Know" is data management, writ broadly, for capturing and unifying people data. "Personalize" is using AI to discover segments, predict propensity, and recommend creative executions. "Engage" can be thought of as journey management, where you orchestrate a customer's interactions with your brand across touchpoints and "measure" their effectiveness.

- *The CDP working model:* There are five requirements to building a successful CDP operating model. You must have the right *team*, consisting of stakeholders from IT, marketing, and analytics. They must employ the right *platform*, which features a "business-friendly" operating model that enables nontechnical users to dive into the data, query it, test out new assumptions, and quickly put the data to work. *Use Cases* must be defined upfront, such that there is alignment between technical and business goals to drive faster executive alignment. The *Methodology* must create a cultural shift based on people data that allows for inquiry, fast results through testing, and rewards data-driven insights. The *Operating Model* requires an ROI framework in which results can easily be shared with executive stakeholders (CEO, COO, CFO) such that success drives continued investment and CDP is a "but, of course" operational expense core to the business.
- *The Center of Excellence model:* The successful COE consists of stakeholders from the *IT/CRM* team who own the data technology and access to it; the *Analytics* team who create the segmentation rules, data models, and ROI framework; and the *Marketing* team who activate the data across every channel. Better data leads to better segmentation. Better segmentation leads to better engagement. Better engagement leads to better data. Rinse and repeat. The real function of the center of excellence is to remove the barriers from that flow, and continue to improve results so more funding can increase the variety and amount of data put into the system, and increase the number of "channels" the data can optimize.
- *A working maturity model:* CDP requires leaping from *touchpoints* to *journeys* to *experiences.* This means moving from highly episodic, ad-hoc campaigns that impact customers on a single channel ... to thinking in terms of sequential journeys that move across several channels ... to iterative, "always-on" marketing where the next experience is determined by the last, often in real time.

CHAPTER 7

Adtech and the Data Management Platform

Advertising consumes most of the marketers' budget in many industries, but it's still often double-siloed, consigned to agency partners, without much data sharing. The best marketers incorporate ad data and insights into their first-party data story. In this chapter, we tell the story of the DMP, how it is ideally suited to handle pseudonymous IDs beyond the cookie, and how to incorporate this data to build a unified user profile spanning known and unknown data. CDMP, anyone?

THE MAGIC COFFEE MAKER

In our previous book about data management, *Data Driven*, one of our favorite stories was featured as the introduction of the book: the aspirational story of Keurig Green Mountain's CIO, Mike Cunningham, who wanted to put a data collection chip in every coffee maker. Mike was way ahead of his time. He theorized (correctly) that such a mechanism could help him get closer to his customers, discover what they were brewing and when, better understand their brand consumption habits, and maybe even power an in-coffee-machine ad network. (Ultimately, Keurig decided not to power DMP-style data collection in its machines, but the thought experiment was powerful.)

Even as a top-100 online retailer, Keurig really has no clue who buys its famous K-cups when at the local supermarket, and really doesn't know the family composition of those who ultimately install a machine in their home (unless they register the unit). And they clearly don't know who's brewing K cups in a hotel or resort. So, like many companies, Keurig is at arm's-length from its most important customers.

Around 20 years ago, a few things converged that brought the data management platform (DMP) – the adtech progenitor of CDP – to the market. Those things were the cookie, a little snippet of indecipherable text internet

131

browsers placed on your computer to remember what happened last time you visited a website, and the coincidental emergence of super-cheap and super-fast data storage thanks to Amazon Web Services.

When our friend Tom Chavez was running advertising at Microsoft's Hotmail division around that time, he started to notice that companies who regularly spent $5–$10 CPMs for targeted advertising were suddenly only willing to pay 50 cents. What happened? Some very smart people started collecting their own cookies, and building audiences of "auto intenders" and "travel intenders," turned the entire online advertising business upside down, invented programmatic advertising, and created a Lumascape of hundreds of adtech companies.

BACKGROUND/EVOLUTION OF THE DMP

Quietly, in the background there was a key piece of technology capturing, unifying, and helping to activate and analyze all of the little cookies and device IDs that powered the ad tech landscape: the DMP. Publishers could realize a 10X price increase selling high value "business readers" from untargeted "run-of-site" ads. The way they carved out valuable audiences from the general reader was through capturing readers' interests as they moved through an app or website. Visiting wsj.com and viewing stock quotes at 5:30a.m. in New York? You were a high net-worth investor. Going on the *New York Times* travel section and looking at the best hotels in Maui? A "luxury travel intender" reveals herself. Big publishers harnessed the power of DMPs first, realizing that deep segmentation of their online audiences yielded more value for advertisers, better campaign results, and more revenue.

Advertisers soon followed, realizing they could use the same mechanics to gather consumer data, and also scour a gigantic pool of other people's cookies and device data (third-party data) through marketplaces like Nielsen's Exelate and Oracle's BlueKai. Consumers, reluctant to pay for most online content, were happy (or, more correctly, impatient enough) to donate their online behavioral data through arcane and bible-length privacy policies to companies willing to collect it. Through these "opt-in" events, billions upon billions of online profiles entered the ecosystem. The typical user has over 20 browser cookies, multiple mobile advertising IDs, and interacts with numerous internet-connected devices like PlayStations, XBoxes and "over-the-top" (OTT) devices like Roku. Each cookie, mobile identifier, and unique device represents a person willing to be monetized by publishers, and targeted by advertisers.

This type of data is almost all of "unknown" users – people addressable by a cookie or "pseudonymous" identity. Why "pseudonymous" rather than truly anonymous? Because, with enough device data (your IP address, device type, browsing behavior, and location), you can be digitally fingerprinted and re-identified as a person. You are never really anonymous on the internet.

That aside (see Chapter 5 for a deeper discussion of online consent and privacy), all of this pseudonymous data about people could be combined to create a very rich profile of people and their behavior. This was an incredible boon to big CPG marketers who rarely had one-to-one relationships with their customers – and a huge advantage for publishers and media companies who profited from connecting advertisers with their audiences.

The wide availability of third-party data played a big role in creating scale and driving more value for both sides. Mom websites without many "travel intenders" could overlap purchased data against their site visitors and find more of them for the big airline advertiser. Auto marketers looking for "moms" in market for the next family car could find millions of them across advertising networks, and bid programmatically in large advertising exchanges to acquire them. In the background the way these data were captured, unified, and sent to the various technologies that powered advertising in the Lumascape? The DMP.

FIVE SOURCES OF VALUE IN DMP

Beyond just helping both sides of the advertising equation manage the common online currency of people (primarily cookies), DMPs powered a great deal of functionality. Those key sources of value look a great deal like what we expect from CDPs today. They are audience *planning*, data *activation*, *personalization*, campaign *optimization*, and delivering *insights*.

With enough audience data, brands like Heineken could figure out how many beer-loving soccer fans there were in a specific area, and target those people with ads for light beer – while suppressing wine drinkers. Big makeup companies like L'Oréal could capture mobile IDs from women visiting their "Makeup Genius" app and immediately target them with offers on Instagram, increasing their category reach. Big CPG brands like Conagra could personalize ads for visitors to Meredith's Allrecipes.com site, and make sure everyone looking at recipes that called for canned tomatoes would see an ad for Hunt's. Kellogg's could figure out the exact amount of monthly ad impressions needed to convert new Family Rewards loyalty members and save $25 million a year on display advertising. And all brands could dig into the entirety of their first-party asset and see what their customers cared about, the websites they frequented, their engagement with online advertising, and more.

The DMP also solved a major problem for all online marketers and publishers. How can you connect the many different devices and cookie IDs together and associate them with an actual person? This represented the "single source of truth" of people when they appeared in a pseudonymous state, before they actually logged in, signed up, or bought a product in e-commerce. The provisioning of "cross-device identity" (CDIM) remains one of the biggest challenges in a world where consumers' device footprint (now an average of eight network-connected devices per person) continues to grow as devices proliferate and we enter the maturing world of the Internet-of-Things.

ADVERTISING AS PART OF THE MARKETING MIX

There's a ton of goodness available and possibly many business school case studies to be had studying the advertising technology sector and its ups and downs over the last 20 odd years. One could easily argue that the premise of the entire industry (the browser cookie) was flawed, and you would not be wrong. But it's harder to argue that online advertising was a mistake, or will not continue to be a vibrant part of omnichannel advertising going forward.

Marketers tend to know a lot about their own customers and, as we have discussed, have been building ever more sophisticated capabilities to use their data to tailor experiences for them that cut across every touchpoint. However, even a brand with 10% market share in a particular category (amazing!) ends up missing 90% of the picture. The observational bias inherent in understanding only your own customers leads to "data-driven" assumptions that create marketing strategies that, because they are based on such a small sample of consumers in general, may be inherently wrong. As our good friend Jon Saurez Davis ("JSD" to his friends) likes to say, "It's amazing how many times you can hit the mark when you're off-target." JSD, who previously ran global media at Kellogg's, likes to cite the example of running a campaign for snacks targeted at Baby Boomers, and finding success with tens of thousands of younger customers instead. In other words, there is value in casting a broader net to capture insights to feed the top of the funnel and sometimes data-driven targets can be too precise to be effective.

In short, marketers will always need to go beyond their own, limited customer data to find and acquire new customers, fill the top of the funnel, and drive revenue. Where are those customers? They are on their mobile devices, social ad networks like Instagram and TikTok, on your website browsing "anonymously," and watching videos on YouTube and Roku. How do you reach them? Advertising. How do you target them? You use a DMP to capture their device ID, and build segments of pseudonymous consumers that look a lot like your limited set of customers.

ROLE OF PSEUDONYMOUS IDS IN THE ENTERPRISE

It seems obvious that there will continue to be a huge role for pseudonymous data in enterprise marketing. Yet, if you read the news, it seems like the DMP has been pronounced dead. So, what gives? As discussed in Chapter 5, the changes in privacy and legislation have decreased the amount and variety of pseudonymous data available (mostly cookies) available for collection. But, there are some fundamental challenges the modern world brings which make it nearly impossible to dismiss the DMP for a long time to come. Do you believe that the number of internet-connected devices will continue to grow over time? That most consumers interact with brands anonymously before they volunteer their name and address to a company? That consumers' digital exhaust of signals from devices and websites can reveal a deep understanding of people's intent? All of those things are true, of course.

As discussed in Chapter 1, if up to 67% of purchases are the culmination of the multi-device journey but 66% of marketers fail to recognize the customer when they switch devices, then it's obvious that the capability to manage "unknown" data alongside "known" data is paramount. So, do you still need a DMP? The answer is "definitely maybe." Companies need the ability to capture, unify, and activate pseudonymous data to connect the customer journey, enrich their knowledge of customers, and reach net-new customers at the top of the funnel. So, they need DMP capabilities and DMP infrastructure. But, in five years will companies license a stand-alone DMP to power their online ads? Probably not. It depends on how DMPs (and other systems) evolve into broader offerings.

ADVERTISING IN "WALLED GARDENS" WITH FIRST-PARTY DATA

Of course, advertising on digital channels has never required a DMP. Ever since Facebook started to sell ads in the mid-2000s – after saying that it never would – social networks and other "walled gardens" have captured more and more of total digital advertising spending around the world. In fact, if you add up all the ad spend that goes to Facebook and Instagram (owned by Facebook), other social media networks, and Google, you're looking at a proportion of around 80%. So, a strong and growing majority. (The so-called "open web" captures the other 20%.)

So-called "walled gardens" offer self-serve tools to execute ad buys within their ecosystems. As a rule, these tools are quite easy to use (again, within the platform's own walls) and are accessible to small and medium-sized businesses (SMB), who make up a majority of their users. Facebook and Google in particular have been extremely successful at capturing SMB ad spend, much of which would have gone to local print and radio in a previous generation.

Even more relevant to our CDP discussion, these ecosystems also offer the ability to execute ad campaigns based upon first-party IDs, such as emails, mobile phone numbers, even names and addresses. These so-called "custom audiences" are sent to the platform, and matched (at a certain rate) to the user base, where there is overlap. Since Facebook for example, sees about 70% of the adult population each month, the match rates are high. The advertiser can also extend this audience by buying look-alikes, which are people the platform believes look like the original list, based on a secret "black box" algorithm.

Using customer audiences built off first-party data in this way, the CDP can define a segment and send it to a platform such as Facebook or Google – and execute an ad campaign. All without requiring a DMP in the mix. Larger advertisers with more complex requirements than the typical SMB will often choose to build and execute these campaigns using a DMP or a combination of DMP and CDP, but the point is that the CDP itself can execute ad campaigns. As long as there is a connection with the walled platform, in this limited sense the CDP begins to look more and more like ... well, a DMP.

END-TO-END JOURNEY MANAGEMENT: THE CDMP

We think DMPs and CDPs are on a crash course and "CDMP" capabilities are required for total, "enterprise-strength" data management. The best parts of DMP (pseudonymous data capture, software-enabled data governance for managing consent, maintaining a real-time profile store, cross-device identity management, and pixel-based activation into advertising endpoints) are all "but, of course" functionality required in CDPs. Over time – and based on how quickly CDPs mature – marketers and publishers will migrate core data management functions away from DMPs and into CDPs.

This enables a single source of truth for customer data (both known and unknown), a single governance platform for managing channel-based consent, a single user interface for handling segmentation, and a single place for activating data. This will allow marketers to truly manage the increasingly complicated, channel-rich, customer journey in which people move from device to device and data modality (known to unknown) in near real time.

This "CDMP" vision is not just a concept. The way people navigate customer journeys makes it a technology requirement. Building one will be harder than it looks and, even after they are widely available, using one will require more than just technical expertise. It will require companies to change the way they operate, integrate their capabilities around customer data, and completely transform their organizations.

CUSTOMER-DRIVEN THINKER: RON AMRAM

We first met Ron Amram when he was managing media for Heineken USA and was looking into leveraging DMP technology to unlock personalization and measurement capabilities to drive sales. Like most mainstream beer brands, Heineken was struggling to maintain its position amidst the 20-year-long boom in craft beer. Despite acquiring Lagunitas Brewing Company in 2015 – one of the most revered brewers of ales and IPAs – the company needed to continue to grow sales of its portfolio, ranging from Heineken and Amstel to Mexico's Sol and Italy's Birra Moretti.

Back in 2014, Ron imagined and implemented a custom "overlap" report that helped Heineken find more beer category buyers – and suppress nonbeer drinkers – and used behavioral data to refine creative approaches to key personas: soccer fans, electronic music fans, craft beer fans, and more. Depicted as a "spider graph," the custom report was so effective at uncovering receptive "category buyers" that we made it a built-in feature of our DMP. We caught up with Ron, who most recently ran global media for Heineken in Amsterdam.

How do you leverage behavioral data to put the customer at the center?

As a marketer, you spend a lot of time thinking about novel approaches to personalization, and the dramatic rise in advertising technology was a wake-up call for many CPG brands. For a long time, the formula for growth was tied to how effective you could be in relatively few channels like TV and print, and you could correlate investment with sales. Over time, as consumers shifted their attention online, the explosion of channels and complexity of being where your customers were, were becoming a technology challenge, and I think we underemphasized creative at the expense of reach and frequency.

A lot of technology has been built to scale messages in advertising and marketing, which is a positive thing, but there are so many other critical touchpoints more impactful for building a brand. Brands earn love by how they work for their customers. We all have stories about our favorite brands and why we love them, whether it's a great experience on a call center line, using a cool mobile phone application, or simply the way a brand responds to a problem. Loyalty and brand love are literally built brick-by-brick in these iterative moments.

As a beer brand, Heineken was mostly at arm's-length from having a one-to-one relationship with customers, so every inference we could make about consumer behavior was critical. Essentially, we were constantly looking for signals which told us what consumers enjoyed, and determining how their behavior would change when stimulus was introduced. We build models to test the impact of weather on purchase, tested different creative and targeting executions based on life stage data, and had highly specific programs around various holidays and seasons where beer consumption was known to be higher. Every brand does this to an extent, but we realized that in order to scale, we needed to connect all of these tactics directly to the path to purchase.

Over time, we developed a discipline for capturing every available signal we could get around consumer behavior, applying it to models which were field-tested and validated, and measuring everything we could. Whether it was leveraging Heineken's close proximity to international soccer, uncovering an opportunity to win younger drinkers who loved EDM festivals, or embracing Heineken's strong multicultural consumer base through personalized messaging – we were constantly looking for the data signals that indicated how customers were entering or leaving categories. By understanding the various stimuli driving behavior, we could try and drive more engagement.

Now that we live in a world where consumers increasingly expect personalization at every turn, it's tempting to try and overengineer marketing and attempt to get to one-to-one engagement. Like many CPGs, we experimented with a number of ways we could have a direct-to-consumer relationship by building new routes to market – like cold beer delivery and home draft systems and the like. However, I have always believed that good personalization does not need to be direct, and usually a subtle approach is just as effective. Remember, contextual and behavioral targeting actually predates digital media!

SUMMARY: ADTECH AND THE DATA MANAGEMENT PLATFORM

- *DMP history:* The ubiquitous browser cookie created the ability to separate people from the websites they visited, and introduced the notion of true "people-based" marketing, albeit based on their pseudonymous or "unknown" data. DMP pioneered many of the core utilities in modern data management: data capture, unification of people and their devices through identity resolution, enrichment through second- and third-party data, modeling, activation, and people-based analytics. If CRM is the father of CDP, then DMP is its fun Uncle.

- *Five sources of value:* DMP also pioneered core sources of value that persist as requirements for modern digital marketing: They are audience *planning*, data *activation*, *personalization*, campaign *optimization*, and delivering *insights*. DMPs established advanced capabilities that expanded the notion of traditional "data management."
- *Importance of advertising in multichannel marketing:* The explosive growth in internet-connected devices and the Internet-of-Things (IoT) means the ability to capture, manage, and activate pseudonymous people data only gets more important in the CDP era. Additionally, the challenges in building a pseudonymous first-party data asset *with consent* make the data all the more powerful and valuable. Channels where customers may not be known such as apps, websites, and display advertising will continue to be core parts of a multichannel journey and require identity management to make them relevant.
- *Role of "pseudonymous" identity:* Being able to match known, PII-based customer data (CRM records, etc.) with unknown device IDs, cookies, and keys is critical to truly get a 360-degree view of the customer, connect a journey that spans multiple channels, and close the loop with analytics. Through their ability to ingest and anonymize CRM data, DMPs came close to delivering this vision – but, due to privacy restrictions, could not provision a contact-level view of customers.
- *DMP evolution:* DMP's natural evolution as a product is to fold into "enterprise" strength CDPs, and deliver the infrastructure that handles pseudonymous data management that continues to operate at the scale of the open web. DMP JavaScript infrastructure for data capture, cross-device identity, tag management, pixel-based data capture, event management, and activation are all core pieces of functionality in "enterprise" CDP. Marketers may not purchase a stand-alone "DMP" 5 years from now, but its infrastructure will power much of enterprise CDP in the future.

CHAPTER 8

Beyond Marketing

Putting Sales, Service, and Commerce Data to Work

Customer data is about more than just marketing, of course. As we have seen, leading enterprises increasingly break down silos between departments. Customer data can unlock engagement across the entire customer journey, from marketing to service to commerce and sales. This chapter presents a number of real-life examples where companies use holistic profiles to improve the customer experience across departments. Customer data is an enterprise-wide asset. The successful enterprise needs to go "beyond marketing" and consider working across sales, service, and e-commerce as critical touchpoints requiring data-driven personalization.

THE EXPANDING ROLE OF CUSTOMER DATA ACROSS THE ENTERPRISE

If we are truly going to "put the customer at the center of everything we do," then the customers' data must be at the center of the various systems we use to communicate with them. As discussed at length in Chapter 1, most companies have built up big walled silos around different systems that store customer data, and Salesforce was no exception. Our first product, Sales Cloud, made the "account" the center of gravity. Everything was related to an account ID as the principal identifier in the system (Figure 8.1).

Later, when we developed Service Cloud as the system of record for customer service and call center interactions, "person" became the currency of identity – everything revolved around the person trying to resolve an issue.

Later, we acquired Exact Target, an email marketing system. Its data model was configured to make "subscriber" the prominent ID. Still later, we

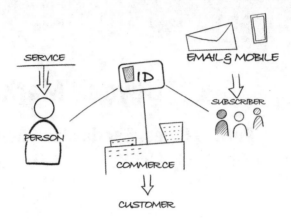

FIGURE 8.1   Different people ID types across clouds.
Source: Courtesy of Salesforce.

acquired a company called DemandWare that provided e-commerce software and renamed it Commerce Cloud. It liked to think of people as "customers" or even just the "bill to" address in an order. All of the different identifiers represent people – their name, email address, or physical address – but each system works slightly differently. Why is this a problem? Take a look at the highly typical, customer journey (Figure 8.2). It goes something like this:

- An office supply company sends an email to a customer promoting deep discounts on office furniture (email system).
- Customer clicks on the offer, goes online, and puts a swivel chair in their e-commerce cart. She gets distracted and does not check out (Commerce system).
- Marketer sends her an email to "complete your purchase" (email system).
- Customer opens the email, but has questions about the exact size of the swivel chair. She calls into the call center and connects with a customer service representative (Service system).
- She ends up going back into her shopping cart and orders the chair (Commerce system).
- Marketing triggers a post-purchase journey, thanking her for her purchase, and sending her shipping details (email system).
- She realizes the order is being sent to her old address, and chats with a customer service rep, who updates her order details (Service system).
- The service agent up-sells her some accessories that are on sale, and creates a new order and updates her customer record (Service and Commerce systems).

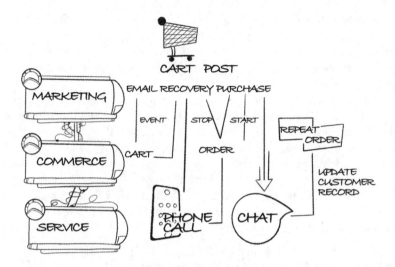

FIGURE 8.2 Connecting a multichannel customer journey.
Source: Courtesy of Salesforce.

We're certain you've been on a journey like this recently, and the experience can either seem really seamless (Delta), or completely disjointed (too many companies to name). In the case of the latter experience, the reason is that the three primary systems the customer is moving between are not connected, or require lots of manual steps to connect. A fast-moving customer can almost always be a step ahead of the experience. "What do you mean you need my order number! I gave it to the last two people on this call!" We've all been there. It doesn't feel good.

In the world of seamless service, there is a single ID connecting people with all of the keys in different systems, and the technical backend looks like this: The abandoned e-commerce cart triggers an event notifying the email system to send an automated "cart recovery" email, the customer's order on the e-commerce site triggers an event to stop the cart recovery journey and start a "new buyer" journey, and the customer's record is automatically updated in the system. This amazing technical ballet happens quietly, in the background, as computers talk to each other and trade information in near real time.

This "backend" functionality is something the chief marketing officer (CMO) has never really had to pay much attention to in the past. But today's customers demand the seamless experience across touchpoints that go beyond marketing. This is what we mean when we talk about the "rise of the chief digital officer" – marketers are now increasingly responsible for the touchpoints delivered to consumers on *nonmarketing* channels like digital commerce and the call center. They want to reward loyalty and drive word of mouth to get the most out of their customers, but it's tough to do when a customer has to repeat their order number three or four times to get the service they need.

Today, the most mission-critical job in marketing is working to increase the ability of the enterprise to identify customers and connect their data across the systems they engage with. You should think about it as protecting your investment. Just as one wouldn't spend $50,000 to buy a new car and fail to insure it, why spend hundreds or even thousands of marketing dollars to acquire a new customer, simply to churn them due to poor personalization?

In this section, we cast a data lens on the various functions customers encounter as they engage with an enterprise, and the benefits of making every touchpoint a function of marketing.

Service: Frontline Engagement with the Customer

How do you turn a $12 per hour call center representative into a $75,000 business development representative? A few years ago, we ran an experiment with a customer to see if data management platforms (DMPs) and call centers could work together. The company, a large hospital group that specialized in cancer care, had a typical sales funnel. They bought lots of broadcast and cable television and radio in key DMAs (designated marketing areas), drove people to their website for more information, and ultimately initiated most of their admissions through an introductory call with a call center rep. A large portion of those calls were "marketing qualified leads" (MQLs) and the company has a high conversion rate for admissions. Pretty typical sales funnel for many companies.

After acquiring a DMP, the company was able to light up some analytics around how different visitors did their research, and started to get some insights on how people were shopping for care online. This was not like other types of purchase consideration. Visitors to their site either were recently diagnosed with cancer, or researching treatment for a loved one. Visitors tended to spend a lot of time on the site, digging deeply into content around patient outcomes, treatment types, different facilities, clinical trial informational, nutritional advice, and much more. What became clear after analyzing the characteristics of people visiting the site alongside the content they consumed, was that there were highly distinct "personas" that were evaluating their care decisions quite differently.

Everyone obviously wanted the highest quality cancer treatment for themselves or their loved one, but looking at the data revealed that people ranked aspects of treatment differently and a dozen different "personas" emerged, based on their priorities. Here are four examples:

- *Analytical:* Those digging deeply in patient outcomes, based on cancer type.
- *Holistic:* Patients who valued the nonmedical aspects of care (diet, mental health) as much as the main treatment.
- *Location:* Those patients whose top priority was access to the facility and proximity to family.
- *Financial:* Those that were focused on insurance coverage and ability to pay for care.

Obviously, most patients cared about all of those aspects of care (and much more), but they were highly focused on one of those key aspects at a certain point of time. Normally, the prospective patients went directly from the website to the 800 number to get more information and schedule a consultation ... and received the same call script from the sales representative, who was primarily concerned with collecting information to put into a form. The call center was world class, and consistently received high survey results for their compassion, fast response times, and clarity, but lacked the ability to personalize those calls.

But what if the call center rep immediately understood the persona type that was calling in, and could read from a personalized script that aligned with the caller's main interests? What if the very first "real-life" interaction a prospective patient had on the phone got their questions they cared about answered more quickly? The company started to link the segmentation they built within their DMP with the call center, and triggered a notification and appropriate script in the call center, such that the rep had a list of key topics to cover during the call, and customized responses to the most frequently asked questions. Customers tended to stay longer in the call, and converted at a greater rate when speaking to an admissions specialist. The company started to get a better understanding of what was important to certain types of patients and their families, and was able to carry their "persona" designation through the entire sales funnel: from creative within advertising, to site content, to emails, the website, the call center, and ultimately the sales rep.

The unification of customers' data across systems, contextual data about their key purchase considerations, and alignment of communications tactics across channels as diverse as website and call center helped this company optimize a process they thought was running at near peak efficiency.

Many companies may never build such a persona-based contextual buyer consideration journey, but the value of connecting the Service and Marketing orgs is indisputable. It can simply start with suppressing known customers with product issues from seeing advertising to drive cost savings. Or employing the same tactic in the opposite direction by targeting those users who had a problem resolved, or gave a high post-call survey response. Most of all, we see service engagements, whether at the call center or via text message or "social service" (engagements on Twitter or Facebook) as one of the most important areas data can be captured and put to work in service of the customer.

Another great use case involves plugging marketing interaction data into the service console to give service reps an opportunity to up-sell and cross-sell customers in a personalized way. "By the way, I see we sent you a coupon for 10% off your next purchase. Do you want to redeem it now?" According to the latest State of Marketing Report:

- 80% of marketing and customer service teams share goals and metrics (up from 53% in 2018);
- 64% of marketing leaders say they now suppress marketing when there is an open customer service case (up from 32% in 2018);
- 79% of marketing and customer services teams have access to the same relevant data (up from 54% in 2018);
- 78% of customer service teams are empowered to sell and market to customers.

These dramatic leaps in connecting the call center to traditional marketing are another reason CDPs are on the rise – the use cases are apparent, effective, and readily available to the enterprise that can connect the customer data to make them happen.

COMMERCE: THE STOREFRONT AND THE NEXUS OF RESPONSE

Another key area for enriching customer data is within e-commerce. In *Data Driven*, we told the story of Pandora, the amazing music streaming service that could guess your age, income, gender, and household composition just by understanding the songs you listened to. If your playlist includes a ton of alternative music, 2000s-era hip hop, and the occasional dip into "Sleepy Time," it's not tough to guess that you are in your mid-30s with a 6-year-old in the house. In much the same way, customers' e-commerce interactions and purchasing habits are just as revealing, and are among the strongest signals – not just of purchase consideration and intent, but also about family composition, income, interests, and more.

Unlike Service, we've watched marketers integrate e-commerce (and in-store purchase) data into their marketing efforts for years. This begins with retargeting (the progenitor of the "shoes following me around the internet" meme), continues into using historical purchase data for modeling ("high propensity buyer"), and naturally evolves into advanced targeting methodologies around category preferences and interests ("snowboard buyer," "eco-conscious," etc.). Given the strength of signal (actual shopping for, or buying of a product), historical data (buys X times a year and spends average of $Y), commerce data is a treasure trove of hard-won people data attributes that make any segmentation strategy exponentially more impactful. Yet, we continually see these key data assets live in isolation of a holistic customer data strategy. What do we mean?

Use of Commerce Data for Modeling and Scoring

At the end of the marketing funnel, after a customer makes a purchase and includes their email and address information, we have plenty of deterministic data to use for targeting and developing propensity models. Pants buyers will need new pants for each season, car buyers will eventually need a new ride, and high net worth buyers of luxury goods will likely continue to buy them until they no longer can. Thanks to this high value, deterministic data set, we can truly know our customers' buying habits and predict their next purchase.

Where commerce data really delivers value, however, is in shaping our understanding of the unknown web visitor, app user, or ad viewer. Almost as soon as pixel-based data collection began, marketers were able to tag their websites and applications such that they could create segments of "yoga pants intenders"' and people who browsed products priced between "$X and $Y" during a session in an e-commerce portal. Marketers would use these strong signals to formulate segments for campaigns and use them extensively for retargeting.

Many marketers never fully connect the data they collect on their known users' purchase behavior with the signals they receive from unknown users. Known buyers get targeted via email early and often; unknown users continue to get retargeted with the products they viewed or left in their cart until they capitulate and buy the product or clear their cookie cache. However, comingling known and unknown purchase data can yield hugely powerful results. The typical browser session can produce dozens of attributes about a visitor. Here's a look at just five of them and what they can tell you about a site or app visitor (Figure 8.3).

So, just by going online and looking at an expensive pair of shoes, I've determined that you are a wealthy female fashion lover in Darien, Connecticut. Overlap those characteristics with hundreds of existing customers who

Unknown Data	Inference
Browsed red high heels between $350 and $700	Female
	High disposable income
	Fashion lover
	Likes color red
IP Address	Lives in CT
CPU / GPU / Screen Resolution	Macbook Pro user
	Professional
Geolocation	Lives within radius of Darien
Goop.com referral URL	High net worth

FIGURE 8.3   Using inference to link common data attributes to insights.
Source: Courtesy of Salesforce.

live in similar zip codes, and purchased similar shoes, and you have a fairly good idea about what ads to serve her, which products to feature on her next website visit, and what price ranges to feature in offers.

By combining the rich, highly granular attributes of unknown visitors with known deterministic customer and purchase data can yield effective predictive models. For example, if we know that visitors who browsed the red shoes more than four times within 7 days were 25% likely to purchase, and 50% of the people who purchased the red shoes went on to purchase an additional $1,000 of merchandise within the next six months, we could calculate a fairly accurate baseline for propensity. If we also knew that living near Darien, Connecticut, increased their purchase probability by 20%, we could further refine our score. This is all pretty easy math for the data science team, but the hard part is tapping into the ever-flowing amount of these signals coming in from different channels such as email engagement, advertising interactions, e-commerce browsing, video watching, call center purchases, and real in-store purchases.

What would a rich profile of customer interaction data mean for call center performance? As above, just like a personalized call center script can create faster time to value and increase engagement, so too can the right commerce data. Imagine the service representative having a tab on her screen that shows the customer's last five e-commerce and in-store purchases, along with any ratings she gave them? The ability for the service agent to go "off script" and engage with customers is obvious: "I noticed you recently bought a pair of our great new red shoes. What did you think of them? (already knows about 5 star rating). Would you be interested in taking 20% off (AI recommended) product today with this exclusive coupon code?" That offer becomes a lot more interesting when the customer feels she is a valued return customer, rather than just another person in the call queue.

Ultimately, the successful data transformation strategy must look at the purchase not as the end of the journey down the funnel, but the seed that can grow into a new top-of-funnel campaign.

SALES: THE B2B CONTEXT, AND WHAT THAT MEANS FOR CUSTOMER DATA

Linking commerce and service systems together in service of better personalization is a no brainer. There are considerable forcing functions that require this connectivity, and a clear and measurable path to ROI for companies that get it right. Most companies who have been successful did not start from a clean slate, nor did they operate from a well-orchestrated "center of excellence" transformation model. As we will discuss below, adding marketing to the mix is the logical next step; advertising, messaging, social, and website interaction data complete the 360-degree customer view and supercharge personalization. But what about sales data?

Alongside (capitals intended) Marketing, Commerce, and Service is another key leg of the table: Sales. Namely, the core system of record of interactions between salespeople and their customers. This is usually a CRM system, and the heart of business-to-business (B2B) marketing. A clean, frequently updated CRM is not only the single "source of truth" for customer data, organized at the account level, but also a treasure trove of predictive data about the health of the sales pipeline, and therefore the business itself.

We think the pipe represents not only the earnest efforts of the sales team to win new business and renew existing customers, but also the ability of the Service Team to reduce churn and up- and cross-sell customers, the Commerce team to remove obstacles between people and purchases, and the Marketing team to fill the top of the funnel with qualified prospects. In keeping with our belief that CDPs are actually the modern manifestation of CRM, it makes sense that there is a single source of truth for an enterprise, with customer data as molecular material that forms the substrate. This has been thought of as a "Business-to-Consumer/B2C CRM" – an interesting, but not entirely valid, point of view. In its first iteration, CDP may well be "B2B CRM" organized around the customer and their engagements with a brand, but even the data from B2B applications has great relevance to customer data transformation.

Sources of Truth

Every enterprise system that has taken a dominant market position recently has been a "source of truth" for a key business function. When you think of the source of truth for the human resources function of a company, you think Workday. When you think about the source of truth for software engineers and how they interact with code, it's Atlassian which makes Jira and Confluence. When you think of "sales," it's Salesforce. These systems create a value multiplier for the companies that create them because they quickly amass scale, and build organic ecosystems around them which are difficult to disrupt. When you have such a "source of truth," you also have a highly valuable input into CDP, which is the core value of connecting "Sales."

The first benefit of bringing B2B CRM data into a B2C-facing CDP effort is the people data that lives within it. The first step is to distill the many different "contacts" in the B2B database into rich "profiles" which not only map many different representations of the customer together (names, addresses, etc.) but add attributes like one's social handle or customer ID (as discussed in Chapter 4). Once the profiles have been established post-resolution, there are some highly impactful ways B2B can be leveraged for B2C "CDP" use cases.

Householding

For many marketers, it's more effective to target households instead of individuals. In many families of five, there is actually only one person who makes the majority of decisions around what groceries to buy, which car to drive, and what vacation to take. Whether it's Mom, Dad, Grandma, there is often a "household CEO" who is the keeper of the budget and key decider in the family. Recently, much work has been done in the pseudonymous space to join groups of identifiers together to make sure an entire "household" goes on the same marketing journey together. It's highly efficient (fewer messages required than individual targeting) and impactful (as all of the purchase influencers are targeted at the same time). But "householding" is even more impactful at the B2B level. Just as one might inhabit a B2C household containing four other people, one might be part of a 50,000-person "household" called Salesforce, as we are. B2B households tell us much about a person based on the size of the company, type of business, and principal location. Within a CRM system, contacts are automatically built into the "household" of the account, which is the principal identifier in the system. When CRM data is leveraged online, for example, "account" becomes a targetable attribute of an ID.

Targetable Attributes

Another key way to use classic B2B CRM data in the CDP is to leverage the ways in which the data has been organized into behavioral attributes. Most CRMs operate within a funnel construct, and will define sales stages from a "first touch" with a customer to "qualification" all the way to "closed/won" after the contract is signed. It makes sense that individuals within an organization that are further "down the sales funnel" have greater consideration for a brand, and many companies will create audiences of higher propensity customers that are targetable outside of the sales channel so they can be influenced across channels like email and display advertising while in a sales cycle. CRM systems that track content engagement (email campaign open rates, website engagement tracked through referral URLs, etc.) can also feed valuable attributes into the CDP as an input into propensity models, which score users based on the impact their engagement has upon purchase.

MARKETING: THE BRAND STEWARDS, REVENUE, AND THE ENGAGEMENT ENGINE

The marketing team has been at the forefront of efforts to extract valuable data from sales, service, and commerce systems for years. Sales data about company type, size, and business title have long been inputs into online B2B campaigns, and companies like Dun and Bradstreet and Bizo (now part of LinkedIn) have been at the forefront of making business data accessible to modern marketers.

In service, advanced marketers have been using call center data for suppression and continue to leverage call center data in increasing amounts. Of course, commerce data has always been integrated into marketing, and businesses like Criteo ($CRTO) thrived for years making a business out of retargeting visitors to e-commerce sites and activating abandoned shopping carts.

In the context of CDPs, we now must pivot our thinking along the lines of the famous John F. Kennedy quote. To wit, "It's not what we can do for marketing, but what marketing can do for us." In other words, how can marketing data be an input into success in the sales, service, and commerce functions?

Vinny Rinaldi, formerly head of media and technology for Hershey's, gave us a great example of how marketing data can be used for cross-team purposes. One of the keys for Hershey's was using digital media to fuel brand consideration, and his team put a lot of effort into building household targets in specific geolocations, near retailers. In lieu of getting actual purchase data from the local gas station or convenience store, Hershey's used location data as a proxy for success: how many more customers were driven to specific retail locations when Hershey's had advertising in market? In cases where Hershey's could prove increased traffic in a local convenience store, the sales team was empowered with the data to show retailers the impact of Hershey's campaigns on foot traffic to help pave the way for conversations about getting larger orders, more shelf space, or preferred placement near end-caps or the checkout area.

Likewise, understanding a customer's engagement with specific website content (as above in the cancer treatment story) or engagement with email can make the difference in a service engagement within the call center. The less-scripted and more personal each customer interaction with the service department can be, the more it equated to tangible equity in the brand relationship.

Ultimately, the marketing team is leading the CDP charge, and many of the initial CDP use cases will involve using cross-cloud data for better targeting or more accurate measurement. However, in terms of long-term CDP success, it behooves the marketer to understand and take advantage of the "give to get" nature of data sharing within the organization and ultimately participation within a center of excellence where every team gets more in value than they individually contribute.

CUSTOMER-DRIVEN THINKER: KUMAR SUBRAMANYAM

Recently celebrating his tenth anniversary at HP (Hewlett-Packard Inc.), Global Head of Marketing Data Sciences, Kumar Subramanyam came into marketing via an increasingly common route: hard-core analytics. A global hardware and software company with an 80-year history, HP faces every customer data challenge imaginable, from a highly complex internal martech footprint and support team to the nuances imposed by multimarket regulations and both B2B and B2C imperatives.

What challenges do you face daily trying to organize and wrangle customer data for marketing across regions and divisions?

> In my role as marketer, my main problem is consistency of data collection. Our data universe is many different assets and technology solutions put together to connect a customer journey. We as humans have evolved from one PC in a household to probably a half-dozen machines in each of our pockets. Connecting activity across these platforms becomes very hard to do. Then once we collect it, how do we know if data conforms to a singular identity? And are we collecting consent in a uniform manner? Sometimes we have data we collect for telemetry, but we realize after the fact that we did not inform the customer of the marketing use. Even beyond identity, we have different personas: consumer and commercial. It's the same person, but a different persona. We have to look at both.

Across the company, there was a data strategy put together. It solved for the "single ID" challenge. But we noticed we did not necessarily solve for universal consent management. For instance, say you just gave consent on your PC for gmail [communications]. Next day you download an app and register the same email address. What if you say "yes" the first time and now you say "no"? What overrides what? Companies that solve this take some "ecosystem ID," like Google or Facebook, and transform it into a singular tracking and consent management approach.

The role of marketing has changed a lot over time. Ten years ago, IT was the center of the universe when it came to asset development, implementation, deploying hardware, services, data assets. Over time, marketing had a need for speed and agility, so it went off and did its own thing, buying and implementing tech. A lot of this was driven by software-as-a-service (SaaS) models. All we had to do was take a credit card and sign up. No infrastructure, no patches, everything is plug and play. IT became more of a maintainer of older assets, hardware, like ERP. Now I think we're at a point where we need more from IT again. We need help with consistent [customer] data flows. IT becomes the glue, the team that sets up common standards.

The importance of first-party data [shared across departments] has skyrocketed. Martech is strongest when it's closer to customer support. The capabilities needed and used by marketing and support are similar. Web is the common medium, web and apps – digital – so the underlying methods we use between them can be maximized to drive value. Of course, the different orgs can be at different levels of maturity. Ours are. We are trying to come up with better integration and storytelling across the customer experience. How do we tie marketing messages to problems or successes in support? How do we translate this into advocacy? The journey goes from buying to post-purchase. For example, we are working toward stopping ads to people with service issues. We're looking at identifying [social] influencers when they contact us. We need to drive a consistent experience, and the journey is the most important element.

SUMMARY: BEYOND MARKETING: PUTTING SALES, SERVICE, AND COMMERCE DATA TO WORK

- *The expanding role of customer data in the enterprise:* The emergence of the CDP category has been a forcing function for enterprise-wide data integration that makes the CMO and her team responsible for personalizing touchpoints that go "beyond marketing" to include service, commerce, and sales interactions. Performing customer resolution to get a common customer ID is important, but so is building the infrastructure to port data between different systems to deliver a seamless experience as customers migrate between channels. There is a new mandate for CMOs to work alongside IT counterparts to deliver a technical backend that connects siloed systems in the service of working orchestration that can personalize every touchpoint customers encounter – in near real time.

- *Service:* Service systems that manage in-person, call center, and social interactions are at the forefront of experience delivery, and ultimately what determines the success of personalization efforts, but today's systems often live in isolation of commerce and marketing data. The connected enterprise – with customer data as its driving force – can bring highly valuable contextual, behavioral, and purchase data to turn low-value call center employees into high-value business development representatives. Connecting commerce and service together is the first priority to drive a steel thread between what people purchase and their satisfaction with the product. Marketing data connected to service extends a conversation that can begin at the top of the funnel all the way through to post-purchase to create end-to-end journeys.

- *Commerce:* Commerce systems offer the strongest and highest fidelity signals of brand consideration, purchase intent, and loyalty – but also can be used in predictive ways to build propensity and lifetime value scores that drive marketing effectiveness. Most enterprises have made rudimentary connections between commerce and marketing (via email marketing, retargeting, etc.) but have not fully leveraged the power of commerce interaction and purchase data in their segmentation and analytics functions. In a world of dwindling third-party marketplace purchase data, brands must prioritize the acquisition and integration of commerce data into the customer profile to drive marketing and even service effectiveness to grow top-line revenue and reduce customer churn.

- *Marketing:* Marketers will lead the CDP charge as initial use cases will feature unified data from sales, service, and commerce driving campaigns, but there are many instances where marketing data can contribute to cross-cloud applications. Marketing analytics data can be used to power sales conversations, and marketing engagement data can be leveraged to better personalize commerce engagements. Ultimately, the marketing team must see CDP efforts in a holistic context, and be prepared to push as much marketing data in the service of nonmarketing use cases, as the data they pull from other clouds to drive success in campaigns and promotions.

CHAPTER 9

Machine Learning and Artificial Intelligence

Customer data has little intrinsic value unless it is put to use. One of the most promising uses for customer data is to make it available to all the magical artificial intelligence (AI) and machine learning (ML) methods that are available for insights and decisions. Leading organizations are those applying advanced analytics to data to gain competitive advantage. We describe the most common types of AI and what's emerging in marketing. How embedded AI and "decision support" by the citizen data scientist are the future. Ultimately, AI will make customer data more useful.

ONCE UPON A TIME . . . IN *SILICON VALLEY*

In Season 4, Episode 4 of HBO's *Silicon Valley*, a story arc was built around an app called "Not Hotdog." An actual app for your iPhone or Android, "Not Hotdog" used an AI image recognition algorithm to determine whether a photo you gave it likely contained a classic hot dog (or not), as in Figure 9.1.

The app was built by Tim Anglade, who worked for the show (among other things), and he generously shared his methods in a fascinating blog post. For details, we recommend the source, full of mustard and drama, and what we'll do in a moment is give you a, um, taste – a nibble – of the way a marketing data scientist might approach this kind of problem using just a laptop, some additional GPUs, and time. But first, a little background on the exciting field of artificial intelligence.

FIGURE 9.1 Tweet depicting results from the "Not Hotdog" app.
Source: Courtesy of Twitter, Paul Stachniak.

DEEP LEARNING AND AI

First described in the 1950s, artificial intelligence is the attempt to make computers do things humans do. It can be divided into so-called "weak" AI, which focuses on specific problems such as interpreting language (i.e. natural language processing [NLP]) and "strong" AI, which attempts to build more general systems, such as Google Brain. It is an umbrella term that includes machine learning, as well as other fields such as symbolic reasoning.

- *Deep learning:* Deep learning is a subset of machine learning that uses artificial neural networks to detect very precise patterns in data (Figure 9.2). Generally requiring massive amounts of info and raw computing power, it was not a widely available technique until recently. It is useful for categorizing unstructured data such as images, text, and speech, and for performing complex tests and making predictions.
- *Artificial neural networks (ANNs):* First described decades ago, ANNs use a large number of neurons or nodes that are arranged into layers. The

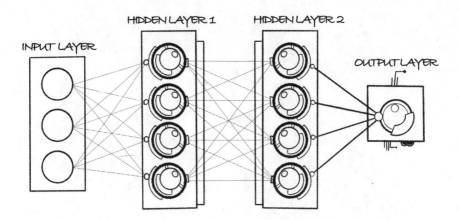

FIGURE 9.2 Depiction of how deep learning works.
Source: Courtesy of Salesforce.

neurons are weighted and re-weighted during the training phase of the modeling process. In the case of deep learning, there are a number of hidden layers between the input and the output nodes. There are many different types of ANNs that are used by marketing data scientists to solve particular problems. For example, so-called convolutional neural networks are particularly useful for recognizing images, e.g. the brand's logo in photos posted on blogs or social networks.

Back to the Hot Dogs

The directive for *Silicon Valley* was to create an app that would run directly on a phone, without requiring a network connection. The entire development lab setup for this fancy piece of AI wizardry (including water bottle) looked like Figure 9.3.

Anglade's post walks through a process of trial and error, typical of these kinds of projects. You'll see here a couple of themes: (1) Google and Facebook are all over AI, subsidizing basic research in extraordinary ways; (2) it's a fast-evolving field, full of wily grad students posting code on Github at midnight; and (3) there's a lot of, as we said, trial and error.

Cast of Characters

Some of the players encountered in the course of the drama:

- *React Native:* This is a popular development framework out of Facebook that was used to build the app itself, the user interface, etc.

FIGURE 9.3 Lab setup to create the app.
Source: Image courtesy of Tim Anglade, published on Medium.com.

- *Google Cloud Platform's Vision API:* This is a very handy service that will take an image as an input and return a set of probabilities and labels that might (or might not) describe the object. This character was let go early on, however, because it wasn't quite accurate enough re: hot dogs (or not).
- *ImageNet:* A legendary repository of labeled images (about 14M at last count), ImageNet is used as raw data to train vision recognition models. These images have been the basis of a yearly competition, held since 2010, to develop the best neural recognition architecture. This contest matters more than the Oscars in certain overeducated circles.
- *TensorFlow and Keras:* These are commonly used open source libraries that can work together. (Libraries are just a collection of prewritten code blocks that can be included in your programs by reference, saving you a lot of time.) TensorFlow was developed by (yes) Google, and it provides ways to train neural networks, among other things. Keras is a library that runs on top of TensorFlow and is used to train and test neural networks.

Anglade also used some open source code offered by a Turkish grad student of the implementation of a technical paper published by Google the day before, as well as some additional techniques to "tune" the model. The program was written in Python.

As usual, a lot of time was spent tweaking the model to make it more accurate and enabling it to handle tricky situations, such as photos at weird angles or photos with hotdog-like things that weren't hotdogs. It seems that collecting and selecting the data (i.e. the images for training) was a major project itself. Any data scientist will attest that building models is almost easy compared to assembling the data.

In the end, the model was trained using 150,000 images (the vast majority of which were "not hotdog") that were run through the network 240 times. This process took about 80 hours, or a long weekend. It's useful to remember that a neural network like the one used by "Not Hotdog" is just a collection of "neurons" and weights. It takes prelabeled images ("hotdog" and "not hotdog") and in a very resource- and time-intensive process tries to figure out what the "hotdog" images have in common. The similarities are translated into a series of weights and filters that can be applied to new images.

What comes out? Just a label (with a probability): Hotdog or Notdog.

CUSTOMER-DRIVEN MACHINE LEARNING AND AI

A gaming company wanted to promote its partnership with a European sports league, so it used network analysis of social platforms to determine overlapping "tribes" to target with advertising. A global computer reseller wanted to make sales teams more efficient by focusing on deals more likely to close, so it built an in-house model to score leads and shortened sales cycle time. A digital commerce fashion brand wanted to improve conversion rates on its websites, so it built a recommendation system based on past purchase data.

As these real examples show, more and more advanced data science is being regularly applied to marketing problems and can be a key application of customer data. The amount of data used by marketers has more than doubled in the past year, according to the Association of National Advertisers. Demand for automated artificial intelligence applications has simultaneously exploded. For example, Salesforce's Einstein machine learning and AI tools saw their adoption and use rates soar almost 186%+ from 2018 to 2020.

Customer data sitting in a data warehouse – even organized and cleansed in a true enterprise-grade customer data platform – serves no real purpose. It must be activated to yield business value. This activation can happen in one of two ways: (1) operational activation, i.e. when the data is put to use in a particular business process, such as personalizing a message; or (2) analytical activation. The latter is arguably the more exciting use for customer data in the future, as advanced machine learning and artificial intelligence – applied to matched and harmonized, real-time customer data – provide the real engine of competitive differentiation.

DATA SCIENCE IN MARKETING

Data science is a hybrid discipline that draws from statistics, mathematics, and computer science. In a marketing context, it can encompass elements of network theory, geography, and even neuroscience. In part, it is a renaming and reorganization of roles that already existed in marketing organizations, consulting firms and agencies, particularly that of the marketing analyst. Indeed, by some estimates more than half of the apparent "explosion" of data scientist titles within enterprises over the past five years is due to retitling.

Data science is about solving business problems, particularly in a marketing context. Typical tasks for a marketing data scientist include:

- *Measurement:* Determining the impact of marketing efforts and ad campaigns.
- *Optimization:* Recommending changes in tactics or spending to improve results.
- *Experiments:* Designing and executing tests to isolate causes.
- *Segmentation:* Identifying groups and subgroups of customers and prospects.
- *Predictive modeling:* Building computer models to improve response rates by providing more personalized content, offers, pricing or other treatments, for example.
- *Storytelling:* Communicating messages derived from data to inspire better decisions.

All good marketing data scientists possess three key attributes: Quantitative skills; some knowledge of their industry; and, above all, curiosity. It is a "horizontal" discipline, meaning that its basic tools can be applied to a wide range of industries and problems. It is common to find successful marketing data scientists who migrated from diverse fields such as finance, healthcare, or academic physics.

In addition to the important work of querying customer data, data preparation, and effective communication, the data scientist's domain can be divided into three general areas:

- *Exploration:* Using statistics and visualization techniques to find patterns in data.
- *Experimentation:* Applying design-of-experiments methods to develop and test hypotheses under controlled conditions.
- *Machine learning and artificial intelligence:* Applying algorithms to build models and make predictions.

Machine Learning Vs. Artificial Intelligence?

There is a secular debate raging about the difference between these two domains, which are not entirely distinct. We define artificial intelligence as any machine-driven process that augments or enhances human decision-making. Machine learning is a subset of artificial intelligence applied to models that learn from experience. In informal practice, the terms are often used to describe a particular group of algorithms, i.e. artificial intelligence is applied to neural networks, and machine learning is applied to more traditional statistical models, such as logistic regression, k-means, etc.

What Does a Marketing Data Scientist Do?

The working data scientist likely spends most of her time locating and cleaning data and performing "feature engineering," or identifying which attributes in the data are more meaningful than others. Among the four domains listed above, the typical practitioner probably concentrates on database queries and data exploration. Since machine learning and AI are largely powered by prewritten computer code, assembled into frameworks called libraries, it is routinized for all but the most complex problems. The data scientist earns her money defining problems, selecting, and exploring data, trying different solutions, and weighing trade-offs among them – not, usually, writing algorithms.

CUSTOMER DATA AND EXPERIMENTAL DESIGN

Although not machine-learning or artificial intelligence, data experimentation is one of the fields of data science that is radically improved by the new era of customer data platforms. Organizing and making available integrated customer data allow data scientists to perform significant experiments that were prohibitively complex and time-consuming in the past.

For example, a national car brand observed a high correlation between viewing an ad on a popular car buying website and visitors to its own website. Although it assumed the ad had an impact, it could not be sure other factors – such as the likelihood that the car-buying website attracts the same people who visit their website – were not responsible. To establish causation, the brand would have to set up a controlled experiment in advance.

In marketing, experimentation is usually applied to improve response to calls to action or other marketing messages. Marketing data scientists often apply experimental methods to do the following:

- test different versions of website or other marketing content
- compare email subject lines and mobile push messages

- develop item recommendation or incentive offers for different groups
- test the impact of creative treatments or media placements for advertising

CUSTOMER DATA, MACHINE LEARNING, AND AI

Machine learning and AI use algorithms that learn from experience to solve problems. Solutions are expressed in the form of models that can be used to make predictions or find underlying structures in data. Both have become more widespread in marketing due to the data explosion, advances in processing speed and scale, and the greater ability of software tools (including excellent free ones), and trained talent.

What Is a Model?

Algorithms used for machine learning build abstract representations of data called models. Typically, models go through two processes, which are often combined:

- training – fitting a model to data
- testing – validating the effectiveness of the fitted model

Labeled Vs. Unlabeled Data

Labeled data is data for which the desired outcome is known, and it is required to build predictive models. For example, a marketer who wanted to build a model to predict whether a customer is likely to unsubscribe from an email list would assemble a list of records from customers who had previously unsubscribed or not. In this case, the label would be "unsubscribed" or "remained," and the analyst's job is to build a model based on historical data that can be used in the future.

Sometimes data is not labeled or the analyst's goal is not to make a prediction. For example, an analyst may have a large number of prospect records, and she may want to apply machine learning to identify segments. Various methods such as algorithmic clustering can be used to identify different groups or determine some other underlying structure in the data.

Fitting a Model to Data

No model is perfect, but some are more useful than others. In the example above, a "perfect" model could be built that simply memorized the dataset; however, it could only be applied to a new record if that record exactly matched a previous example. Such a model is said to be too rigid to generalize well on out-of-sample (or new) data. On the other hand, a model that mimicked a coin flip would be equally right (or wrong) against any new data but is, by definition, no better than chance. The analyst must continually balance between the two extremes of memorizing the training data (known as overfitting) and building a weak model (known as underfitting).

Most ML/AI problems fall into one of two categories:

- supervised – using labeled data to build models that make predictions
- unsupervised – applying methods to unlabeled data to identify structures

In either case, the data used can be numerical or categorical (e.g. state of residence).

Making Predictions

Predictive models are widely used in marketing. They are an example of supervised learning because they use labeled historical data to build a model that can be applied to make a prediction about new data. These predictions can take the form of an actual numerical value (regression) or – perhaps more often – are used to classify customers and prospects (classification).

Regression

Regression models use numerical data to make a numerical prediction of a desired value. Examples include:

- Estimate the lifetime value (LTV) of a new customer based on a few months of purchases.
- Predict the number of incremental website orders to expect after an advertising campaign.
- Determine the best frequency to send emails based on historical open rates.

Classification

Rather than predict a numerical value, categorical models attempt to classify or label something. Examples include:

- Predict whether someone will or will not click on a digital video advertisement.
- Determine whether someone is likely or unlikely to purchase a particular brand or type of product.
- Identify B2B sales leads who are more likely to respond to a pitch.

Finding Structure

Another use for machine learning is to probe data and identify structure that is not obvious to the unaided analyst. Structure can be defined as any underlying organization that filters out meaningless or random variations.

Clustering

Finding structure in numerical data generally involves creating groups or clusters that have some internal similarity while being relatively distinct from other groups. Examples include:

- Discover different groups of visitors to a marketing website based on browsing behavior.
- Determine different types of prospects based on demographics and buying patterns.
- Separate high-value customers into subgroups based on preferred product types.

Dimensionality Reduction

Beyond clustering and similarity measures, a variety of complex methods are used to detect underlying structure within categorical (or combined numerical and categorical) datasets. Marketing data scientists treading here usually need a lot of information, heavy computing power, and special training. Examples include:

- Determine which items to recommend to a customer based on his similarity to other customers.
- Find evidence of brand affinity on social networks based on identifying logos in photographs.
- Divide customer comments into different topics based on linguistic analysis.

Neural Networks

In addition to the statistical methods outlined above, a newer class of artificial intelligence and so-called deep learning model is increasingly being applied to marketing problems. These methods are based on a set of complex algorithms that train networks of nodes in various ways, particularly to mimic functions of the human brain. Such networks are more suited to address highly nuanced and data-intensive tasks such as image recognition (e.g. "Where is the cat in this picture?"), machine translation (e.g. "*Où est le chat?*" becomes "Where is the cat?"), and call-center voice transcription.

APPLYING MACHINE LEARNING AND AI IN MARKETING

Two of the most interesting ways machine learning has been used in marketing have been the areas of segmentation and attribution. Early experiments over the past several years have yielded promising results, but each will find a new life in the CDP era. Meanwhile, there are a number of other areas of AI that offer exciting potential benefits for the savvy marketer.

For example, Salesforce Einstein (the tag given to the company's AI and ML features and services) offers the following advanced features to marketers, among others:

- *Image Recognition:* recognizing brand logos in social network posts; tagging images with categories (e.g. "footwear").
- *Natural Language Processing:* copy insights to help improve email subject-line performance.
- *Predictive Models:* predicting best time to send an email or message; best frequency for messages.
- *Contribution Analysis:* revealing which factors contribute to a desired outcome (e.g. which "touches" impacted a sale).

When Salesforce surveyed thousands of marketers around the globe for its latest State of Marketing report (April 2020), we found that marketing was the #1 use case for AI. In 2018, only 29% of marketers said they were using AI. Now, 84% report using it. For most brands, marketing will remain the top use case for AI, and the best-performing teams were found to be twice as likely to have a fully defined AI strategy.

In that survey, the top uses for AI among marketers (with percentage of respondents) were:

- Personalize individual channel experiences (78%).
- Improve customer segmentation/lookalike audience modeling (77%).
- Automate interactions over social channels/messaging apps (76%).
- Drive next best actions in real time (76%).
- Surface insights from data (76%).

Let's take a look at a few of the most commonly used AI and ML-driven uses for marketers, bearing in mind we are still at the beginning of the AI revolution.

Machine-Learned Segmentation

One of the most common pitfalls of the modern enterprise is how data silos create duplication in customer segmentation. Over the years, brands acquire different systems that work with customer data, and require them to organize people differently. Buy a DMP, and organize your customers by segments of pseudonymous IDs and cookies. Buy an email service provider (ESP), and organize your customers with lists of contacts. Data Warehouse? Build a master list of all of your customers with dozens of attributes. Advertise on Facebook? Have your agency import your contact lists, and build lookalike models within the social advertising network.

Just as there needs to be a single source of truth for people data, there must exist a single place to access that data for the purposes of segmentation. A single reference point – especially for marketing – makes things like multichannel journey delivery and analytics possible.

Despite living in an era with more data-driven marketing and advertising possibilities than ever existed, most enterprises have a decidedly arcane method of working with people data, their most precious business asset. Segments are created, expensive campaigns are built and activated, results are gathered. Segments are "optimized," and sent back into the market to test new theories around how changes to audience composition impact outcomes. Even in a landscape that features near real-time reporting, A/B testing, and modeled attribution, segmentation for most marketers is a matter of trial and error, based largely on our (sometimes biased) assumptions of what should work.

Sure, "travel intenders" tend to travel more than others, and maybe that "auto intender" really is in the market for a new minivan. Why should we only be able to find out for sure after the campaign money is spent? Given a combination of a rich, granular set of customer and campaign performance data, we should be able to determine the best segments *before a campaign is ever run*. This concept is called machine-learned segmentation, essentially a way to overlap thousands of people data attributes against campaign performance data and find the things that really make people buy.

It's like adding artificial intelligence to the old "beer and diapers" theory. In case you are unfamiliar with this marketing chestnut, it's an urban legend about a consultant who discovers, through basket analysis, that beer and diapers tend to have a high purchase correlation – a surprising insight. The reason? Mom sends Dad out to the store to get some diapers and, while he's there, he grabs a six-pack of beer for himself. Whether it's true or not (some argue that this statistically unproven "insight" actually caused a major retailer to stock beer and diapers together, validating the theory), it would be amazing to have an automated way to get the occasional "beer and diapers" moment of insights, but incredibly useful to fine-tune the small correlations among data attributes that create a higher propensity to buy.

Machine-learned segmentation has been a DMP feature for some time, and relatively successful for brands that have a large scale of consumer data with highly granular attributes. CDPs will take this AI application to the next level. Whereas pioneering DMP segmentation was restricted to pseudonymous keys and used a great deal of modeled (read: inaccurate) third-party data, CDPs will connect people data attributes with more "real-life" touchpoints, such as in-store and e-commerce purchase data, thus ML models will have a richer set of attributes to learn from.

Machine-Learned Attribution

"Machine-learned segmentation" is just a single example of the power of mass computation for marketing. How about attribution? As we discuss at length in Chapter 10, there are any number of ways digital data have created unique ways to measure and attribute success to a multichannel journey. In today's world, the accuracy of most models depends on the values you assign to different interactions. If a marketer values the last interaction a consumer had before they purchased, then "last touch" attribution is the prevailing model used. No matter how sophisticated a fractional attribution model may be, the problem has always been the complexity of modern journeys, and the amount of data they create.

Think about a typical digital campaign: there are dozens of segments, several creatives, multiple DSPs connecting to hundreds – perhaps thousands – of websites, several different landing pages, and other interactions in between the first click on an ad and a purchase. The amount of unique customer journeys between A and Z can number in the thousands, such that no human being could elicit a working theory from the data, due to the sheer scale of results the combinatorial values create. But machines can.

The advantage of living in a complex world is the availability of complex analysis and, if machine learning is good for anything, its finding statistically relevant deviations in large sets of data. By looking at hundreds of different journeys, machine learning can assign values to various touchpoints (solving the main problem of human beings guessing which channels work), and also look at the most effective sequences of events that lead to a conversion. Seeing the top five most effective journeys out of thousands would fine-tune a brand's ability to provision such a prescriptive journey – one in which success was more or less statistically guaranteed.

This capability has been pioneered in early versions in DMPs, built in-house in a few major brands, and offered as a data science service through major consultancies. It's obvious that machine learning is the key to unlocking more accurate attribution, but the problem was never conceptual – it has always been about the fidelity and scale of data available to feed the machine. It's the classic attribution conundrum: a brand spends $10M on broadcast television and $10M on Google search, and awards 100% of the attribution credit to search, even though the great TV ads originated the demand. It's hard to measure what you don't see.

Where CDPs come in is the ability to set down a stable substrate of people data as the yardstick against which performance data is measured. People data changes much more slowly than events, so measuring multiple, different campaigns over time against a relatively stable denominator of people data is the key to making comparisons relevant. But the real difference between early experiments in machine-learned attribution was the amount of high-quality data the CDP will bring to the table (purchase, sales, call center, loyalty, etc.) versus the data such systems tried to learn from in the past (advertising and website interactions). We believe CDP data, combined with new algorithmic approaches to journey-based sequential attribution, will herald in a new era of measurement, and make media mix modeling and multitouch attribution a real science.

Image Recognition and Natural Language Processing (NLP)

Two of the most exciting areas of current development in artificial intelligence for marketing are image recognition and natural language processing (NLP). As our opening story about *Silicon Valley* illustrated, the availability of rapid processors, large libraries of images, and innovative deep learning algorithms have combined to push both fields far beyond what was thought possible even a half-decade ago. From being an impossible feat for a computer, the quintessential "human" tasks of recognizing and naming images and of performing advanced language tasks such as translation and even composition are increasingly real.

For marketers, the uses of image recognition and NLP are emerging. Initial applications for both are already being used, sometimes with dramatically positive results. However, results are mixed, based on internal capabilities, computing power, and business use cases. We feel safe in saying that AI and marketing are currently in an "early dating" scenario.

Current uses for *image recognition* include:

- *Social media:* recognizing brand logos and products in social posts, including context (for measurement and sentiment analysis).
- *E-commerce:* automating formerly manual tasks such as product image labeling, classification, sorting and inventorying for e-commerce applications.
- *Recommendations:* making images, including both product and experience images, available to recommendation algorithms for optimized content recommendations on websites, mobile apps, and email.
- *Personalization:* automating testing-and-learning processes to include content and products on websites and mobile apps.

- *Search and visual search:* automating and optimizing search results on brand websites and applications, including the use of visual cues in "top rank" results and grouping items by visual characteristics.

Current uses for NLP in marketing include:

- *Social media and email:* computer-aided text editing, e.g. algorithms, can review text created by a social media manager or email marketer and recommend improvements to boost response rates, based on analysis of previous response data.
- *Customer experience:* NLP algorithms can read and summarize text and verbal raw feedback from customers and prospects, e.g. call center logs and website response forms with open text fields; these summaries can inform direct customer service, responses, or experience improvements.
- *Content creation:* NLP can be used to autogenerate (or robo-write) text, including email subject lines and text fields on websites or e-commerce storefronts. This automated writing is based on analysis of previous response data, and will often require review by a human editor.
- *Chat-bots:* Already widely used in service contexts, the application of chat-bots to automate text chats on websites, apps, and storefronts can be extended to cross-sell, up-sell, voice-of-customer, and other marketing goals.
- *Voice applications:* Marketers can use NLP that decodes and creates voice communications for various applications, such as emerging commerce or service channels.

IMPORTANCE OF CUSTOMER DATA FOR AI

One of the great advances in marketing over the past decade has been the rapid adoption of data lakes which give brands the ability to capture, collect, and store an almost unlimited amount of data for analysis. Almost every big enterprise maintains a data warehouse or lake, and it tends to be a sort of "catchall" environment. Customer generates a click-path? Great! Store it in the data lake. Log level data, loyalty point redemptions, historical purchase data, survey data, biometric data, clicks, views, social data – it can be collected and stored, and queries run against it.

Having such a rich data environment spawned the data science era, and put many statistics majors to work over the past decade. We remember in the early days of programmatic advertising when the best demand side platforms (DSPs) would do their "AI optimizations" with a room full of statisticians running SQL queries in Microsoft Access. (It actually worked pretty well.)

The emergence of cheaper storage, better and faster cloud infrastructure, and more open source tools (Spark, Kafka, etc.) has democratized Big Data analytics, and made data modeling and scoring accessible to the masses. It's odd to encounter an enterprise that doesn't leverage some level of modeled data to build lifetime value (LTV) scores or propensity models for every customer in their database.

This is being done at scale today, but the main problem is where this work is being done. Most data lakes are not natively connected to many other marketing systems an enterprise owns – and getting modeled data to the endpoints of activation for advertising and marketing is an IT exercise that requires automating data ingestion, opening up infrequent "batch windows", and aligning data lake customer data to the information models used by other systems. In other words, the insights tend to exist in isolation of the opportunities to use them. Better speed and more connectivity are the keys to unlocking the value created through the yeoman's work of modeling and scoring.

While it's unlikely enterprises will abandon their data warehouse environments in favor of making the CDP their ultimate single source of truth for customer data immediately, over time, this is precisely what must happen to bring the source of modeled data closer to where it can have the most impact: activation channels and analytics systems. Data warehouses, lakes, CRMs, and mobile device management (MDM) systems are great places to store and model customer data, but were not necessarily designed to activate and connect to the multitude of systems that have been built over the last 20 years to activate it (see the "Martech Landscape"). CDPs, on the other hand, because they are being built initially for marketing and advertising use cases, lead with the idea that the customer data craves connection with systems of activation, and must be extensible enough to anticipate future connection opportunities that do not yet exist.

We believe that, over time, as the CDP becomes the single source of truth for customer data, *period* (not just marketing and advertising data), being able to deliver rich computed attributes across a people data asset is what will ultimately separate the winners from the losers. If data capture, unification, and activation are table stakes – and scale and speed tied to the public cloud infrastructure they are built upon – CDP's core differentiator will be the intelligence built inside the system. Initially, this will manifest itself in the ease of enriching customer data with computed attributes to calculate lifetime value and propensity for action.

AI/ML IN THE ORGANIZATION: DATA SCIENCE TEAMS

Data science is a differentiating discipline, increasingly separating more successful marketing organizations from the also-rans. A recent survey of data-driven marketers revealed that the most successful marketers enjoyed larger teams and higher proportional spending on analytics teams and consultants. Even as 69% of marketers say they either have or are planning to build an analytics center of excellence, leading marketers also allocated almost 30% of their analytics budgets to external service providers.

How can marketers make use of the talent sitting inside and outside company walls? Suggestions include:

- Don't assume that all data scientists are equal – determine who the traditional marketing analysts are and who are more advanced modelers.
- Provide opportunities for data scientists to learn on the job and explore ideas that may be speculative – they are curious people.
- Understand the basic domains of data science and think about their application to your business.
- Look at your strategic priorities in light of the things data science might bring to it. For example, if you're unhappy with your current segmentation scheme, see what a clustering model uncovers.
- Don't drag-and-drop data scientists into a problem. Although they do work alone, marketing analysts need help defining precise business needs and trade-offs.
- Respect the process of data science and its limits. Many problems take time to solve, and there are many problems that cannot be solved.

Marketing and data science are only now in Act One of their operatic collaboration. Great things lie ahead. There will come a time when analytical techniques are built into most workflows and machine-driven decisions are commonplace. At such a time, data science will no longer be a separate activity but the essence of marketing.

CUSTOMER-DRIVEN THINKER: ALYSIA BORSA

There is probably no company in the world that knows more about women and family living than Meredith Corporation. Through its broad portfolio of 40-plus media brands such as *People*, *allrecipes*, *Parents*, *Better Homes & Gardens*, and *Real Simple*, the company has specialized in bringing audiences of the "household CEO" (moms) to advertisers since 1902. We first met Alysia Borsa in 2015, when she was pioneering a data-sharing use case that enabled ConAgra, maker of Hunt's canned tomatoes, to understand their target consumers and then personalize ads for visitors looking up recipes for pasta sauce, chilli, and the like.

As chief data officer, Alysia understood the value of Meredith's combined data assets, and also its value. We understand this today as "second-party data sharing" – a prescient approach, considering the looming demise of third-party, cookie-based data. Ultimately Meredith's forward leaning, data-centric posture was a major factor in transforming the company from a print-based publisher to a digital powerhouse, as it shocked the publishing world by acquiring Time, Inc. in early 2018. Today the company reaches more than 190 million consumers across multiple platforms and 94% of all US women through its combined platform. As EVP and Chief Business and Data Officer, Alysia continues to innovate.

How could you make Meredith consumers accessible to big advertisers without putting their privacy at risk?

One of the early insights we had around the power of customer data was through scaling the way we exposed advertisers to our audience assets through a data management platform. We have a very special relationship with our consumers, and really understand not only their demographics and online behavior, but also their interests and intent – including advertising. Data is a core asset to Meredith, something we think can be valued on the balance sheet. For us, customer data is about understanding our audience and predicting consumer trends to develop new content, new consumer products, and also drive more revenue by connecting advertisers to our consumers.

For example, our advertisers can use our predictive trends and survey a panel of consumers to directly create a target segment for testing and execution. This type of in-depth audience targeting and testing has resulted in up to four times better performance on their media campaigns on our sites. The capability to do this starts with the ability to identify our 190M+ customers across their known and unknown data, such as connecting a known subscriber with their online web and mobile identifiers.

We also need to connect that identity with the core data assets we own: content and experiences across publications that we have categorized into a taxonomy covering over 12,000 unique terms, and a real-time ability to capture billions of intent signals. This creates billions of data sets. Using machine learning, we now have the ability to understand our consumers' unique relationship with our brands, and use that to customize the content, offers, and advertising they see across our portfolio – and do it in real time. Consumers move quickly, and we realized we needed the power to continually ingest, segment, and analyze our customer data to make sure that we could provision the right experiences based on the moment. Through this, we have created 800+ segments based on our predictive insights and scoring to show greater propensity to consume a certain type of content, or buy a certain category of product.

Our customers, like CPG company Clorox and Napa Valley wine company Chateau Ste. Michelle, are using the rich consumer trends data – also bringing their own proprietary data – to overlap their audiences with over 800+ segments in our Data Studio platform to automatically find audiences with a high propensity to consider their brand. Today, as advertisers struggle with the "post-cookie" era, and third-party data becomes less available, our ability to come to the table with a high quality, proprietary data asset is a big differentiator.

SUMMARY: MACHINE LEARNING AND ARTIFICIAL INTELLIGENCE

- *Data science in marketing:* Artificial intelligence and a subset of AI called machine learning (ML) are the disciplines of training computer models and simulations that can learn from experience. Data science is the discipline that includes the use of analytical tools and techniques, including software, to improve and understand many business domains, including marketing. Marketers are increasingly applying AI and ML in their data science efforts to get more value from customer data and improve outcomes.
- *Customer data and experimental design:* Analysis cannot be done without good data, and this is particularly true of AI and ML, which require more and cleaner data in order to succeed. So, the customer data revolution described in this book is a prerequisite to a thriving analytics program. Of course, some important data science is done outside the realms of AI and ML, including measurement and the design-of-experiments, which enables marketers to test and improve experiences and campaigns.
- *Making predictions and finding structure:* A key use of machine learning in particular is to build predictive models. These models are widely used to improve product and content recommendations on websites, mobile apps, and email, as well as to improve the response to offers and discounts. Another use of ML models is to find structure in otherwise obscure or opaque data. A common example of the latter in marketing is to discover customer segments (or clusters) with attributes in common that are not easily discovered or practical using traditional statistical or manual methods.

- *Machine learning:* We believe CDP data, combined with new algorithmic approaches to journey-based sequential attribution will herald in a new era of measurement, and make media mix modeling and multitouch attribution a real science.
- *Modeling and scoring:* As the CDP becomes the single source of truth for customer data (not just marketing and advertising data), being able to deliver rich computed attributes across a people data asset is what will ultimately separate the winners from the losers. If data capture, unification, and activation are table stakes – and scale and speed tied to the public cloud infrastructure they are built upon – CDP's core differentiator will be the intelligence built inside the system. Initially, this will manifest itself in the ease of enriching customer data with computed attributes to calculate lifetime value and propensity for action.
- *AI and ML in the organization:* Data science is a differentiating discipline, increasingly separating more successful marketing organizations from the also-rans. A recent survey of data-driven marketers revealed that the most successful marketers enjoyed larger teams and higher proportional spending on analytics teams and consultants. Marketing and data science are only now in Act One of their operatic collaboration. Great things lie ahead. There will come a time when analytical techniques are built into most workflows and machine-driven decisions are commonplace. At such a time, data science will no longer be a separate activity but the essence of marketing.

CHAPTER 10

Orchestrating a Personalized Customer Journey

This chapter makes the "engagement" part of the data platform more tangible. Customers are each on their own journey with your company, and it takes many forms. At any point, their needs, requirements, expectations, and tolerance will vary. Good customer experience (CX) requires you to know as much as you can about their context and history so you can provide the right experience across marketing, service, and commerce. We describe journey builder tools, RTIM, and other methods to automate these engagements.

THE RISE OF CONTEXT MARKETING

The hoariest old chestnut in addressable marketing is certainly "right person, right message, right time" (or any number of variations on this theme), and it's for a good reason. People tend to react to marketing more favorably when they are targeted well, in the right frame of mind, and ready to buy. Send us as many emails as you want just after we bought a car, and you are wasting your time. Send us a great financing offer right before we are heading to the auto dealership, and you have our undivided attention.

Perhaps the most seminal work on consumer marketing, Byron Sharp's *How Brands Grow* (Oxford University Press, 2010), argued that customer sentiment could be manipulated based on a simple formula: the *mental availability* of a brand in the consumer's brain, and the *physical availability* of the product at the store. Big CPG companies like Proctor and Gamble wrote the first playbooks on this, and executed upon these precepts with an almost religious zealotry. Soak massive reach channels like TV and print with ads for Tide detergent, and make sure the product had the best placement in supermarket shelves and customers practically had boxes of Tide in their shopping carts before they knew what they were reaching for! In a nutshell, Sharp posited that brand consideration was not a scientific exercise with customers, who hardly considered the differentiating factors between Tide and Gain. Brands were emotional things, and people instinctively gravitated toward them through the workings of their mammalian brains.

Sharp was not wrong. Brands are as important as ever, and people are willing to pay a premium for the ones that comport with their self-identity and positively trigger their subconscious mind. Sharp also looked at loyalty programs, and concluded that they were not as effective as previously thought, citing the fact that 72% of Coke drinkers also bought Pepsi. People were more likely to be brand loyal in the presence of a great deal. Constant promotion was needed to fill the "leaky bucket" of lapsing customers with new ones, making "penetration" into the product category as important as, or more important than, cutting prices. At the end of the day, brands that were "always-on," readily available where the consumers were buying, and consistent with messaging won the day.

But how does Sharp hold up in modern times, in a world where consumers have real-time access to pricing data, and almost unlimited choice immediately available on their mobile phones, just a click away? Brands that want to earn "mental availability" by being everywhere their consumers are can no longer overinvest in mass reach channels like TV – they must be on Facebook, Instagram, Pinterest, TikTok, and dozens of other channels, making scaled penetration a costly and near impossible affair. And "physical availability" is no longer a function of having the best placement in a handful of retail stores, since every consumer has 10,000 retail outlets just a click away in e-commerce.

While Sharp's precepts for brand success still hold true, the methodology in activating those concepts in marketing has changed dramatically. Brands must be prepared to make themselves known on hundreds of channels, and make themselves available to buy seamlessly online – and do this in real time, so as to be relevant and available in the moment the consumer wants to engage. This is what "customers are in control" means. Over the last twenty years, this dynamic is responsible for the rise of context marketing, and the growth of over 8,000 marketing and advertising technology tools to help brands go from using mass reach media to drive people to stores to using technology to manage dozens of channels to drive people to a mix of in-store and online outlets.

But brands cannot find the "right person" without the capability of ingesting and connecting known and unknown people data, nor deliver the "right message" without being able to sense what always-on, fast-moving consumers care about, nor understand the "right time" without transforming from simple funnel-stage analysis into real-time journey analysis. Sounds like a problem for customer data platforms to solve! If you think about the promise of customer data platforms (CDPs), what they are being built for is to help brands automate the process of delivering on context marketing: to sense consumer behavior and respond to consumers' desire to engage with brands at the time and pace of their choosing. We think of this capability as orchestration or journey management.

PRESCRIPTIVE JOURNEYS

Even as customers spread out across dozens of channels and engaged with brands in ever more real-time ways, the one channel of marketing that always seemed to deliver consistent value was email. Once a brand had the implicit permission of an "opt-in" or entered their information after a purchase, a brand owned a reliable channel of communication for delivering information, and soliciting a response.

In 1978, a man named Gary Thuerk used a precursor of the internet called Arpanet to message 400 contacts a promotion for DEC computers, and created $13 million in sales from a single email message. Thuerk, a man completely ahead of his time, may still hold the record for most effective email campaign but he is now known as the "Father of SPAM" (his novel approach worked, but also generated many complaints from recipients). Nonetheless, the era of email marketing was born. Over time, the advent of the internet and services like Hotmail and AOL brought email to millions, and the evolution of handheld devices and smartphones took email from desktop to ubiquity. By 2010, marketers were segmenting their email lists, using contextual and behavioral attributes to microtarget customers, and starting to automate campaigns. Enter "customer journey management" or orchestration, the ability to prescriptively provision a series of interactions based on a customer's stage in a process.

The ability to manage messaging-based journeys is now so ubiquitous that our 2020 State of Marketing report cited the email service provider (ESP) as the second most popular data management solution, right behind CRM systems. Most customers tend to behave similarly, so there is a great deal of efficiency and effectiveness in automating common customer journeys. The typical post-purchase journey starts with an order confirmation email, follow-up with shipping details, a confirmation of delivery, and culminates in a post-purchase survey and the invitation to buy again. There are product return journeys, loyalty journeys, and customer service journeys that align the typical stages in a customer-driven process to the right messages and interactions that people expect. Today, almost a decade after these more sophisticated capabilities emerged, basic journey automation has become a science and is considered "table stakes" capability for enterprise marketers.

The role of the CDP in prescriptive journey building is to close the gap between the data needed to effectively deliver the experience. Most retailers have mastered plugging in shipping data from UPS or FedEx in their "Your Order Is on the Way" emails via publicly available APIs. But coordinating data from a phone call ("I ordered the wrong size") to the e-commerce system ("cancel the order!") and email system ("here's a return label for your order") involves the ability to connect customer data between two usually siloed systems. The CDP's role is to unify the people data underlying the three systems – and do it at the speed in which the customer is interacting with all three departments. By piping customer and event data seamlessly between systems in near real time, CDPs will bring a level of precision and refinement to the process of prescriptive journeys, enabling marketers to spend less time connecting pipes and more time building ever more granular journeys for different experiences.

Today, the intelligence that powers much of this automation is found in the email systems themselves (see our discussion of AI for email in Chapter 9). When email channel data lived in isolation of service, sales, or commerce, it seemed obvious to embed intelligence closer to the endpoint of delivery. With the emergence of CDPs, we will see more intelligence baked into the customer data itself, and delivered to the endpoints, such that a messaging campaign, for example, has metadata about a customer's loyalty status, past purchase history, and most recent interactions across commerce and service. Going forward, ESPs must configure their systems to rapidly ingest richer sets of customer data and apply them to create relevant experiences that can be triggered based on real-time events.

PREDICTIVE JOURNEYS

As we discussed in Chapter 6, there is a stepwise progression from going from touchpoints to journeys to experiences. If automating journeys is "touchpoint" marketing, then being able to deliver better journeys based on prediction is true "journey"-based marketing. But how do you manage a funnel that no longer traverses a known path, where customers are bouncing between advertising, email, app experiences, and more? It's all about being able to use the learnings of past interactions to predict the next best action.

Take the typical email campaign. A customer comes onto a website, signs up for a generous offer (10% off), puts a product in the shopping cart, and ... walks away. While we don't know the specific reason, we can guess that one of three things happened: (1) the customer got distracted by work or home, or didn't have time to complete the transaction and will come back later; (2) the customer had reservations about the cost and decided the product was too expensive, and abandoned their cart; or possibly the shipping costs were not considered; and (3) the customer left to try and find a better deal elsewhere. In each instance, we can start a customer journey that addresses each of these scenarios by offering a reminder, a deeper "new customer" discount, or free shipping on the first order. Predictive journeys look back on all past paths to purchase from similar customers with similar products (based on location, price, time of day, and other factors) and recommend the message with the highest propensity to close the transaction.

Moreover, intelligent journeys can use rules-based methodology to send customers down a path that advances over a prescribed time. Different customers can receive different subject lines, different "call to action" messages and offers, and click into different web experiences.

Also, predictive journeys can move customers between channels. Didn't open the last three emails? Nurture this user with ads on Facebook or Instagram until they reengage. Not responding to an abandoned cart email? Try the message on SMS. Expanding the availability of creative channels, and managing the delivery of interactions over time have given marketers a way to automate experimentation. Additionally, every new predictive journey throws off data that feeds algorithms that are hungry to validate their theories.

At Salesforce, we have innovated in developing the ability to perform "persona splits" that can be used to build journeys based on contact-level data, and "engagement splits" which segment journeys based on the channel we predict consumers are likely to engage on.

While predictive journey capabilities were once initiated mostly in messaging (primarily the email channel), capabilities have expanded to include being able to automatically initiate a journey from a call center interaction, or start a journey based on one's segment membership in a DMP. Leveraging AI-based prediction to provision journeys that cut across multiple channels is an art form that can increase conversion rates, reduce churn, and tether previously disconnected touchpoints like service and commerce to the steel thread of a marketing campaign. When seen enough times, journeys can be automated to account for the large majority of customers and scenarios.

CDPs can make journeys better by enriching the most critical input into the decision tree: the amount of data one has on the customer on the receiving end of it. By connecting service (how many call center interactions, any open cases?), marketing (what is the customer's receptivity to offers?), and commerce (what is the customer's lifetime value and propensity to purchase?), journeys can be fine-tuned to select the highest value channels and messages, and the right sequence of engagement over time. But what about customers we don't yet understand, who are interacting with brands rapidly?

REAL-TIME INTERACTION MANAGEMENT (RTIM) JOURNEYS

On the spectrum of touchpoints to journeys to experiences, the category of real-time interaction management (RTIM) software gets marketers as close as they come to being able to deliver iterative, "in the moment" experiences that are always on. RTIM is defined as "enterprise marketing technology that delivers contextually relevant experiences, value, and utility at the appropriate moment in the customer life cycle via preferred customer touchpoints." Wait. That sounds exactly like the journey capabilities we described above. Well, yes and no.

The typical journey management system is built on email as the primary channel, which requires the customer to opt in to marketing at some point, and be "known," but doesn't cover customers who are interacting with a website or app for the first time as "unknown" entities. Also, typical journeys are built over hours and days, and customers often move between channels (social advertising and website) within seconds. By ingesting interaction data in real time, and maintaining a real-time customer profile store, RTIM tools are able to make personalization decisions immediately.

Of course, tag management companies have been capturing real-time intent signals from customers for many years, and using those signals for personalization. DMPs have many similar capabilities, and web personalization companies have been optimizing website experiences in real time as well. So, what's new about RTIM? It's really about speed, intelligence, and channel coordination. The right RTIM system should be able to deliver the next best action (NBA) or next best offer (NBO) at the right moment, and work between channels based on the entire context of the customer including their recent behavior, past history, preferences, and other factors, such as time of day, weather conditions, or location. This is contextual marketing, tuned to be hyperaware and real-time.

RTIM operates primarily based on behavior. If the customer looks at these three products, we should show him this product next, based on what similar customers typically purchase. Or, if the customer clicked on an offer for 10% off on shoes, show her this color, based on her browsing behavior. RTIM also operates based on context. The customer browsing on a mobile app from a New York City subway may be on her way to work, and may be in a mindset to consume shorter form content than when logging into a website from a laptop at home. Or think about the national coffee chain trying to personalize a campaign based on weather. Cold and rainy locations get offers for hot cappuccino drinks, and hot and sunny locations get a promotion for iced frappuccinos.

Even without leveraging tons of additional contextual data, RTIM can lift conversion rates by simply bringing users back to the last page they visited when they left a website or app – or help users continue their experience when they come back to complete a car purchase, do research on a flight, or finally check out their shopping cart.

Because many popular RTIM systems maintain a real-time profile store of customer data, some have positioned themselves as "engagement"-type CDPs. This is not incorrect; most effective RTIM tools have built robust data capture, store, and analytics capabilities in order to maximize their understanding of context to maximize their ability to optimize experiences. (At Salesforce, we recently acquired such a company, Evergage, to power our Interaction Studio product, and provide the real-time "engagement" capabilities for our customer data platform.)

Marketers ultimately need the capability to build predictive journeys that happen over longer periods of time (journey building) and the ability to manage interactions in real time across channels (RTIM). The role of the CDP will be in connecting both systems through letting each system access a rich, real-time customer profile store that cuts across pseudonymous data (real-time interactions with media, advertising, and content) and PII-based data from multiple known sources (purchase history, service history, marketing interaction data, etc.).

CUSTOMER-DRIVEN THINKER: LAURA LISOWSKI COX

As she tells the story, Laura Lisowski Cox got the idea to start a skin care company because she was frustrated by the lack of healthy products available for her husband. Launched in 2016 by Cox and co-founder Mia Saini Duchnowski, Oars + Alps designs and markets high-end deodorants, cleansers, and moisturizers aimed at men on the move. The pair saw their start-up picked up by Target in 2018 and, according to media reports, they were acquired by S. C. Johnson a year later. As CMO, Cox has seen it all: shoestring budgets, lots of tests, building a customer database and a library of insights.

How did you approach the customer journey – and how has that changed as your startup grew into a division of a consumer products juggernaut?

> The role of our website has changed dramatically since we started the company. At first, it was our only "storefront." We focused on driving people to our site, serving the right product and message to increase the likelihood that they would complete a purchase, and then ensuring the flow from landing page to checkout and payment method was seamless. We would analyze what type of person we drove to our site, what message or image would compel them to come to the site, and what pages they landed on. For example, in 2016, we found a close-up product image that was held by a person on a dark background time and time again outperformed.

We made a costly mistake – this was early on, thankfully – where we drove messaging around this one particular product. It had the highest Return on Ad Spend (ROAS). However, as we started to build up our customer data and segmentation, we found people that purchased that product had the lowest repeat rate and lifetime value of all our products. Clearly that was not a good way to build a business. So, we quickly pivoted to a different product that had a higher repeat purchase rate and customer lifetime value – even though it had a slightly higher customer acquisition cost (CAC). That insight had a direct impact on all of our messaging, creative concepts, and even product extensions.

As we tried to continue growing, it became clear we had to move beyond our website. As we went into brick and mortar, we discovered that the retail shopper is different than our website shopper. In the early days on our website, it was mostly men buying for themselves. In-store within our category, the majority of purchases are done by the mom, wife, concerned sister, and so on. So, we had to try a different approach in-store and learn how to entice the female buyer if they haven't heard of the brand. We tested different messaging and images for retail in our survey panel. It was amazing how much preference varied based on a simple gender or customer/prospect split. We realized that in retail we had to prioritize the female shopper who was buying for her household who had never heard of our brand.

As we slowly expanded, our website became the center for data intelligence, testing, validation, and customer service. If we have a new product, we launch it first on our dot-com. If there's a problem, we want to know before it's available in Target. If we see the same set of questions appear in our customer service email, chat, and text, then we'll develop education content around it, optimized for keywords.

Given our shift to omnichannel, we have moved away from mostly lower-funnel media – like search, email, paid social, affiliate – to drive immediate sales. We have increased our media mix to include upper-funnel media to drive brand awareness and consideration – for example, connected TV. As a digital native brand and team, I have a preference for digital channels. We can target specific audiences and quickly receive validation such as lift in branded search queries. While we continue to run tests such as lift in ad recall to identify which video to push in connected TV, a lot of the initial insight in messaging, product, comes from our website.

I love what I do – and the intersection of psychology and economics. The study of human behavior on a macro level. To other entrepreneurs, I'd say be sure your customer data is accessible, linked with all the moving pieces in the digital space. And, of course, interpret it all with skepticism.

SUMMARY: ORCHESTRATING A PERSONALIZED CUSTOMER JOURNEY

- *Rise of context marketing:* Brands must be prepared to make themselves known on hundreds of channels, and make themselves available to buy seamlessly online – and do this in real time, so as to be relevant and available in the moment the consumer wants to engage. This is what "customers are in control" means. But brands cannot find the "right person" without the capability of ingesting and connecting known and unknown people data, nor deliver the "right message" without being able to sense what always-on, fast-moving consumers care about, nor understand the "right time" without transforming from simple funnel-stage analysis into real-time journey analysis. This capability is called "orchestration" or journey management, and has several different modalities: prescriptive, predictive, and real-time.
- *Prescriptive journeys:* Prescriptive journeys build experiences over time across channels and are based on previous interactions. The role of the CDP in prescriptive journey building is to close the gap between the data needed to effectively deliver the experience. The CDP's role is to unify the people data underlying the three systems– and do it at the speed at which the customer is interacting with all three departments. By piping customer and event data seamlessly between systems in near real time, CDPs will bring a level of precision and refinement to the process of pre-scriptive journeys, enabling marketers to spend less time connecting pipes and more time building ever more granular journeys for different experiences. We are entering an era in which much of the intelligence required to deliver such journeys will live in the CDP, rather than in separate email or personalization systems.
- *Predictive journeys:* While predictive journey capabilities were once initi-ated mostly in messaging (primarily the email channel), capabilities have expanded to include being able to automatically initiate a journey from a call center interaction, or start a journey based on one's segment member-ship in a DMP. Leveraging AI-based prediction to provision journeys that cut across multiple channels is an art form that can increase conversion rates, reduce churn, and tether previously disconnected touchpoints like service and commerce to the steel thread of a marketing campaign. When seen enough times, journeys can be automated to account for the large majority of customers and scenarios. CDPs can make journeys better by enriching the most critical input into the decision tree: the amount of data one has on the customer on the receiving end of it.
- *Real-time interaction management journeys (RTIM):* On the spectrum of touchpoints to journeys to experiences, the category of real-time

interaction management (RTIM) software gets marketers as close as they come to being able to deliver iterative, "in the moment" experiences that are always on. Because many popular RTIM systems maintain a real-time profile store of customer data, some have positioned themselves as "engagement"-type CDPs. Most effective RTIM tools have built robust data capture, store, and analytics capabilities in order to maximize their understanding of context to maximize their ability to optimize experiences.

- *Conclusion:* Marketers ultimately need the capability to build predictive journeys that happen over longer periods of time (journey building) and the ability to manage interactions in real time across channels (RTIM). The role of the CDP will be in connecting both systems through letting each system access a rich, real-time customer profile store that cuts across pseudonymous data (real-time interactions with media, advertising, and content) and PII-based data from multiple known sources (purchase history, service history, marketing interaction data, etc.).

CHAPTER 11

Connected Data for Analytics

In this chapter, we discuss how customer data can be harnessed to visualize, measure, and optimize your marketing campaigns – and, more broadly, to optimize your day-to-day operations. We discuss key topics in marketing analytics for a customer-driven organization: how to think about "success"; how to ensure you're collecting the right data; how to integrate and harmonize it (using tools like Datorama); how to build effective visualizations (using tools like Tableau); and how to optimize operations, either manually (using KPIs) or automagically via Datorama or data science.

CUSTOMER DATA FOR MARKETING ANALYTICS

When one of the authors was working at a digital marketing agency around 2008, his job was fairly routine. He did something called "measurement," which today would probably be called "data science" (giving him a retroactive promotion). It was what it sounds like: he would pull data from various different sources, such as ad server logs, search ad reports, email systems, and social platforms; cut and paste them into Excel; do some reformatting and combining in Excel; take the final aggregate data and re-cut and re-paste it into a dashboard template that had been designed by the art department and that did not vary at all each month. This dashboard was then presented to the client, with commentary (Figure 11.1). The whole process was a full-time job.

In fact, the agency he worked at employed about 80 full-time college-educated people like him simply to organize data and move it around in Excel, for a handful of Fortune 100 clients. There were statisticians with PhDs employed at the agency – two of them, in an agency of 500, known for its analytical prowess – but they were reserved for months-long, intense data mining projects that involved data that were months (and even years) old. Nothing was "real-time" at that time!

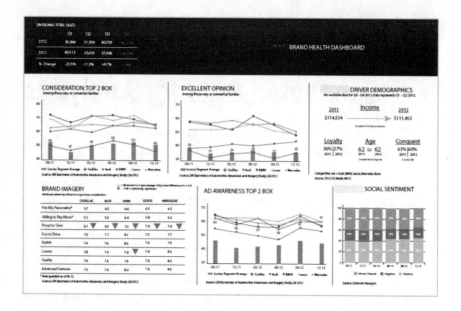

FIGURE 11.1   An example of an early "brand health" analytics dashboard for a major US luxury auto brand.

Marketing analytics has changed a lot since then. Although marketing analysts still generate roll-up reports and campaign recaps for management, increasingly these are automated and analysts are called on to do real-time analysis, on-the-fly decision support, in-the-moment optimizations and advanced tasks, such as building models and developing detailed customer insights. Much of the value provided by the enterprise customer data platform is precisely its ability to enable and support the new breed of marketing analyst, as well as democratizing basic analytics more broadly through declarative user interfaces (UIs) and drag-and-drop interfaces.

Rather than static queries and manual report-building, today's marketing analytics professional looks much like analytics professionals in other departments, including finance. They use a framework such as in Figure 11.2 to execute their work. As you can see, "Data" is at the center of everything – specifically a Customer 360 view of customer and account data.

Marketing leaders are under pressure to be more accountable, defend marketing performance, optimize the marketing mix, and demonstrate the business value of their function. They need rapid access to information and insight to make more informed decisions, plan strategically, and measure return on marketing investments. Timely information and insights into

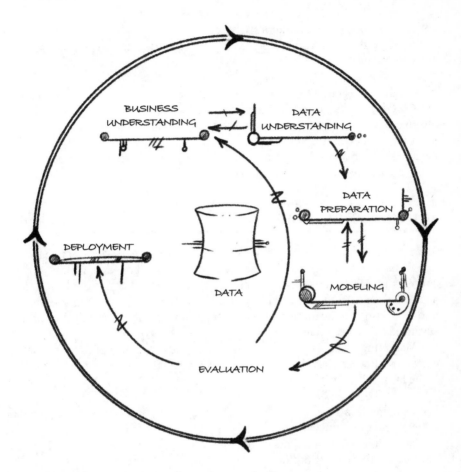

FIGURE 11.2 Value chain of data in business intelligence.
Source: Courtesy of Salesforce.

markets, competitors, customers, and programs are needed for marketers to successfully manage, execute, and improve their work.

By making timely, accurate, and harmonized customer data available across the marketing organization, the new generation of enterprise-grade customer data platforms promises to give chief marketing officer (CMOs) and their teams a competitive edge.

In general, CMOs are responsible for making sure organizations do three things well:

■ Understand markets and customers.

- Create strategy and marketing assets.
- Manage all the functions required to execute marketing and programs and operations.

Analytical capabilities and information sources are essential to help the CMO understand and manage effectively. Deep market understanding informs strategic planning, and customer insights build effective acquisition, retention, and communication strategies. Managing a modern marketing machine requires continuous analysis of programs, people, and processes, built on a strong foundation of available customer data.

ANALYTICAL CAPABILITIES

A raft of analytical capabilities are required to support the CMO's insights initiatives. These range from basic reporting to predictive modeling and optimization. Data science as a discipline is becoming ever more relevant to marketing, and techniques (and even talent) are increasingly being ported into marketing applications from more traditional business intelligence and advanced analytics milieu.

Marketing organizations must ensure that they have the appropriate analytical resources available to support all relevant analytical capabilities. Some of the most critical categories of support include:

- segmentation
- customer lifetime value
- campaign and channel measurement
- media mix and attribution
- predictive and propensity modeling
- social analytics
- dashboarding and visualization

ANALYTICS DATA SOURCES

As we have seen repeatedly throughout this book, one of the biggest challenges for CMOs is data fragmentation across silos within marketing; within the company but external to marketing; and outside the company with partners, distributors, agencies, and other suppliers. A sound data integration and metadata strategy is required to ensure accurate, reliable, and consistent analysis, and derived insights. The CMO may want to have the marketing operations director or another dedicated resource work directly with the chief information officer (CIO) and IT to develop a cohesive data strategy for marketing to support its analytical requirements. (See Chapter 6 for more on customer data management within the enterprise.)

Enterprises have as many different matrices of data sources for marketing as there are enterprises; every one is unique. Common sources have been mentioned throughout *Customer Data Platforms*. For analytics, additional data sources might include:

- third-party data overlays and appends
- voice-of-customer data, including call center output
- product and pricing data (e.g. point-of-sale and store systems and e-commerce platforms)
- loyalty systems
- trade promotion and event analytics solutions
- operations systems, including marketing resource management (MRM) and digital asset management (DAM) tools

BEYOND THE BASICS

Ongoing improvements in data availability and processing speed, and more usable (and useful) software tools, combined with digital transformation, have forced advanced analytical methods into the day-to-day consciousness of many marketing analysts and agency practitioners.

Advanced marketing analytics is distinguished from traditional methods in using:

- *Multiple channels:* Collecting data from all relevant consumer touchpoints, including websites, mobile apps, email, social channels, advertising, content marketing, and public digital displays.
- *New data sources:* Incorporation of nontraditional data sources, including location, social network relationships, text and speech analysis, voice of the customer, and sources related to the Internet-of-Things (IoT).
- *Greater scale:* Applying analytics to nonrelational database and big data stores, including in-memory and noSQL.
- *Real-time analysis:* Moving from analysis of data at rest, in a historical view, to analysis of data in motion, including trigger and anomaly detection, and some forms of complex event processing.
- *Predictive models:* Using the vast toolbox of predictive analytics (e.g. machine learning) to improve customer experience, broadly defined, particularly around next-best-offer and content recommendations, brand and churn propensity, profitability, and lifetime value.

- *More data types:* Incorporating complex combinations of information around what people are (demographics), what they do (behaviors), and what they think and feel (psychographic and attitudinal).

KEY TYPES OF ANALYTICS

In the following sections, we go through the key types of analytics employed by enterprise marketers.

Marketing/Email Analytics

Many marketers spend a lot of their marketing efforts trying to up-sell and cross-sell to their existing customer base through email campaigns. As we discussed above, email marketing tends to become fairly predictable, given list accuracy and the consistent quality of campaign creative. At its most basic, marketers get a sense of how many people opened an email (open rate), clicked an offer inside the message (click-through rate), and opted out of future campaigns. Other key performance indicators (KPIs) include list growth, deliverability, and unsubscribe rates. More sophisticated marketers layer in demographics, applying a people-based layer against performance to see how age, gender, and location impact campaign performance. Most advanced email marketers also run a number of A/B tests across multiple creative executions to better understand how a particular headline, product offer, background color, or image impact engagement. Going a step further, email marketers could run analytics across historical campaigns to better understand how certain groups respond to receiving email offers at different times of day or based on their device.

The game changer for standard email analytics is to go beyond what many marketers see in a common journey analysis (email opens, website visits, etc.) and start to measure things like e-commerce and call center interactions alongside messaging touchpoints. Similar to DMP analytics, most channel marketing managers suffer from observational bias: they can only measure what they see, and most see only the interactions their email service provider (ESP) can deliver. The CDP has the ability, through unifying touchpoints that go "beyond marketing" (for a bank, things like branch visits and ATM withdrawals, as an example) to broaden the spectrum of digital and offline touchpoints to fill in the gaps of a journey between email interactions. When seen in a broader context, messaging interactions become highly valuable and valid contributors to multitouch models.

DMP Analytics

Data management platforms (DMPs) have highly granular analytics that can go beyond pure campaign performance and "slice" analytics by vendor and segment. How did this campaign perform for a particular group (male versus female) or a vendor (Yahoo versus Google)? Before DMPs organized people by segment, most marketers only had the most basic view of performance in channels like display media, measuring things like impressions and clicks, usually in retrospect and in aggregate. The innovation in analytics was to bring the "people layer" of data into every report. All of a sudden, marketers could overlap the entirety of their first-party data asset against different media outlets. Kellogg's could discover that 30% of their campaigns targeted to Moms were actually reaching Dads, or that they could find the same "Moms" on a general interest site far less expensively than buying on "Moms.com."

Additionally, DMPs allowed marketers to discover which audiences converted faster, based on their exposure to advertising, and manage the delivery of cross-channel advertising. One of the biggest insights early DMP users discovered was that there was a definite "sweet spot" in monthly ad delivery. People tended to click, buy, or "convert" when seeing between 5–20 ad impressions per month. Less than that was ineffective, as people tend to need multiple impressions of the same ad creative to enter into brand consideration. More than that? A total waste of money, as people became "banner blind" and ignored ads they saw over and over again. The DMP's ability to capture device data and ride along with advertising campaigns via a tracking pixel made advertising analytics more granular than ever, and offered the ability to slice and dice the numbers by a person's segmentation.

The DMP's highly granular, "people-based" viewpoint changed the game in digital media, as marketers started to look beyond vendor-based attribution (Yahoo! did better than AOL) and started to look at one's segment as the arbiter of value. As people quickly migrated from site to site, it didn't matter so much whether an ad was seen on one particular site as much as the fact that the hotel ad was properly targeted to a real "travel intender." Of course, DMPs were limited by their reliance on pseudonymous data, which suffer from observational bias around what they could measure (mostly clicks and impressions). Although most DMP owners could upload (anonymized) rich PII-based data from CRM databases, DMPs tended to remain in the hands of digital teams and their agencies, and analytics was mostly a media consideration.

The CDP that can unify people data from both pseudonymous and PII-based sources (a "CDMP," if you will) will immediately widen the aperture of analytics by introducing attributes that common media analytics never really considered, such as historical purchase data, call center interactions, and loyalty data. When tied to addressable media interaction, and measured at the segment level, CDP data becomes the most valuable predictor of marketing performance.

Multitouch Attribution (MTA)

Some marketers are pretty good at combining things like DMP and email analytics together to get a more holistic sense of performance across multiple addressable channels like display, mobile, video, email, SMS, and push notifications. But what about social media advertising, addressable television (over-the-top, OTT), trade promotions, and the like? How about print, radio, outdoor ads, and broadcast TV spots? Which channels drive more performance than others? How do they work in combination? Which impression, at what time, is valued more than another? The discipline of "multitouch attribution" or MTA is part science and part witchcraft but, once agreed on as the source of truth for marketing success, very hard to displace as a working model.

"Multitouch" models generally consider the impact of one or more customer interactions that lead to a KPI (sale, download, click, or other metric). Because of data availability, they tend to be digital-only in scope. Multitouch models are meant to bring more clarity than traditional "single touch" models that most marketers still rely upon: giving attribution to either the first interaction a consumer has with a brand (a search result, for example) or the last touch someone had with a brand. Because so many online interactions begin and end within Google (often search), MTA is meant to assign value to the interactions across the journey, taking into account emails, website visits, video views, and even (in more sophisticated models) in-store visits.

MTA models take several different approaches. A "linear" attribution model assigns equal value to every touchpoint along the way. For example, if there are four interactions, each "touch" is credited 25% of the total. "U-shaped" models favor the first and last touches more than the rest. In this scenario, when there are four touchpoints, the first and last touches get 40% credit, and the middle two get 10% each. "Time decay" models value each touchpoint that is closer to the sale with more value. In this instance, the first touchpoint might be worth 10%, the second 15%, the third 25%, and the last 50%. Algorithmic models use machine learning to determine an appropriate weighting – and there is little agreement among practitioners which machine learning model to use.

Here, CDP data may be the input required to fix decades of failed attempts at MTA by bringing more granular interaction data, thereby making more touchpoints truly addressable. Survey data that feeds broadcast data on ad recall ("do you remember seeing an ad for this product?") gets more powerful and verifiable when matched against subscriber data. In-store purchase data that can be aligned with addressable media interaction data becomes a valid KPI. Other addressable interactions (call center, sales) can fill in the gaps of an attribution journey. Arguably, many of the CDP-derived touchpoints are more valuable, because they happen in "real life" rather than on the internet. It's not that companies are not doing highly sophisticated work bringing offline data into multitouch attribution models today – it's that the effort required to integrate the data from disparate systems to create a unified profile and snap different interactions into a working, scaled data model is not worth the expense, time, or effort. CDP changes all of that. It may save MTA.

Media Mix Modeling (MMM)

Media mix modeling, or MMM, can be thought of as MTA's aggregated cousin. Instead of granular, people-based data, MMM models are built at a higher level (e.g. campaign), and they tend to work well for companies that do a lot of offline (TV, print, terrestrial radio) media as well as digital. Media mix modeling often looks beyond the immediate time period, considering several years' worth of media spending, and can offer a 10,000-foot view of how things like promotions or seasonality affected sales. Most CPG and retail companies have built robust MMM practices over time, and found them reliable sources of directional attribution for hard-to-measure offline sales, and barometers of soft metrics like brand equity. The ability to load these models with years' worth of historical data unveils trends that are harder to see closer up (within a campaign's timeframe), but are constrained by the infrequency of reporting, the inability to measure things like creative's impact on performance, and a lack of granularity.

While the CDP may be the ultimate boon for making MTA more science than witchcraft, MMM will survive as long as marketers are willing to make investments in nonaddressable media. As proprietary ecosystems – aka "walled gardens" – proliferate, MMM may necessarily displace MTA as the weapon of choice even for digital campaign optimization. The reason: "walled gardens," almost by definition, do not release user-level data. So, the data available to marketers will be increasingly of the aggregate variety, pushing measurement away from log files and user-level analytics such as MTA.

Ultimately, media mix models will become a highly valuable, aggregate-level input into CDP analytics, akin to what FLOC ("federated learning of cohorts") analysis brings to the table in the Google ecosystem. By starting with a directional roadmap of years' worth of channel-based measurement, CDPs can fill in the gaps with addressable, people-based insights to validate and improve existing models.

Marketing Analytics Platforms

What about measuring social advertising, search campaigns, and customer programs bought directly from publishers? It seems like every channel and partner has a separate report. We experience this at Salesforce in marketing. We buy plenty of banner advertising through several DSPs on the open web, buy search ads on Google, run social media advertising on LinkedIn, and have a lot of custom programs with big publishers like the *Wall Street Journal* and similar business publications. Each channel offers tons of great analytics about our reach; interactions with our ads through impressions, click-throughs, or video engagements; and overall effectiveness.

Essentially, anything measurable found its way into a massive spreadsheet, with multiple tabs, where we kept track of all of our channel-based campaigns. Each one had a different campaign name and field names that identified similar things by different names ("Impressions" might be "IMPS" or "IMP_COUNT" or "IMP_TOT"). Putting the tabs together in a way that makes sense required lots of Excel macros, manual field mapping, and human intervention. If you have ever been on a team responsible for trying to unify marketing analytics, then you understand the pain (see our agency experience, above).

The pain of manual data munging and human analysis leads to a lot of smart people doing the lower-order work of unification, incomplete analysis due to limited powers of manual observation, and extreme lag times in leveraging analytics data to optimize campaigns. The answer to the problem starts with a great ETL (extract, transform, load) capability to ingest and unify data, a scaled set of APIs (application programming interfaces) to collect campaign data in real-time, and the power of machine learning and other AI tools to find the winners and losers across dozens of campaigns, creative executions, and vendors.

Yesterday's approach was to build marketing performance dashboards that helped analysts see all of their campaigns in aggregate, and exposing key reports (top channel, top creative, top segment) to inform periodic optimizations. Marketers could see how campaigns were pacing over their lifespan, keep track of KPIs, and set alerts to see when a campaign fell below a specified KPI, such as click-rate. Data that contributed to such dashboards was usually imported in batch mode, via CSV files, or generated via pixel-based data collection. Most systems relied on careful prepping of the data into a common taxonomy and mapping common field names took lots of manual work. We did some of this work for a large agency and their telecom client back in 2011 and can attest to the heavy lifting required "behind the curtain" to produce the pretty, colorful dashboards. Updates were infrequent, as were optimizations based on the insights the reports suggested.

What has changed over the past decade is the impact of artificial intelligence on data capture (smartly fitting disparate data sets together in a persistent model), analysis (deep learning to surface anomalies in the data), and activation (automated optimization recommendations). AI and machine learning have transformed reporting dashboards into intelligence tools that increase time to value by automating the process of data unification, building data models, and making optimization available hourly rather than weekly or monthly.

This is increasingly critical in a world which features nearly 10,000 marketing and advertising technology tools, and the continual introduction of new addressable channels. Having a scaled platform with a library of API connections into the most common platforms is table stakes, but having a platform with a flexible API infrastructure, open to new connections and rapidly updating old ones as they depreciate and are replaced is the new requirement. On the analytics side, whereas dashboards could only munge and visualize data for manual analysis, AI brings scale and speed to model building, by evolving dynamic models as more data comes into the system.

Just as the CDP unifies people data, the right marketing analytics dashboard unifies cross-channel interaction data. The combination of the two will create exponential value. As above, with DMP analytics, the fidelity of a brand's people data asset is the secret to opening the aperture of observation to turn reports into insights that drive performance. The ability to overlap a segment composed of highly granular people data (purchase, loyalty, location, etc.) against higher granular media interaction data (opens, views, clicks, downloads, etc.) will yield more insights that result in actionable optimizations.

Just as CDP data will enhance the marketing analytics platform's ability to provide finer measurement, real-time analytics data ingested back into the CDP will enrich segment data, creating a virtuous cycle of data enrichment. Machine learning models need to constantly feed on granular data to get smarter, and benefit from fidelity in the underlying data – so creating a steel-threaded connection between CDP and analytics confers a unique advantage.

Enterprise Analytics/BI

CDPs' initial appeal was to marketers, but they are evolving beyond marketing use cases as they enter adolescence. Just as a unified "people data" asset can enrich and inform activation and analytics for the multichannel marketer, CDP capabilities can enrich the enterprise's understanding of other business challenges. Business intelligence (BI) platforms go beyond marketing analytics through combining data mining, visualization, data tools, and infrastructure to help organizations get a comprehensive view of holistic enterprise data to drive change, eliminate inefficiencies, and adapt to market changes. We call this "enterprise" analytics to distinguish it from marketing analytics (as above).

The category of BI emerged in the 1960s, primarily as a way to share data across organizations or disparate teams, evolved in the 1980s alongside computer models (the "intelligence" part), and have since evolved to include dashboarding and visual analysis. More modern tools include the ability for business users (rather than IT experts) to use the system via self-service, better data governance capabilities, and faster query speeds. Enterprise analytics concerns itself with statistical and visual analysis of data that may include, but is not limited to, sales, data, inventory, supply chain data, weather data, biometric data, and more. With the right BI tool, using data to visualize and analyze Big Data, maps, surveys, and time series analysis becomes automated and interactive.

Where do enterprise analytics and CDP intersect? In *Data Driven*, we shared the story of how Campbell's Soup Company has been using weather data to direct its marketing budgets for over 70 years. People tend to buy more soup when a storm is coming, and Campbell's pioneered the idea of leveraging local weather data to target advertising. This started with radio, but evolved to television and more addressable channels over time. With a DMP, access to third-party weather data, and the ability to do location-based targeting, Campbell's had a highly efficient way to generate demand in stores that had the highest propensity to sell soup.

Building on that example, think what a company could accomplish by going beyond those data attributes and adding enterprise-grade insights. As an example, targeting by weather is interesting, but adding in stores with high inventory availability ensures demand generation matches available products on the shelf. Furthermore, some locations consider "foul weather" in very different ways. One inch of snow in Atlanta can shut down the entire city, but is a beach day in Fargo. For an airline, mapping typical marketing analytics data alongside loyalty points data might reveal the different points at which a customer might be more receptive to an offer to redeem their points.

Ultimately, while marketing analytics tools will always be directed at the marketing persona, the right BI tool can be positioned to serve multiple stakeholders across the organization. CDP will make enterprise analytics more robust and ultimately, may be the default tool for visualizing customer data in multiple ways that go beyond marketing.

CUSTOMER-DRIVEN THINKER: VINNY RINALDI

We first met Vinny Rinaldi at his agency, Dentsu Aegis, where he was the in-house data expert, helping Merkle, a CRM agency, integrate into the agency network. In this role, he was at the forefront of the CDP evolution, combining sales data to influence marketing outcomes, and soon thereafter he went to work transforming how Hershey's, a company founded in the 1880s, sells chocolate. He currently is principal, programmatic partner manager at Amazon, and was formerly the Head of Addressable Media and Technology of the Hershey Company.

For companies that sell candy bars and chocolate, there is no bigger season than Halloween. Like Black Friday, this holiday can make or break the financial year. But, like most CPG companies who do benefit from a direct, one-to-one, customer relationship, attribution was a challenge. For the 2017 season, Vinny challenged his leadership to "think like a direct-to-consumer," leveraging local sales data, combined with media data in a data lake, and see how close the company could get to a true attribution model. This is the story of how a better attribution model turned a relatively small media budget into $4.5 million in incremental sales.

How did you combine sales and marketing data to win the candy Super Bowl?

After joining the Hershey Company in Q4 2017 as the Head of Addressable media, I reviewed the recent performance of Halloween, the "Super Bowl" of the confection category, in early November. During the review, I noticed impressions, clicks, and video views were our main KPIs for seasonal performance, I knew there needed to be some changes. By only understanding how many people or households saw your ad and watched a 15-second video was not enough to correlate back to an actual sale. If we measured impressions in a certain market, we could then start to monitor sales growth and household penetration growth by the DMA (Designated Market Area). Being new to the company, I set out to understand who in the organization would be willing to start a task force with me to focus on this project.

The hypothesis was if we could analyze the data we ingest as a company from a sales perspective, we should be able to correlate media metrics back to business results, which is not an easy feat when your immediate team doesn't own the retail aspect of the sales cycle. Knowing we had some time, I put together a group of three people, representing three separate groups within the company, that had access to customer data to build out a new process.

Throughout Q1 2018, we put together a plan that outlined how merging media data and sales data together would represent incremental growth for the business. We then presented our solution to "Win the Season" to senior leadership for approval. Being able to match media data with unit sales data by location would put Hershey at the forefront of media-buying principles within the CPG space. Our team became fascinated with the Direct-to-Consumer businesses' mindsets of testing and learning, but in near real time with actual sales metrics, so we adopted the mantra, "Think Like a DTC, Act Like a CPG."

The foundation of our business was predicated on sales data across some of the largest brick and mortar retailers in the US and aggregated into a single data lake. Three of those retailers made up greater than 50% of unit sales, with one of them being the majority at greater than 30%. We felt confident that if we utilized the baseline of our largest customer, we could build a model that would allow us to reflect incremental growth for the business. Over the next six months leading up to Halloween, we continued to pressure test the system with similar forms of testing. We started out with running a match market test, during the "S'mores Season" running primarily in the summer. The test consisted of creating a test and control environment, where we ensured market size and sales were of equal sizing for the cleanest results possible. We then built creative messaging for the respective platforms in digital, and shut off all other digital mediums for a 14-day period. After we ran three studies, what we learned was the testing markets with a media presence, continued to have a lift over the control at 3% or greater each time. Although this was at a smaller scale, we felt confident we could replicate and scale this model. The framework of the test was set to run weekly campaigns, for the five weeks leading up to October 31. Each Monday, we would measure the previous week's sales by zip code at our largest customer, and then analyze where we saw underperforming markets. Before the Halloween Season started, the company already knew how many units we sold to our customers (retailers).

Our focus was ensuring as much of our product sold through, before retailers severely discounted our product on November 1, to move seasonal units off the shelf. For the campaign, we picked markets that performed at less than 80% against the national average of sell through. In the process we streamlined, we could assess a market list, send data into our programmatic platforms and be live within an 8-hour day. For reference, a typical campaign launch ranged from five to seven business days. Once Halloween ended, we were able to look at the campaign to understand the test/control variables of the markets we spent budget against. Each week we were able to identify markets that we turned on with media presence and never came back on the weekly market list through the campaign. We also found markets where we turned on media one week and they reached the 80% average, but then two weeks later that market came back onto our list, after the media was turned off.

At the end of the season, we were able to attribute approximately $4.5 million in incremental sales to the business on an $850,000 media budget, netting out to a $5.29 ROI. After we implemented this strategy during Halloween season, we were able to replicate this framework six weeks later to drive holiday sales, then Valentine's Day sales, and lastly the Easter season. We were able to collaborate with multiple organizations creating faster, more efficient workflows. This was a project that required managing multiple stakeholders across multiple organizations, creating a positive outcome and solving a critical business need, while marrying media data with business data.

SUMMARY: CONNECTED DATA FOR ANALYTICS

- *Customer data and marketing analytics:* Analytics has evolved from a CMO support function to a capability at the center of modern marketing. Analytics teams help their organizations to understand, target and measure performance, improve ROI, and continually optimize results. As a result of digital transformation, marketing analysts increasingly require the data scale, scope, speed, and accuracy provided by the enterprise CDP.
- *Email analytics:* Channel marketing managers suffer from observational bias: they can only measure what they see, and most see the interactions their ESP can deliver. The CDP has the ability, through unifying touchpoints that go "beyond marketing," to broaden the spectrum of digital and offline touchpoints to fill in the gaps of a journey between email interactions. When seen in a broader context, messaging interactions become highly valuable and valid contributors to multitouch models.
- *DMP analytics:* The CDP that can unify people data from both pseudonymous and PII-based sources (a "CDMP," if you will) will immediately widen the aperture of analytics by introducing attributes that common media analytics never really considered, such as historical purchase data, call center interactions, and loyalty data. When tied to addressable media interaction, and measured at the segment level, CDP data becomes the most valuable predictor of marketing performance.

- *Multitouch attribution:* CDP data may be the input required to fix decades of failed attempts at MTA by bringing more granular interaction data by making more touchpoints truly addressable. Arguably, many of the CDP-derived touchpoints are more valuable, because they happen in "real life" rather than on the internet. Ultimately, CDP may revive the moribund MTA category by bringing scale and speed to the underlying data that drive model creation and validation.

- *Media mix modeling:* Media mix models can offer a high-level view of how things like promotions or seasonality affect sales and will become a highly valuable, aggregate-level input into CDP analytics. By starting with a directional roadmap of years' worth of channel-based measurement, CDPs can fill in the gaps with addressable, people-based insights to validate and improve existing models.

- *Marketing analytics platforms:* Marketing performance dashboards are being replaced by AI-driven marketing analytics platforms. AI brings scale and speed to model building, by evolving dynamic models as more data comes into the system. Just as CDP data will enhance the marketing analytics platform's ability to provide finer measurement, real-time analytics data ingested back into the CDP will enrich segment data, creating a virtuous cycle of data enrichment.

- *Enterprise analytics:* BI tools are positioned to serve multiple stakeholders across the organization: sales, IT, marketing, and customer service, to name a few. CDPs will make enterprise analytics more robust and ultimately may be the default tool for visualizing customer data in multiple ways that go beyond marketing. As the CDP itself evolves to go from the *single source of truth of people data for marketing users* to the *single source of customer truth period*, enterprise BI tools will make the CDP their primary source of people data.

CHAPTER 12

Summary and Looking Ahead

SUMMARY

Thanks for taking this ride with us. We thank you, and we have a feeling your customers will also thank you in the years to come. By making an effort to understand the fast-moving world of data integration, management, and use – to say nothing of the consequential matters of org design, analytics, and AI – you have proved that you care about your customers' experiences.

Customer data is a topic that transcends any marketing technology soup-of-the-day. As long as companies exist that want to deliver relevant and timely experiences to individuals and accounts, there will be a need to integrate, organize, analyze, and use customer data. Channels and customer behaviors will change, technology will get smarter and faster and cheaper, analytics and insights will expand beyond the boundaries of our imaginations – but customer data remains at the highly competitive core of everything else.

Let's take a moment to revisit where we've been on our journey with you in *Customer Data Platforms* and then make a few predictions about what happens next.

We opened with the "Pizza Problem," providing a vivid example of the outsize returns that marketers can make by implementing simple automation and personalization protocols. For Casey's in the great Midwest, all it took was an ability to match people with their preferred pizzas in their email reminders, and a great customer-and-brand relationship was built based on better plumbing: nuts-and-bolts data integration, management, and use. We admitted becoming an Amazon-killer (or pick-your-own-rival-killer) isn't easy, but it's increasingly within reach.

In Chapter 1, we described the different categories of customer data. There is "known" data, that is, data that is tied to a form of personally identifiable information (PII), such as an email or name and address. Known data may belong to customers or prospects, but it is so called because you can potentially tie it to a person in the real world. On the other hand, "unknown" data is linked to a proxy or pseudonymous ID, such as a browser cookie or MAID or encrypted email address (HEM), and it can't be tied to a real-world individual.

People themselves are linked to both types of IDs, and we explained that the successful modern marketer will need to be able to navigate – and link – both worlds successfully.

Then, in Chapter 2, we took a brief trip back through the history of marketing technology, showing how today's data-driven digital marketer is the direct heir to advances made by direct marketers and direct mail practitioners. We looked at the rise of key technologies such as email, relational databases, and SQL that allowed marketers to automate and speed up many previously manual tasks. However, we also traced the phenomenon of application pile-up, as new channels such as mobile and social media and so on arose and acquired their own applications, each of which built a customer database. The result was a siloed landscape and the disconcerting "Frankenstacks" that too many of us have to manage.

Responding to the proliferation of isolated, purpose-built marketing and other-tech systems in their portfolio, CMOs and their colleagues said: Enough. Thus, came the phenomenon – around 2016 or so – of the customer data platform. At first, largely theoretical and aspirational, the CDP described a natural desire to ingest data from these multiple siloed systems and organize it in a central location – the CDP itself – in order to make it available for common uses, such as analytics, decisions, and activation to channels such as email, websites, and social networks. Chapter 3 presented our description of the two types of CDP: Insights CDPs (a single-view-of-the-customer), and Engagement CDPs (enabling real-time personalization). We made the case that a true Enterprise CDP must combine both into an overarching platform that spans unknown and known data and both insights and engagement capabilities.

Chapter 4 started our deeper dive into the practical workings of our Enterprise CDP. After introducing you to an intrepid group of marketers in the Midwest in the 1960s that foreshadowed many of the solutions of today (and had a heaven-sent 80% response rate), we laid out the five pillars of the ideal CDP. These were: (1) data ingestion from any common source and format; (2) data harmonization, or the ability to format and cleanse this data; (3) identity management, allowing users to tie information about customers together accurately; (4) segmentation in a user-friendly, drag-and-drop interface, as well as other analytics; and (5) activation, or the ability to send decisions and instructions wherever they need to go for use.

Of course, customer data is heavily intertwined these days with regulations, consumer privacy preferences, data use rights and practices, consent, and security. That was the topic of Chapter 5, which described the various "privacy paradoxes" and how to approach them. On the one hand, consumers increasingly require a personalized, relevant, one-to-one experience across platforms; but they're also increasingly wary about sharing the data required to build such experiences. Then there is the odd phenomenon that consumers are not good at understanding the tradeoffs between data and experiences: we cannot assess risks and rewards easily. We described government regulatory regimes around the world and what's going on with web browsers, and we closed with some tactics to resolve the "paradoxes."

In Chapter 6, we changed our focus to the organizational. Digital transformation requires different departments throughout the enterprise to work together in new ways and perfect mutual processes. Customer data may be the focus of this book, but it's only one component of ultimate success. Leading companies will integrate their organizations as much as they integrate their data. We described the "center of excellence" model, and showed how spinning up a central group with responsibility for the customer data tech transformation can serve as an anchor in the roiling sea of change. And we presented a maturity model showing how organizations can crawl-walk-run their restructuring efforts.

Early on, the CDP was often confused with the Data Management Platform (DMP), which arose more than a decade ago to handle the complexities of programmatic advertising. The DMP and advertising more broadly were the topic of Chapter 7. We described how the DMP differs from the CDP, as generally defined: the former treats pseudonymous IDs at great scale, while the latter deals with known IDs at customer-size scale. Then we made a case that the future of the customer data environment, encompassing both known and unknown data, will have to include elements of both DMP and CDP.

Although marketers were the first to champion the CDP category, customer data itself has many uses outside of marketing. And digital transformation promises to erase enterprise boundaries – or, more realistically, lower them a bit – so there's no logical reason why CDPs should remain a marketing solution. In Chapter 8, we described the ways in which we've seen marketing work more closely with service (as the frontline engagers with customers), commerce (the storefront in the digital sphere), sales (in a B2B context), and partners. Rather than organizational and departmental definitions, we see evidence that the most successful companies are those that put the customer at the center, organizing around customer requirements, with a clean and cross-divisional unified customer view at the center.

Customers told us that the most important applications for the CDP are analytical: segmentation, building predictive models, closed-loop measurement. In Chapter 9, we show that one of the most exciting capabilities unlocked by an accurate customer view is artificial intelligence (AI). With clean and voluminous customer data, gathered with consent, organizations can start to think about applying more advanced AI and machine learning (ML) tools to solve harder problems. These might include building more useful segmentation schemas, developing more powerful next-best-action or next-best-offer models, and even delving into areas such as image recognition or natural language processing.

In Chapter 10, we described the ways that customer data and analytics can be applied to journeys and orchestration. Figuring out the right sequence and timing of messages, offers, and content is very much a part of delivering on the promise of the "right message at the right time." The ability to automate message sequences using simple manual logic (if-this-then-that) was a component of marketing automation and multichannel campaign management systems. Like other marketing technologies, these systems often addressed only one or two channels and used customer data resident in the system. By separating customer data from decisions and journeys, the CDP promises to enable new capabilities such as predictive journeys (using AI/ML to decide what to do next) and more decisions made in real time.

Finally, we wrapped up in Chapter 11 by looking at the important area of analytics. Customer data sitting in a warehouse somewhere, no matter how clean and accurate it is, has no real value. It is first put to use through pointing analytical tools and methods at it, to inform insights and decisions and actions. We described the key types of analytics that are enhanced by better customer data, including email and DMP analytics. We visited holistic measurement approaches such as multitouch attribution (MTA) and marketing mix modeling (MMM) and showed how they were improved. And we outlined the role of more traditional disciplines, such as business intelligence (BI) in the new world of customer-driven analytics.

Change is the only constant, particularly in marketing. What's next?

LOOKING AHEAD

At Salesforce, we start many presentations with a "forward-looking statement," meant to inform customers that they should make their investment decisions with us on the basis of what we have available today, not the future-facing innovation and product roadmap items we talk about. It is good advice – even the best-planned and intentioned development ideas in software are bets on the future. As we've seen throughout *Customer Data Platforms*, technology moves fast and customers move even faster.

The data management space has moved pretty slowly over the past 40 years, especially when it comes to marketing-specific applications. Even as the Martech Landscape Map has evolved from a few hundred logos to 8,000, the power underlying all of those clever apps has remained *people data*. The companies that can capture, unify, activate, and analyze it will put their customers at the center of everything they do, and will win. Enterprises that fail to adapt, and move slower than their customers will fail during the Fourth Industrial Revolution. It's really that simple.

Today, what we are witnessing in this latest era of data management is the collision of a number of trends: cheap data storage, highly available open source big data software, a hot venture capital market chasing software-as-a-service businesses, and the emergence of a "digital first" imperative.

CDP is not a fad. CDPs are merely the latest boulder uncovered in the chronostratigraphy of customer data management – a brief but exciting epoch during a 30-year CRM era that really accelerated in the 1990s, when Salesforce first put it in the Cloud. That said, CDP is perhaps the most exciting and promising stage of this long journey – a time where the ubiquity, speed, and scale of technology can actually deliver on the powerful customer-facing use cases marketers and entrepreneurs can dream up.

So, where is it going? We'll make a few predictions:

CATEGORY SHAKE-OUT!

We think the category of CDPs will be defined by the bigger players like Salesforce, Microsoft, and Adobe that are building "enterprise" versions of CDP, as we defined them in Chapter 3. Over the last decade there has been a tendency, especially among large enterprises, to consolidate their technology stacks and reduce the number of vendors and data sources that need integration. This trend will only intensify as the harsh light of CDP evaluations reveals just how fragmented and siloed most marketectures have become. CMOs and CDOs who want to partner with their CIO and CTO counterparts will have to balance their data-driven ambitions with the reality of existing "stacks." Most companies will choose to align their CDP efforts where the weight of their customer data resides currently: either the CRM system or marketing cloud data store.

Therefore, we see the dominance of enterprise strength – mostly marketing-cloud-based players – as inevitable, but can see a future where an extremely capable, extremely small set of pure-play providers can offer a best-of-breed, technology-forward alternative. If companies are likely to move forward with CDPs from the big cloud players to further consolidate their existing investments, there is an interesting niche for smaller, nimble companies that create CDP-adjacent offerings in the areas of data enrichment, portability, and data orchestration. The bottom line? Today's independent CDPs create just another data silo in large enterprise marketecture, promising data unification but actually offering more fragmentation. Most will fade away, or quickly pivot to become applications that fill in the "white space" unoccupied by larger players.

AGGREGATE-LEVEL DATA AND "FLOCTIMIZATION"

We are seeing a trend that is not going away anytime soon: the move from user-level data analytics to aggregate-level data. Thanks to the continued rise of walled-garden data environments like Google, Facebook, Amazon, Apple, and others – and continuing privacy legislation by governments – we are in an era where properly collected and consented-into first-party data is more valuable than it's ever been. Like any other product, the laws of supply and demand apply – less third-party marketplace data and more restrictions on data collection make every customer ID three times as valuable (another reason why investments in CDP are more important than ever).

Marketers are going to require their CDPs to become experts in making the aggregate-level data that Google and Facebook can give them, such as "Federated Learning of Cohorts" (FLOC) or another method available to map against one's first-party data such that they become valuable for analytics, insights, and optimization. That means the early battles in CDPs will be won by companies that can offer *data provisioning services* (for replacing third-party marketplace data with second-party partner data); and the ability to use such technology for *clean-room data sharing* to suck insights out of walled gardens. CDPs that can do this without running afoul of privacy concerns can build specific applications for leveraging aggregate-level data for insights and even targeting (perhaps creating a "FLOCtimization" platform that leverages CDP data to recommend different cohorts for targeting in Google, or uses purchase data from Amazon to append buyer propensity score to user profiles, as examples).

A FRESH START FOR MULTITOUCH ATTRIBUTION

As we discussed above, multitouch attribution has always been a flawed science, marred by observational bias, incomplete data, and offering insights that are directional at best. The death of the cookie has taken what was a positive move forward for attribution (more user-level data), and turned recent advances into liabilities. MTA and other measurement disciplines have also been overly dependent on digital marketing touchpoints (clicks, email opens, video views, etc.), and biased in favor of things a pixel can capture. As we discussed in Chapter 11: more available people data, from sources with more fidelity than marketing data (sales, service, and commerce), analyzed through AI – and deployed not just in dashboards but as real, actionable, optimization signals – will forever change the game in attribution. What we didn't talk about was the impact this change will have on marketing in general.

The combination of more user-level insights on "real-life" touchpoints like call center, e-commerce, and sales interactions – combined with addressable marketing data – will change the way analysts value "touches." The real-time availability of such data, tied to a persistent person ID, will unleash AI with the ability to fine-tune models with precision. And the availability of broader, more frequent access to aggregate-level data from walled gardens will serve as validation for more traditional survey- and panel-based measurement. These three fast-moving trends position CDPs to disrupt a $4 billion market and change the way we measure success in marketing (and ultimately force the adoption of "nonmarketing" touchpoints that are tied to customer data).

AI FINALLY TAKES OVER

What do we mean? As discussed in Chapter 9, we are well on our way to a marketing future dominated by machine learning and artificial intelligence. What has been holding it back? Lots of clean, prepped data. We talked about the power of open-source libraries and tools that can bring an unprecedented level of intelligence and scale to marketing. If they are so valuable, why did Google make TensorFlow, perhaps the world's most sophisticated artificial intelligence algorithm library, free? It turns out, algorithms are only as good as the amount of data they work on! In the same way, CDPs are only as useful as the amount of customer data they process.

CDP's ability to unify customer data and enrich them with attributes gives data-hungry machines the fuel they need to solve big problems through finding tiny deviations in data. How does it impact marketing? In the near future, we will see entire sectors fundamentally changed by AI running on clean, well-structured CDP datasets. AI will analyze months' or years' worth of campaigns and automatically create media plans – further transforming the media agency sector. It will automatically match customers with personalized offers on channels based on their past purchase history, marketing interactions, and real-time propensity to buy – eliminating much of the value of DSPs, SSPs, and other "programmatic" tools, further upending the adtech sector.

It's an exciting future, but one in which most of the "smarts" live inside the CDP itself, rather than the endpoints where data is delivered. In the new world, systems that simply catch and apply CDP data to various channels become less valuable and more commoditized – and must become more symbiotic with the "source of truth" where customer data resides. In this sense, CDPs start to overlap many of the categories within the martech landscape, and ultimately subsume many.

THE FUTURE

We end where we began: a vision for a connected customer profile. The need to have a single view of the customer isn't new, and there's no reason to think it will ever go away. The more marketing changes, the more it stays the same. Every department in the enterprise goes through its phases of growth and contraction, innovation, and retrenchment. Technology marches on, and consumer behaviors and expectations remain forever difficult to predict. We hope we've convinced you that the CDP – while an exciting and innovative category – is not exactly new: it stands in a long line of once equally new categories such as CRM, marketing automation, multichannel campaign management, even data lakes, and marts.

As we look forward, then, we see marketers needing their unified view as much as they do now; we see them applying more and more advanced analytical models, and differentiating more on their insights; and we see them needing to reach consumers on whatever platform they happen to prefer. (Hello, voice: Do we hear you talking?) So, much stays the same. To the extent that customer behavior is as unpredictable as tech innovations, we can confidently say that the CDP will have to grow more flexible, more adaptable, more agile – not less. More connectors, more flexible data models, more outbound integrations. Easier-to-use interfaces with clicks and not code (although with code too).

We believe in the platform vision. As the person who first identified the CDP, David Raab, told us, it's fairly certain that every martech stack in the future will have a box labeled "CDP." This is because every marketer needs a unified user profile, updated in real time, accessible via a standard set of protocols. What sits above this data layer will have to adapt to the user's needs and the warp and woof of the market itself, as well as new inventions. We believe the future will see a universe of more and more marketing applications, not fewer. The inventor of the Martech Logo Map, Scott Brinker, told us as much when he asked the rhetorical question: "Who complains there are too many apps in the App Store? No one, that's who."

We see a world where citizen developers use low code and no code tools to spin up apps in an afternoon to fill gaps in their current stacks, to do something better than they do it now, or because they're inspired by a new idea nobody has had before. It's a world where a million apps bloom overnight – and we welcome them warmly. All is good as long as there is a coherent, secure, privacy-first, scaled platform underneath it all. A platform that is powered by a trusted, accurate, and persistent customer profile that puts it all to work.

That's the promise of the customer data platform. We can't wait to greet the future, now.

Further Reading

Check out these useful reports from Salesforce:

- Three Principles to Help You Rethink Your Approach to Customer Data
- Customer 360 Audiences Product Information
- Demystifying the Future of Customer Data and CDPs
- What Is a CDP?
- Build a Business Case for CDP
- How to Buy a CDP
- How to Handle Change Management Around a CDP
- Customer Data Management Trail

Acknowledgments

As the old saying goes, it's not really "work" when you are doing what you love, and we are very grateful to work for a company that allows people to pursue their passions – including the odd ones like writing a feature-length book on data technology. To that end, we would like to thank our colleagues at Salesforce, starting with our main sponsors, Adam Blitzer, the CEO of Salesforce Digital 360 and Dan Farber, SVP of Communications. Getting a major public company to let you publish a book is not easy, but Adam and Dan sure make it seem like it. Stephanie Buscemi, our CMO, and John Taschek, SVP of Market Strategy, gave some much-appreciated support.

We'd never have been able to write this book without the fellowship and support of our friends who actually build data technology (rather than just write about it) – people like product leader Robin Grochol and engineering guru Muralidhar Krishnaprasad. We also got a lot of technical assistance from some great product people inside the company – folks who have built their fair share of DMPs, CDPs, and other marketing platforms. They are Bradley Wright, John Taschek, Matthew Westover, Katrin Ribant, Gabrielle Tao, and Patrick Barrett. Our marketing ohana really helped us too, starting with Shannon Duffy and Bobby Jania, who supported our efforts. We also got a lot of help from our neighbors from the 18th floor of Bryant Park, Paul Cordasco and Chris Jacob. And a very special *merci* to Katrin Ribant, SVP of Product Management, co-founder of Datorama and strategic advisor to the CDP team during its critical early phase.

From a content perspective, we had a ton of great customers sit down and share their digital transformation challenges and successes. These included Ron Amram, former head of global media at Heineken and current senior director of global media at Mars; Alysia Borsa, the chief digital officer of Meredith Corporation; Vinny Rinaldi, formerly at Hershey Corporation and now at Amazon; Laura Lisowski Cox, the co-founder and CMO of skin care brand Oars + Alps; Kumar Subramanyam, Global Head of Marketing Data Sciences at Hewlett-Packard (HP); Sebastian Baltruszewicz, CPG Product Owner for Consumer Data & eCRM at RB (Reckitt Benckiser); Brad Feinberg, North America V.P. of Media & Consumer Engagement at Molson Coors; Danielle Comito, Global Group Marketing Director of Boston Scientific; and Art Sebastian, VP of Digital Experience at Casey's General Stores.

We also benefited from talking to the pros in the CDP space – opinion leaders like Kevin Mannion, the chief strategy officer of research firm Advertiser Perceptions; Scott "Chief Martech" Brinker, who allowed us to use his wonderful "Martech 5000" landscape; and David Raab, the inventor of the "CDP" moniker and leader of the CDP Institute.

A special thanks also to Michael Auth, a great illustrator who brought his creativity to our marketecture. Jennifer Uram shepherded our contracts. And of course we also want to thank the great team at Wiley, including our editor Jeanenne Ray, Sally Baker, and our copy editor Susan Dunsmore.

About the Authors

Martin Kihn is SVP of Strategy for Salesforce Marketing Cloud, where he provides market guidance and product insights for the world's #1 Marketing Cloud. Before joining Salesforce, he led the data-driven marketing practice as Research VP at Gartner, focusing on marketing data integration, and cross-channel, predictive, and attribution analytics. Two-time winner of analyst awards, he was the firm's most-read blogger and a frequent speaker on marketing strategy. After earning his MBA from Columbia Business School, he worked for a time as a management consultant – an experience described in his book, *House of Lies*, which was the basis for a Showtime series. He is the author of two other memoirs, and his work has appeared in *Forbes*, *Fast Company*, the *New York Times*, *New York*, *AdExchanger*, and other publications.

Chris O'Hara leads global product marketing for Salesforce's Data & Identity group, which includes Customer 360 Audiences, a customer data platform. A veteran of data technology, Chris joined Salesforce after the acquisition of data management platform Krux in 2016, where he held senior sales, strategy, and marketing roles. Chris is the author of *Data Driven: Harnessing Data and AI to Reinvent Customer Engagement* (McGraw-Hill), a recipient of the Axiom Silver Medal for best Business Technology Book. Chris is also the author of six popular books about food and drink, including *Great American Beer* (Random House), a look at how marketing transformed mass-produced beer into some of the world's most iconic brands. Chris and his books have appeared on the NBC *Today Show*, the CBS *Early Show*, the Food Network, *Forbes*, *Glamour*, and *Playboy*.

Index

Page references in *italics* refer to figures.

A

A/B testing routines, 38
Acquire (CDP component), *50*,
    50–51
Activation (data management step),
    83–85
Acxiom, 31
Ad Age, 63
AdExchanger, 48–49
Adobe, 47, *48*, 205
Advertiser Perceptions, 24–26, 47
Advertising
  ad blocking technology, 92
  ad receptivity, 6
  adtech (programmatic advertising)
    (*See* Data management
    platforms (DMPs)
  customer data conundrum
    response of, 24–26
  internet design and, 92
  marketers' top challenges, *12* (*See
    also* Customer data)
  as part of marketing mix, 134
  predictive, 23–24, 26
  in "walled gardens" with
    first-party data, 135–136
  See also Marketing
Advertising Research Foundation
    (ARE), 6, 92

Amazon, 3, 97, 132
America Online, 32
Amram, Ron, 137–138
Analytics, 185–200
advanced marketing analytics,
    189–190
  aggregate-level data trend, 206
  analytical capabilities, 188
  Analytics (CDP component), *50*,
    50–51
  data management platforms
    (DMPs) for, 191–192
  data sources for, 188–189
  disconnected data, 6–7
  enterprise analytics/business
    intelligence (BI), 195–196
  historical perspective of,
    185–188, *186*, *187*
  marketing analytics platforms,
    194–195
  marketing/email analytics, 190
  media mix modeling (MMM),
    193
  multitouch attribution (MTA),
    192–193, 206–207
  overview, 10, 189–190, 204
  Rinaldi on, 197–199
Anglade, Tim, 155, 157–159
AppExchange, 116

Apple
  Identifier for Advertisers (IDFA),
    94–95, 101–102
  Intelligent Tracking Prevention
    (ITP), 94
  Safari, 93, 94, 101
Application programming interfaces
    (APIs)
  data management example, 70–71
  defined, 44
  for engagement activation, 86
Arpanet, 177
Artificial intelligence (AI). *See*
    Machine learning (ML) and
    artificial intelligence (AI)
Artificial neural networks (ANNs),
    156–157
Attitude. *See* Consumers and
    customers
Attributes, segmentation and, 82–83,
    83
Attribution, machine-learned, 165,
    167–168
Audience Studio (Salesforce), *20*
Automation
  defined, 35
  early CRM and marketing
    automation, 35–38, *36*, *37*

B
Baltruszewicz, Sebastian, 103–104
Batch processing (data collection), 73
Beberg, Dwayne, 69–71
"Beer and diapers" theory, 166
Behavior
  behavioral data, 137–138
  behavioral segmentation, 81
  real-time interaction management
    (RTIM) and, 13, 180–181
  See also Consumers and customers
Benefits segmentation, 81
BlueKai (Oracle), 91–92, 96, 132

Borsa, Alysia, 171–173
Brinker, Scott (ChiefMarTech), 40,
    40, 44–45, 63, 109–110
Business Automation (magazine),
    29
Business intelligence (BI), 195–196
Business-user friendly UI, 62–63

C
California Consumer Privacy Act
    (CCPA), 5, 9, 17, 95, 100, 105
Call centers, 144–146
Campaign management
  automation with campaign
    database, *37*
  campaign management tools,
    74–85
  cross-channel campaign
    management, 52
  ideal marketing architecture and,
    43, 43–44
  multi-channel campaign
    management (MCCM), 86
  See also Marketing
Campbell's Soup Company, 196
CAN-SPAM, 32
Casey's, 1–2, 201
Categorical models, 163
CDP Center of Excellence Model,
    119–128
  analytics, 122–123
  core responsibilities and process
    of, 123–124, *124*
  IT/CRM, 120–122
  marketing, 120
  overview, *119*
  working maturity model for,
    124–128, *125*, *127*
  See also Customer-driven
    marketing
CDP Working Model, 114–119
  methodology, 117

operating model, 118–119
overview, *115*
platform, 116
team for, 114–116
use cases, 116–117
Censuswide survey, 6
CHAID (decision tree), 82–83
Channels
  advanced marketing analytics and, 189
  coordination stages, 126
  engagement with, 111–112
  predictive journeys to move customers between, 179
Chat-bots, 169
Chavez, Tom, 132
Chief marketing officers (CMOs)
  executive support of, 118–119
  identifying customers across enterprise, 143–144 (*See also* Customer data as enterprise-wide asset)
  IT/CRM teams and, 120–122
  on regulatory requirements, 99–100, *100*
  responsibilities of, 187–188
ChiefMarTech. *See* Brinker, Scott
Chrome (Google), 93–95, *94*, 101
Chromium (Google), 93
Cloud (Google), 158
Cloud Information Model (Salesforce), 76
Clusters, 82–83, 164
Coca-Cola, 4
Codd, E. F., 34
Comcast, 14
Commerce Cloud, 142
Consent, 91–105
  Baltruszewicz on, 103–104
  consumers on, 96–99
  corporate ethics and, 93, 98

cross-device identity management (CDIM) and, 19–20, *20*
demographics and, 102–103
international/cultural attitudes on, 99–100, *100*
IT/CRM and privacy, 121–122
overview, 9, 104–105, 202–203
privacy concerns and, 91–92
privacy paradox and, 100–101
"Unsubscribe" rules, 32
web browsers and standards bodies on, 93–96, *94*
Consumers and customers
  average number of devices used by, 77, 134
  campaigns (customer lists) and, 37 (*See also* Campaign management)
  consent and trust of, 96–99 (*See also* Consent)
  consumer behavior, 13, 81, 137–138, 180–181
  custom audiences, 136
  customer-driven thinking for CDPs, 44–45, 65–66
  customer engagement channels, 32–35, *33* (*See also* Customer data management, history)
  customer experience and natural language processing (NLP), 169
  customer numbers, 34–35
  customer resolution, 15–16
  customer value segmentation, 81
  loyalty of, 3, 53, 82, 176
  new customer cost, 14
  on regulatory requirements, 99–100, *100*
  resistance toward data collection, 4–6, 92
  trust by, 5, 6, 96–99

Consumers and customers
(*Continued*)
   See also Consent; Customer data;
     Customer-driven marketing;
     Customer journey; Customer
     relationship management
     (CRM); Regulation
Consumer Technology Association,
   77
Content creation, natural language
   processing (NLP) for, 169
Context marketing, 175–177
Conway's Law, 115
Cookies
   adtech and data management
     platform, 131–135, 138–139
   consent and privacy issues, 92, 93
   cross-device identity management
     (CDIM), 19–20, *20*
   unknown data and, 16–18, *17*
Corporate ethics, 93, 98
Cox, Laura Lisowski, 181–182
CPM (cost per mille), 14
Cross-device identity management
   (CDIM), 19–20, *20*, 79, 134
Cunningham, Mike, 131–132
Custom audiences, 136
Customer data, 11–27
   advertising and marketing
     agencies' response to, 24–26
   cross-device identity management
     (CDIM), 19–20, *20*
   customer relationship
     management (CRM), defined,
     15
   customer resolution, 15–16
   data onboarding, 21–22
   data portability, 15, 16
   experimental design for, 160–162
     (*See also* Machine learning
     (ML) and artificial intelligence
     (AI))

   golden records of, 14–16, 24–26
   importance for AI, 169–170
   known and unknown data,
     connecting, 20–21, *21*
   known data, defined, 14
   marketers' top challenges and, *12*
   for marketing analytics, 185–188,
     186, *187* (*See also* Analytics)
   modeling and scoring for, 147–149,
     148, 162–163
   organization of (*See* Data
     management)
   overview, 9, 26–27, 201–202
   silo problem, 11–13, *13*, 22–24, *23*
   unknown data, defined, 16–18, *17*
   See also Customer data as
     enterprise-wide asset;
     Customer data management,
     history; Customer Data
     Platforms (CDP); Known data;
     Unknown data
Customer data as enterprise-wide
   asset, 141–154
   commerce and customer data,
     146–149, *148*
   customer data and role across
     enterprise, 141–146, *142*, *143*
   marketing data for cross-team
     purposes, 151–152
   overview, 9, 10, 153–154, 203
   sales and customer data, 149–151
   Subramanyam on, 152–153
Customer data management,
   history, 29–46
   analytics and historical
     perspective, 185–188, *186*, *187*
   Brinker on, 44–45
   customer engagement channels,
     32–35, *33*
   direct mail and email, 31–32
   direct marketing (DM) history,
     29–31, *30*

early CRM and marketing
automation, 35–38, *36*, *37*
marketecture and, 41–44, *42*, *43*
modern-day landscape, 49, *49*
multi-channel marketing and
growth of digital, 38–40
overview, 9, 45–46, 202
Customer data management
platforms (CDMP), 62, 136–137
Customer Data Platform Institute, 49
Customer Data Platforms (CDP),
47–67
as anonymous to known, 8
capabilities of, 54–57, *55*, *58*
CDP data, machine learning, and
artificial intelligence, 168 (*See
also* Machine learning (ML)
and artificial intelligence (AI))
companies used for, *48*
customer-driven thinking and,
44–45, 65–66
customer relationship
management (CRM) and, 7, 8,
51, 51–52
data management platforms
(DMP) and, 47
defining category of, 52–54, *61*
enterprise CDP (*See* Data
management)
future of, 204–208
idealized feature set of, 49–51, *50*
insights and engagement for, 8–9
need for, 47–49
overview, 9, 66–67, 202
platform ecosystem as, 54, 63, 64,
64
prescriptive journey building with,
178 (*See also* Customer
journey)
three types of, *58*, 58–63
See also CDP Center of Excellence
Model; CDP Working Model;

Customer data as
enterprise-wide asset
Customer-driven marketing,
107–129
CDP working model of, 114–119,
115
Center of Excellence (COE) model
of, *119*, 119–124, *124*
Know, Personalize, Engage, and
Measure with, 107–114, *108*
organizational transformation and,
114
overview, 9, 128–129, 203
working maturity model of,
124–128, *125*, *127*
Customer journey, 175–184
from anonymous to known, 8
connecting known and unknown
data for, 20–21, *21*
context marketing and, 175–177
Cox on, 181–182
data management platform (DMP)
and journey management,
136–137
depiction of, *142*, 142–144, *143* (*See
also* Customer data as
enterprise-wide asset)
engagement maturity and, *127*,
127–128
for enterprise-grade CDP, 8
Journey Builder (Salesforce), 85
journey management, 112–113
management (orchestration) of,
177
overview, 10, 183–184, 204
predictive journeys, 178–179
prescriptive journeys, 177–178
real-time interaction management
(RTIM) journeys, 13, 180–181
Customer relationship management
(CRM)
CDP as expansion of, 7, 8

Customer relationship management
(CRM) (*Continued*)
  defined, 15
  early CRM and marketing
    automation, 35–38, *36*, *37*
  history of, 51, *51*
  inception of software for, 35

D
Dashboards *vs.* platforms, 194–195
Data
  aggregate-level data trend, 206
  collection and CDP capabilities,
    54–55, *55*
  cookies, 16–20, *17*, *20*, 92, 93,
    131–135, 138–139
  data analytics (*See* Analytics)
  database marketing, 35
  data-driven marketing (*See*
    Customer data management,
    history)
  data ingestion and CDP
    requirements, 53, 70, 72–74
  data munging, 15, 122, 123, 194
  data onboarding, 21–22
  data portability, 15, 16
  data sources for analytics, 188–189
    (*See also* Analytics)
  storage of, 170
  transformation use case, 116–117
  See also Analytics; Customer data;
    Personalization of data
Data Driven (O'Hara, Chavez, and
  Vaidya), 18, 131, 146, 196
Data management, 69–89
  CDP capabilities for, *55*, 55–56
  data pipeline elements for, *71*,
    71–72
  example, 69–71
  Feinberg on, 86–88
  overview, 9, 88–89, 202
  spheres of influence for, 85–86
  steps for, *72*, 72–84
    activation, 83–85
    data harmonization, 74–76, *75*,
      76
    data ingestion, 53, 70, 72–74
    identity management, 76–80, *78*,
      80
    segmentation, 81–83, *83*, *84*
Data management platforms (DMPs)
  advertising as part of marketing
    mix, 134
  advertising in "walled gardens"
    with first-party data, 135–136
  Amram on, 137–138
  for analytics, 191–192
  background/evolution of, 132–133
  for call centers, 144–146
  customer data management
    platforms (CDMP), 62, 136–137
  example of, 131–132
  journey management and, 136–137
  overview, 10, 138–139, 203
  pseudonymous IDS and, 135
  rise of CDP platform and, 47, 57,
    131–139
  sources of value in, 133–134
  unknown data and, 16–18
Data science
  analytics historical perspective
    and, 185–188, *186*, *187*
  CDP requirements and, 53
  data scientists' role in marketing
    organizations, 161, 170–171
  location targeting, 79
  marketing functions of, 161
  for measurement, 160
  measuring (and optimizing) for
    customer-driven marketing,
    107, *108*, 113–114
  See also Machine learning (ML)
    and artificial intelligence (AI)
Datorama (Salesforce), 71, 122

DEC, 177
Decision trees, 82–83
Deep learning, 156, *157*
Delivery (CDP component), *50*,
    50–51
Delta, 112
Demandware, 142
Demographics, privacy tactics and,
    102–103
Dentsu Aegis, 197–199
Devices
    average number of devices used by
        customers, 77, 134
    device matching, 79
    unknown data and, 16–18, *17*
Digital Command Center (Land O'
    Lakes), 69–70
Digital transformation. *See*
    Customer-driven marketing
Dimensionality reduction, 164
Direct mail, 31–32
Direct marketing (DM), 29–31, *30*
Disconnected data, 6–7
Duchnowski, Mia Saini, 181–182

E
Edelman Trust Barometer, 6
Edge browser (Microsoft), 93
Einstein (Salesforce), 159, 165
Email
    analytics, 190
    data beyond email, 37
    email service providers (ESP) as
        data management solution,
        177–178
    historical perspective of direct mail
        and, 31–32
    for machine learning and artificial
        intelligence, 161–163, 165, 166,
        168–169
    personalization and, 109–110
    See also Customer journey

Engagement, system of
    as CDP type, *58*, 60
    data management example, 70
    engagement activation, 85–86
    engagement maturity stages,
        126–128, *127*
    engaging ("the right channel") for
        customer-driven marketing,
        107, *108*, 111–113
    for enterprise-grade CDP, 8–9
    ideal marketing architecture
        (martech stack) and, *43*, 43–44
Enhanced Tracking Prevention (ETP,
    Mozilla), 94
Enterprise analytics/business
    intelligence (BI), 195–196
Enterprise holistic CDP, *58*, 62–63
Epsilon, 31
Ethics, corporate, 93, 98
European Interactive Digital
    Advertising Alliance (EIDAA),
    100
European Union (EU). *See* General
    Data Protection Regulation
    (GDPR)
Exact Target, 141–142
Executive support, importance of,
    118–119
Expose (CDP component),
    50, 50–51

F
Facebook, 3, 38–40, 97, 98
Feedback loops, 38
Feinberg, Brad, 86–88
Firefox (Mozilla), 93, 94
First-party data, 6, 91, 135–136. *See
    also* Consent
First-person sharing, 102
FLOCtimization, 206
Forrester, 92
Frankenstack martech, 41–42, *42*

G

Gartner, 7

General Data Protection Regulation (GDPR)

brand information and, 104

consent and, 32, 59

consumer trust and, 99, 100

data collection methodology and, 117

personalization issues and, 5, 9

privacy and, 101–102

"Seven Principles" of, 95–96

unknown data and, 17

Geographic segmentation, 81

Golden records of customer data, 14–16, 24–26

Google

AdID, 94–95

Chrome, 93–95, *94*, 101

Chromium, 93

Cloud, 158

H

Hacking Marketing (Brinker), 44–45

Harmonization (data management step), 74–76, *75*, *76*

Harris Poll, 99

Harvard Business Review, 5–6

HBO, "Not Hotdog" app and, 155, *156*, 157–159, *158*

Heineken, 133, 137–138

Hershey's, 151–152, 197–199

Hewlett-Packard (HP), 152–153

Hotmail (Microsoft), 132

Householding, 150

How Brands Grow (Sharp), 175–177

Human resources. *See* Team

Hype cycle, 49

I

IBM, 29, 30, 34, 38

Identifier for Advertisers (IDFA, Apple), 94–95, 101–102

Identity management

benefits of, 77–78

CDP requirements for, 53

as data management step, overview, 76–77

in practice, 79, *80*

spectrum of identity, *78*, 78–79

See also Customer data; Data management

ImageNet, 158

Image recognition, 168–169

Information flows, 102

Information models, *75*, 75–76

Ingestion (data management step), 53, 70, 72–74

Insight, system of

as CDP type, *58*, 58–59

for enterprise-grade CDP, 8–9

Instagram, 39

Integration. *See* Harmonization (data management step)

Integration gap, 49

Intelligent Tracking Prevention (ITP, Apple), 94

Interbrand, 3

"Internet Trends Report" (Meeker), 14

IT/CRM teams, 120–122

J

Journey Builder (Salesforce), 85

Journey management, 112–113

K

Keras, 158

Keurig Green Mountain, 131–132

Kihn, Martin, 18, 131, 146, 196
Known data
  co-mingling known and unknown
    data, 147–149, *148*
  defined, 14
  knowing ("the right person") for
    customer-driven marketing,
    107–109, *108*
  known and unknown data,
    connecting, 20–21, *21*
  unifying with unknown data, 62

L
Labeled data, unlabeled *vs.,* 162
Land O' Lakes, 69–71
Legal issues. *See* Consent;
    Regulation
Lifetime value (LTV) modeling, 14,
    30
LinkedIn, 97
LiveRamp, 21
Location targeting, 79
Loyalty
  CDP requirements and, 53
  customer journey and brand
    loyalty, 176
  decline of, 3
  loyalty segmentation, 82
Lumascape, 53, 63, 132, 133

M
Machine learning (ML) and artificial
    intelligence (AI), 155–174
  AI, defined, 156, 161
  AI future and, 207
  applied in marketing, 165–169
  Borsa on, 171–173
  CDP capabilities for, *55,* 57
  clusters, 82–83
  customer data and experimental
    design, 160–162

customer data importance for,
    169–170
customer data modeled for,
    162–164
customer-driven, 159
data science in marketing,
    160–161, 170–171
deep learning, defined, 156–157
example, 155, *156,* 157–159, *158*
ML, defined, 156, 161
overview, 10, 173–174, 203
Mannion, Kevin, 24–26
Manual attributes, segmentation
    and, 82–83
Maple's Seed Company, 31
Marketecture
  CDP as martech category, 49
  Frankenstack martech, 41–42, *42*
  ideal marketing architecture,
    42–44, *43*
  Lumascape, 53, 63, 132, 133
  Martech Landscape Map, 40, *40,*
    63, 109–110
  martech layer cake, 107, *108* (*See
    also* Customer-driven
    marketing)
  "second golden age of martech,"
    64, *64*
Marketing
  advertising as part of marketing
    mix, 134
  beyond marketing (*See* Customer
    data as enterprise-wide asset)
  campaign management, 37, *37, 43,*
    43–44, 52, 74–85, 86
  channels, 11–112, 126, 179, 189
  chief marketing officers (CMOs),
    99–100, *100,* 118–119, 120–122,
    143–144, 187–188
  context marketing, 175–177 (*See
    also* Customer journey)
  predictive, 23–24, 26

Marketing (*Continued*)
See also Customer-driven marketing; Marketecture
Marketing technology history. *See* Customer data management, history
"Marketing Technology Landscape" logo map (Brinker), 40, *40*, 63, 109–110
Match rates, 22
Measurement. *See* Data science
Media mix modeling (MMM), 193
Meeker, Mary, 14
Mental availability, 175–177
Meredith Corporation, 171–173
Merkle, 197
Messaging, personalization and, 109–110
Methodology, *115*, 117
Microsoft, 93, 132, 205
Mobile Marketing Association, 125
Modeling
  customer data for modeling and scoring, 147–149, *148*
  fitting model to data, 162–163
  models, defined, 162
  See also Predictive modeling
Molson Coors, 86–88
Montgomery Ward, 31
"MOSST" study (Mobile Marketing Association), 125
Mozilla, 93, 94
Mulesoft Connectivity Benchmark Report, 54
Multi-channel marketing
  growth of digital marketing and, 38–40
  multi-channel campaign management (MCCM), 86
Multitouch attribution (MTA), 192–193, 206–207
Munging, 15, 122, 123, 194

Mutually exclusive and collectively exhaustive (MECE) fields, 76

N
Natural language processing (NLP), 168–169
Net promoter score (NPS), 23
Netscape, 32
Neural networks, 164
Nielsen, 77, 132
Normalization, CDP requirements and, 53
"Not Hotdog" app, 155, *156*, 157–159, *158*

O
Oars + Alps, 181–182
Observational bias, 22
Occasion segmentation, 81
Ogilvy, David, 32
O'Hara, Chris, 18, 131, 146, 196
One-to-one (1:1) marketing
  defining, 3
  direct mail as, 31
  for personalization, 2
  "Share a Coke" (Coca-Cola) example, 4
Online-offline authentication, 79
Online-offline matching, 79
Operating model, *115*, 118–119
Optimization
  data science for, 160
  ideal marketing architecture and, 43, *43*
Oracle
  analytics, 122
  BlueKai, 91–92, 96, 132
  CDP of, 47, *48*
  relational database of, 34–36
Organizational perspective. *See* Customer-driven marketing

P

Pandora, 146

Personalization of data, 1–10
  Customer Data Platforms (CDP)
    for, 7–9
  customer expectations and, 1–4
  customer resistance and, 4–6, 92
  defining, 3
  personalizing ("the right
    message") for customer-driven
    marketing, 107, *108*, 109–110
  roadblocks to, 4–5

Personally identifiable information
  (PII), 14, 31

Persona splits, 179

Pew Research Center, 97, 102

Piggybacking, 92

Pixels, 92

Platform ecosystems
  in CDP working model, *115*, 116
  customer data platforms (CDP) as,
    63, 64, *64*
  marketing analytics and, 194–195
  overview, 44–45

Predictive modeling
  advanced marketing analytics and,
    189
  categorical models, 163
  CDP for, overview, 23–24, 26 (*See
    also* Customer Data Platforms
    (CDP))
  data science for, 160
  early use of, 30
  engagement activation and, 86
  overview, 163
  predictive customer journeys,
    178–179
  regression models, 163

Prescriptive customer journeys,
  177–178

Price sensitivity segmentation, 82

Prime (Amazon), 3

Privacy. *See* Consent

Process (CDP component), *50*, 50–51

Product preferences segmentation,
  82

Profile building, CDP requirements
  and, 53, 55, *56*

Pseudonymous data, defined, 18n.
  See also Unknown data

Psychographic segmentation, 81

Punch cards, *33*, 33–34

R

Raab, David, 49, 65–66, 208

Rational choice theory, 101

Real-time analysis, 189

Real-time event-based marketing, 86

Real-time interaction management
  (RTIM), 13, 180–181

Reckitt Benckiser (RB), 103–104

Regression models, 163

Regulation
  California Consumer Privacy Act
    (CCPA), 5, 9, 17, 95, 100, 105
  consumer protection legislation, 32
  increased regulation, 5
  unknown data and, 17
  See also Consent; General Data
    Protection Regulation (GDPR)

Requests for proposals (RFPs), CDP
  requirements and, 52–54, *61*

Rinaldi, Vinny, 151–152, 197–199

S

Safari (Apple), 93, 94, 101

Sales. *See* Customer data as
  enterprise-wide asset

Sales Cloud, 141

Salesforce
  analytics, 122
  Audience Studio, *20*
  CDP future and, 205
  CDP of, 47, *48*

Salesforce (*Continued*)
    Cloud Information Model (CIM),
      76
    customer data stored by, 141
    customer relationship
      management (CRM) software
      inception and, 35
    Customer 360 Audiences, *80*, *84*
    Datorama and, 71, 122
    Einstein, 159, 165
    forward-looking statements by, 204
    Journey Builder, 85
    Marketing Cloud, 85
    persona splits performed by, 179
    as "source of truth," 150
    "State of Marketing Report," 5, 8,
      11, 73, 146, 177
    "State of the Connected
      Consumer," 3, 96, 97
    surveys of, 2–3
Sankaraiah, Chakra, 69–70
SAP, 205
S.C. Johnson, 181
Schmitt, Alfred, 30–31
Sears catalog, 31
Sebastian, Art, 1–2
Segmentation
    CDP capabilities for, *55*, 56–57
    CDP requirements and, 52
    data management step, 81–83, *83*,
      84
    data science for, 160
    engagement maturity stages,
      126–128, *127*
    machine learning and artificial
      intelligence in, 165–169
Service Cloud, 116
"Share a Coke" (Coca-Cola), 4
Sharp, Byron, 175–177
Siebel Systems, 35
Silicon Valley (HBO), "Not Hotdog"
    app and, 155, *156*, 157–159, *158*

Silos of data, as problem, 11–13, *13*,
    22–24, *23*
SKU (shop-keeping units), 34–35
Social media
    marketing analytics for, 194–195
    natural language processing
      (NLP), 169
    *See also individual social media
      company names*
Society of the Divine Savior, 29–31,
    30, 33
"Source of truth," 150
"State of Marketing Report"
    (Salesforce), 5, 8, 11, 73, 146, 177
"State of the Connected Consumer"
    (Salesforce), 3, 96, 97
Stitch Fix, 97
Storytelling, data science for, 160
Stream processing (data collection),
    73
Structure, finding, 164
Structured Query Language (SQL),
    34–37, 39
Suarez Davis, Jon, 134
Subramanyam, Kumar, 152–153

T
Target, 181
Team
    data scientists' role in marketing
      organizations, 161, 170–171
    IT/CRM teams, 120–122
    marketing data for cross-team
      purposes, 151–152
    people at center of CDP working
      model, 114–116, *115*, *119*,
      119–123
    siloed customer data and, 11–13,
      13, 22–24, *23*
    See also Chief marketing officers
      (CMOs); Customer data as
      enterprise-wide asset

TechCrunch, 91
TensorFlow, 158
Thuerk, Gary, 177
Time, Inc., 172
Touchpoint marketing, 127, *127*
Touchpoints of customer data. *See*
    Customer data as
    enterprise-wide asset
Transparency, privacy tactics and,
    102
Trust
  consent and consumer trust,
    96–100, *100*
  consumer decline in, 5, 6

U
Unica (IBM), 36
Unknown data
  adtech and data management
    platform, 131–139
  co-mingling known and unknown
    data, 147–149, *148*
  defined, 16–18, *17*

known and unknown data,
    connecting, 20–21, *21*
  pseudonymous data, defined, 18n
  unifying with known data, 62
Unlabeled data, labeled *vs.,* 162
Use cases, *115*, 116–117
User interface (UI)
  business-user friendly UI,
    62–63
  improvement of, 37–38
User-match deployment, 79
Use segmentation, 82

V
Voice applications, natural language
    processing (NLP), 169

W
"Walled gardens," 135–136, 193
Web browsers, on consent, 93–95, *94*
Wehner, David, 98
World Wide Web Consortium
    (W3C), 93